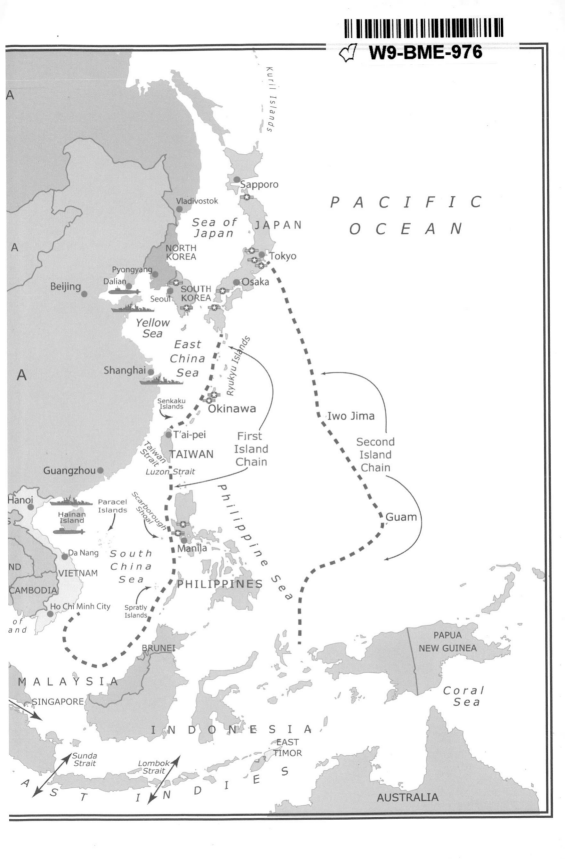

MORE PRAISE FOR *CROUCHING TIGER*

"Navarro makes a compelling case that trouble lies ahead in Asia, mainly because China is going to attempt to dominate that region the way the United States dominates the Western Hemisphere. China, in other words, is going to imitate Uncle Sam. *Crouching Tiger* is not only clearly and concisely written, but it also addresses almost every issue related to the question of whether China can rise peacefully. And that includes the counterarguments to Navarro's position. This book is ideally suited for a wide audience."

> —John J. Mearsheimer, R. Wendell Harrison Distinguished Service Professor
> of Political Science, University of Chicago

"A brilliant and clear-headed analysis of America's general short-sightedness on China—including allowing US multinationals to utilize offshore production in order to benefit from Beijing's export subsidies, sweatshops, forced labor, currency manipulation, and absent environmental controls. Of equal note is the frank unmasking of the kowtowing of the US media to China, rampant academic self-censorship, and, at dead center stage, the growing Chinese military threat now bearing down on Asia."

> —Hon. David Kilgour, JD, former Canadian Secretary of State for Asia-Pacific

"Penetrating the mystique of a rapidly reemerging China and its implications for global peace has seldom been as easy or as intriguing as the exegesis provided by Peter Navarro in *Crouching Tiger*. Posing forty-five salient questions, Navarro deputizes his readers to join his step-by-step Sherlockian investigation into whether it is possible—and ultimately why it is important to try—to avoid conflict with China."

> —Patrick M. Cronin, DPhil, senior director, Asia-Pacific Security Program

"There is still so much about 'geopolitical China' that the world needs to understand and appreciate—especially the country's military agenda and capabilities—and *Crouching Tiger* by Peter Navarro fills in many of the blanks. China's global agenda and the means China now has in hand to achieve this agenda are the main themes of the book, and thankfully so. Navarro is brilliantly informed, meticulous with his research, fair with his use of experts, and thoughtful and balanced in his conclusions. *Crouching Tiger* will be a mainstay of the foreign-policy community for years to come."

> —Leo Hindery Jr., member, Council on Foreign Relations;
> cochair, Task Force on Jobs Creation; and founder, Jobs First

"Peter Navarro's provocative study thinks the unthinkable: a great power war between the United States and China in the not-so-distant future. Navarro systematically examines the underlying causes, the immediate triggers, and the possible trajectories of such a hypothetical conflict. In the process, he drives home the imperative to keep the peace through American strength. What sets this book apart from the booming literature on China's rise is its appeal to the wider public. By drawing attention to the risks of a Sino-American strategic rivalry, Navarro's work should spur much-needed debate on one of the most consequential challenges facing the United States."

> —Toshi Yoshihara, John A. van Beuren Chair of Asia-Pacific Studies,
> US Naval War College, and coauthor, *Red Star over the Pacific:*
> *China's Rise and the Challenge to US Maritime Strategy*

"*Crouching Tiger* weaves together history, economics, geopolitics, ancient Chinese doctrines, and modern military strategy to assess the challenge of China's military rise and its one-hundred-year quest for global supremacy. It should be read by everyone, from Pentagon strategists and members of Congress to American citizens and taxpayers."

> —Michael Pillsbury, director, Center on Chinese Strategy at the
> Hudson Institute; member, the Council on Foreign Relations and the
> International Institute for Strategic Studies; and author,
> *The Hundred-Year Marathon: China's Secret Strategy to*
> *Replace America as the Global Superpower*

"It feels incongruous to call a book with such sobering content a fun read, but Peter Navarro pulls it off with this engagingly written work. Nor is *Crouching Tiger* a one-sided account of China's rise and its implications for Asian peace and security; Navarro taps a wide range of opinion among 'China Hands' in order to give a balanced perspective. Even if you don't end up agreeing with the author's conclusions, the journey through his observations and analysis will provoke you into thinking about Asian affairs in new ways. That's no small accomplishment."

> —James Holmes, PhD, professor of strategy, Naval War College,
> and coauthor of *Red Star over the Pacific*

"Navarro's prescient analysis in *Death by China* of Beijing's mercantilist attack on America's manufacturing base—dismissed by some as alarmist—has become the conventional wisdom. In *Crouching Tiger*, Navarro's crystal ball is working overtime as he vividly paints a disturbingly accurate portrait of the trouble ahead for the US-China military relationship. To ignore his message—and his brilliantly incisive call to action—is to do so at America's peril."

> —Dana Rohrabacher, congressman (R-CA)

"While the world's attention has been rightly focused on the Middle East over the past two decades, Peter Navarro's *Crouching Tiger* provides compelling and unvarnished insight into the capabilities and intentions of China's global rise, the most important challenge to US national security and international peace for the next century. I strongly encourage the American public to read this critically important work as our future depends on an informed electorate."

> —Jim Fanell, retired US Navy intelligence officer, former director of
> intelligence and information operations for the US Pacific Fleet,
> and creator and moderator of the Red Star Rising list service

"Peter Navarro's *Crouching Tiger* is an excellent description of China's emerging global challenge to freedom and American interests."

> —Richard D. Fisher Jr., senior fellow,
> International Assessment and Strategy Center

"*Crouching Tiger* is a must read for anyone interested in world affairs or the future of our nation."

> —Greg Autry, assistant professor of clinical entrepreneurship,
> University of Southern California, and coauthor, *Death by China*

Crouching
TIGER

What CHINA'S MILITARISM

Means for the WORLD

Peter Navarro

Prometheus Books

59 John Glenn Drive
Amherst, New York 14228

Published 2015 by Prometheus Books

Cover image of tiger © insima/Shutterstock.com
Cover image of Chinese art element © istockphoto.com/yukipon
Cover design by Jacqueline Nasso Cooke

All maps are from Peter Navarro, *Crouching Tiger: Will There Be War with China?* www. crouchingtiger.net (documentary film series from DBC Productions, forthcoming 2016).

Inquiries should be addressed to
Prometheus Books
59 John Glenn Drive
Amherst, New York 14228
VOICE: 716–691–0133
FAX: 716–691–0137
WWW.PROMETHEUSBOOKS.COM

19 18 17   5 4 3

Library of Congress Cataloging-in-Publication Data Pending

Printed in the United States of America

To Captain James E. Fanell,
for his unwavering courage and unyielding commitment
to a deeper mission

The question at hand is simple and profound:
Can China rise peacefully? My answer is no.

—Professor John Mearsheimer,
"Why China's Rise Will Not Be Peaceful," 2004

CONTENTS

ACKNOWLEDGMENTS

Much of the source material for this book is derived from what is a very extensive English and Chinese literature—scholarly, journalistic, and government-sourced. However, the "detective story" you are about to begin could not have been crafted without the help of a large number of experts who graciously agreed to sit down in front of a camera for in-depth interviews with the author. These experts, all of whom appear in the companion documentary film series to this book, include:

- Michael Auslin and Dan Blumenthal, American Enterprise Institute
- Professor Greg Autry, University of Southern California
- Richard Bush and Michael O'Hanlon, Brookings Institution
- Gordon G. Chang, author, *The Coming Collapse of China*
- Kurt Campbell, former US Assistant Secretary of State
- Dean Cheng, Heritage Foundation
- Bernard Cole and T. X. Hammes, National Defense University
- Patrick Cronin, Center for a New American Security
- Seth Cropsey, Hudson Institute
- Richard Fisher and Ed Timperlake, International Assessment and Strategy Center
- Professor Aaron Friedberg, Princeton University
- Professors Amitai Etzioni and Charles Glaser, George Washington University
- Bill Gertz, senior editor, *Free Beacon*
- Bonnie Glaser and Michael Green, Center for Strategic and International Studies
- Professors Lyle Goldstein, James Holmes, and Toshi Yoshihara, US Naval War College
- Professor Stefan Halper, University of Cambridge
- Dr. Phillip Karber, president, Potomac Foundation
- Stephanie Kleine-Ahlbrandt, US Institute of Peace
- Professor David Lampton, Johns Hopkins University

- Professor John Mearsheimer, University of Chicago
- Commissioners Pat Mulloy, Dan Slane, and Michael Wessel, US-China Economic and Security Review Commission
- Michael Pillsbury, author, *The Hundred-Year Marathon*
- Sheila Smith, Council on Foreign Relations
- Mark Stokes, executive director, Project 49 Institute
- Ashley Tellis, Carnegie Endowment for International Peace

I wish to deeply thank each of these individuals for their generous gift of time, their incredible patience with me and my film crew, and most of all, for bringing a diversity, richness, and balance to the investigation with their keen expertise and often markedly contrasting points of view. Excerpts from these interviews may be accessed from this book's official website: www.crouchingtiger.net.

Foreword

CHINA'S EXISTENTIAL CHALLENGE TO THE WORLD

by Gordon G. Chang

My friend, Peter Navarro, has written the ultimate "geopolitical detective story." It is a compelling narrative about the country posing the greatest challenge to the United States—and to the international system that has created prosperity for the world for seven decades.

That country, of course, is the People's Republic of China, the ultimate Communist super state, and *Crouching Tiger* asks the right question: What will the international community do to meet Beijing's fundamental assault on peace and stability in the most economically vibrant part of the world?

Navarro also asks this question at the right time. With each passing day, an increasingly emboldened China is using its new-found economic power and military might to grab territory, violate trade rules, proliferate nuclear-weapons technology, support rogue regimes, cyberattack free societies, flout norms, and undermine international institutions.

Why is Beijing acting so provocatively now, shedding any remaining pretense of a "peaceful rise"? Simply because Chinese Communist Party leaders think they own the century; they are sure the United States is in terminal decline, and they believe no one will oppose them.

And there is one more reason. At home, the Communist Party is insecure, facing unprecedented internal challenges, both economic and political. Unfortunately for the world, these internal problems create serious external consequences. For more than three decades the Communist Party has relied on the continual delivery of prosperity as the primary basis of its legitimacy. Now that China can no longer reliably create growth, it is falling back on its last resort: a militant and revanchist nationalism.

As Beijing has continued to lash out, it has set itself against its neighbors, the United States, and the international community. Today, as *Crouching Tiger* details, there are far too many triggers for a once unthinkable, but now increasingly imaginable, war—from the "wild child" of North Korea and proud democracy of Taiwan, to the strategic reefs and islands in the East and South China Seas.

Regrettably, the United States, the world's guarantor of security, has not risen to meet this unprecedented challenge. From the Oval Office to the halls of Congress and across the suites of corporate America, our political and corporate leaders have not wanted to confront the fact that China, despite our efforts, does not want to enmesh itself in the community of nations.

Instead, US diplomacy, over the course of decades, has tried to walk many fine lines. It has, for instance, tried to "engage" the Chinese, maintaining good relations with them, while also seeking to cajole and constrain Beijing from time to time. America has also reassured allies like Japan and friends like Taiwan but has, at the same time, been concerned about emboldening these critical Asian partners with too much backing.

Ely Ratner, who served on the State Department's China desk, has borrowed an apt sailing metaphor and likened this inconsistent-looking process to "tacking." Yet what we thought was our diplomatic subtlety and carefulness, the Chinese have merely perceived as weakness and irresolution. As a result, our policy has failed.

Today, Chinese rulers, fueled by a toxic mix of historical grievance and arrogance, are trying to redraw the map of Asia through coercion and force, expanding into the lands and waters of others. As they have pursued outlandish claims like those defined by their infamous "nine-dash line," they have destabilized their periphery—from the Himalayas in the south to the waters of the East China Sea in the north. And with their new partnership with Russia and assistance to client and rogue states like North Korea and Iran, the Chinese have taken on not just their neighbors but the world as well. It is an existential challenge that inexplicably the international community has largely ignored.

With *Crouching Tiger*, however, we can no longer say we have not been warned. We can also no longer claim there is no alternative way forward. For within these razor-sharp pages, there is not just the geopolitical world's most important mystery revealed and unraveled. There is also hope in the ultimate pathways to peace that this detective story unveils.

In fact, this is a broader struggle playing out across the world, not just between Beijing and Washington, but also between America's open and democratic architecture and China's closed and authoritarian system. Only one of these visions can ultimately prevail. So much is at stake.

Gordon G. Chang is a contributor at Forbes.com, a blogger at the *World Affairs Journal*, a frequent cohost on the John Batchelor Show, and a two-term trustee of Cornell University. He has given briefings at the US National Intelligence Council, the Central Intelligence Agency, the State Department, and the Pentagon and has spoken on the China question in Beijing, Shanghai, Taipei, Hong Kong, New Delhi, Seoul, Singapore, Tokyo, The Hague, London, Ottawa, Toronto, and Vancouver. His website is www.gordonchang.com.

PROLOGUE

In the Gobi Desert, on the northern rim of the People's Republic of China, there sits a target on the cold and barren landscape that conforms almost perfectly to the size and shape of an American aircraft carrier. China's vaunted Second Artillery Corps is now using this target to perfect the delivery of a radically game-changing antiship ballistic missile that has only one purpose—drive the US Pacific Fleet out of Asian waters.[1]

Over a thousand miles away, at the Xichang Satellite Launch Center in Sichuan Province, military strategists are testing an equally game-changing suite of antisatellite weapons like the ground-based Dong Neng-2 high-Earth-orbit missile. It is designed to literally ram American satellites out of the sky—and thereby neutralize the US strategic advantage in space.[2]

Meanwhile in China's southernmost province—picturesque Hainan Island—Chinese engineers have fashioned a massive underground submarine base right out of a James Bond novel. From this base, submerged Jin-class nuclear subs can slip out undetected, armed with intercontinental ballistic missiles—like the Julang-2—capable of destroying any city in the world.[3]

And even as the United States has committed by treaty with Russia to significantly reduce nuclear warhead stockpiles, China continues to develop its Underground Great Wall. This maze of tunnels, up to three thousand miles long, now houses a rapidly growing arsenal of nuclear-tipped ballistic missiles aimed not just at the United States but also at other countries, like India, Japan, the Philippines, and Vietnam, with which China has increasingly contentious territorial disputes.[4]

Why is China rapidly developing such offensive capabilities if, as its leaders have repeatedly claimed, China seeks only a peaceful rise?[5] This may well be *the* most important question of our nuclear-tipped times. That is why this book is, at its core, a geopolitical detective story; and your mission is to help solve this broader mystery: Will there be war with China?

To that end, each chapter that follows will provide an important clue presented in the form of a key question leading off the chapter. Each question will then be followed by possible answers across the range of opinion and thought with the considerable help of our stable of experts.

Through this Sherlockian process, we, together, should be able to come to some key conclusions about the prospects of war or peace. The broader mission, of course, is to raise general public awareness about an increasing danger and provide possible pathways to peace, thereby hopefully changing the course of a history which at this point appears grimly and inexorably headed for conflict—and perhaps even a nuclear cliff.

Part 1

THE BEST OR WORST
OF INTENTIONS?

Chapter 1

THE THUCYDIDES TRAP MEETS THE "SECURITY DILEMMA"

Question: Based on the historical record, how likely is war between a rising power like China and an established superpower like the United States?

1. Very likely
2. Very unlikely

W ill a rapidly rising China play the upstart Athens to America's wary Sparta as both plunge headlong into the infamous "Thucydides Trap"?[1] This is the historical conceit of our first question. The Thucydides Trap dates back thousands of years to the Peloponnesian War—famously chronicled in the Greek classic, *The History of the Peloponnesian War*. As the author Thucydides wrote of this quite-literal Greek tragedy: "What made war inevitable was the growth of Athenian power and the fear which this caused in Sparta."[2]

Like America of today, Sparta in the fifth century BCE was the reigning superpower and hegemon when Athens came bursting onto the scene and quickly emerged as the preeminent civilization of its time. As Harvard University scholar Graham Allison has observed:

This dramatic rise shocked Sparta [and] fear compelled its leaders to respond. Threat and counter-threat produced competition, then confrontation and finally conflict. At the end of 30 years of war, both states had been destroyed.[3]

Fast-forward to the nineteenth century, and we see another classic case of two great powers falling into the Thucydides Trap. That's when Kaiser Wilhelm's Imperial Germany emerged to challenge the hegemony of a

British Empire that had ruled the waves—and thereby the world—for more than a century. Ominously, the grim result of this particular clash between a rising power and an established power was the slaughter of millions of soldiers and civilians in the first true "world war."

Of course, two anecdotes hardly prove a theory. That's why this particular statistic is particularly alarming: Across the broad swath of world history, in fully eleven of the fifteen times since 1500 that a rising power like China faced an established power like the United States, war resulted more than 70 percent of the time.[4] On that basis alone, no sensible speculator would want to put big money on China's peaceful rise over the next several decades.

As to exactly why Athens versus Sparta and Germany versus Great Britain and a host of other rising versus established power pairings seem to inevitably plunge into war, University of Chicago professor John Mearsheimer has produced arguably the most convincing theory of what he calls the "tragedy of great-power politics."[5]

Mearsheimer's theory rests on three key assumptions.[6] The first is that the global system is *anarchic* rather than hierarchical—meaning there is no higher authority than nations. The important implication of this "no night watchman" assumption is that if a nation gets into trouble, it can't dial 9-1-1 for help. Therefore, it must take steps to protect itself by building military *capabilities*.

That all nations build up such military capabilities—the weapons of war—is the second key assumption of Mearsheimer's theory. However, while one nation can easily determine the capabilities of a rival nation by counting its airplanes, guns, ships, and other weapons, it is far more difficult to know its rival's *intentions*. Is that rival country developing military capabilities simply to defend itself or, alternatively, does it have conquest in mind?

That, in fact, is the third key assumption of Mearsheimer's theory; namely, it is difficult or impossible to know a nation's true intentions. It is precisely this opaqueness of a country's intentions coupled with the lack of a night watchman to call upon if one is in trouble that leads to the same kind of fear that Sparta began to have of Athens, Europe had of both Kaiser Wilhelm's imperium and Adolph Hitler's Third Reich, and many nations in Asia, along with the United States, are now experiencing when it comes to a rising authoritarian China.

Not surprisingly, such existential fear, in turn, leads nations to increase their own capabilities so as to be able to defend themselves against a rising nation. The result is a vicious escalatory spiral captured in yet another famous construct of international relations theory—the so-called security dilemma. The typical trajectory of the "security dilemma" is an arms race that inexorably ratchets up until an actual shooting war erupts, often as a result of some miscalculation or random event, for example, the assassination of Archduke Franz Ferdinand in Sarajevo that triggered World War I.

The final piece of Mearsheimer's "tragedy of great-power politics" that seems most applicable to the case of a rising China is the inference that, as a matter of survival, all big countries will seek to be the preponderant global power or "hegemon." Explains Mearsheimer:

> The key to understanding how China and the United States are likely to behave is to understand that in an anarchic world, there is a very powerful incentive to become as powerful a state as possible. And the reason is you can never be certain that another state won't grow to be powerful and have malign intentions towards you. So if you end up one day next door to a very powerful, hostile state—picture yourself living next door to Imperial Germany or Nazi Germany or Imperial Japan—you want to make sure you're much more powerful because if that state decides it's going to play rough, there's no higher authority to pull your chestnuts out of the fire. So the best way to be secure in an anarchic system is to be a regional hegemon, to dominate your area of the world to the point where nobody can cause you any trouble.[7]

From this vantage point, Mearsheimer concludes that as China seeks to be Asia's hegemon, the United States must also attempt to prevent China from gaining power at America's expense. In other words, in Mearsheimer's tragedy, it's "game on," and this old, great-power game in a new Asian bottle is not likely to end pretty.

✳✳✳✳✳

It would appear from this analysis that the answer to the question leading off this chapter—How likely is war with China, based on the historical record?—is "very likely" indeed. That said, it would be a huge mistake to extrapolate an inevitable future war with China from the vainglorious mistakes of the past.

For this reason alone, we must not end our detective story so quickly. Instead, we must come down from the thirty-thousand-foot heights of great-power politics to do our own "boots on the ground" examination of China's intentions.

If, in fact, we can do what Professor Mearsheimer says cannot be done—determine unequivocally that China's intentions behind its military buildup are in fact benign—we will have solved our mystery by concluding that war is definitely not in the cards or stars. If, however, China's intentions are malign—or if there is at least some confusion about what those intentions are amongst the United States and its allies in Asia—then we have a problem we must probe further. To work through this puzzle, let's turn next to the three main reasons typically given for China's military buildup—two of which are arguably quite benign, but one of which raises very real concerns.

Chapter 2

CHINA'S CENTURY OF HUMILIATION AND ITS HOMELAND-PROTECTION IMPERATIVE

Question: Which countries have invaded China
over the past two hundred years?

1. France
2. Germany
3. Great Britain
4. Japan
5. Russia
6. The United States
7. All of the above

I f you are not Chinese or a student of Asian history, you may be surprised to learn that the correct answer to this question is actually "all of the above."[1] In fact, China's fear of being dominated by foreign powers and its pursuit of homeland protection are the most obvious reasons why it is seeking to build up its military. China's concerns in these dimensions are both fully justified and deeply rooted in its so-called century of humiliation.

This "century of humiliation" began in 1839 with Britain's first opium war against China. It ran through the end of the Second Sino-Japanese War in 1945 and featured everything China fears today—from military domination and naval blockades to massive landgrabs, equally massive war reparations, repeated assaults on Chinese sovereignty, and the slaughter of millions of Chinese citizens.

Prior to 1839, dating back to the 1600s, an imperial China, through a succession of emperors, was the undisputed superpower in Asia. Vassal states, which regularly paid tribute to China's dynastic rulers, included Burma and Vietnam in Southeast Asia, Nepal on China's western flanks, and Korea and Japan in East Asia. By 1683, a dynastic China had also conquered a critical gateway to the Pacific Ocean—the island of Taiwan.[2] China's undisputed regional hegemony would, however, come to an abrupt and inglorious end in 1839 once Britain and its powerful navy forced China's emperor to cede the territories of Hong Kong and Kowloon— along with effective control of all of China's major ports.

Over time, the British Empire would also wrest Nepal from China's sphere of influence and colonize Burma. Czarist Russia would militarily coerce China into surrendering a large chunk of its northeast territory— along with its strategic access to the Sea of Japan. And Imperial French forces would use, among other tactics, a naval blockade of Taiwan to force China to turn over control of all of northern Vietnam to France—thus paving the way for French hegemony in Indochina.

Despite these humiliations, the worst was yet to come as China's once-loyal vassal Japan was quickly emerging from two centuries of isolation; and unlike China, the Land of the Rising Sun was eagerly embracing the new technologies of modern warfare. By 1894, under cover of the First Sino-Japanese war, Imperial Japanese forces would assume *de facto* control of the Korean Peninsula while taking the prize of Taiwan as a spoil of war. In hostilities that set the stage for the Second Sino-Japanese War, Japan would then seize mineral-rich Manchuria in 1932 under cover of the puppet state of Manchukuo. By 1940, Japan's brutal occupation would encompass most of eastern China and all of China's major ports. China's "century of humiliation" would come to an end only with the defeat of Japan by Allied Forces in 1945.

Throughout this "century of humiliation," it wasn't just the loss of so much territory that so deeply scarred the Chinese psyche. It was also the sheer brutality of the foreign powers themselves.

For example, during the Boxer Rebellion between 1899 and 1901, when Chinese citizens rose up to protest the foreign occupation, a full twenty thousand troops from an eight-nation alliance (including the United States) stormed into Beijing and crushed the uprising. In what newspapers of the time described as an "orgy of looting," this German-led expeditionary force committed numerous atrocities; rape, particularly by French and Russian troops, was so prevalent that thousands of Chinese women committed suicide just to avoid it. As a prelude to the atrocities committed in the 1930s, Japanese soldiers were likewise reported to be particularly skillful in the beheading of Chinese men suspected of being Boxers.[3]

✱✱✱✱✱

Given this indelible history of humiliation, it should hardly be surprising that the China of today wants to develop a military force powerful enough to avoid the kind of wanton imperialistic abuses it suffered for more than 100 one hundred years. But this homeland-protection rationale for China's military buildup is not the end of our detective story—it is simply the beginning.

Chapter 3

ESCAPING A "MALACCA DILEMMA" AND GUARDING TRADE ROUTES

Question: Is China rapidly building up its military to guard the trading routes and global investments it needs for robust economic growth?

1. No
2. Yes

The answer to this simple question—they will get much harder—is of course yes. China's imperative to protect its trading routes begins with what former Chinese president Hu Jintao once described as China's "Malacca Dilemma." Here, a little economic history is in order.

For the first three decades after its communist revolution in 1949, the People's Republic of China subsisted as a backward agrarian nation that traded very little with the world. During this autarkic phase, China had no need to import foreign oil—it had its own significant reserves, relatively few cars, and very little manufacturing.

In 1978, then vice premier Deng Xiaoping began to create an entirely different reality with what he called China's "second revolution."[1] This economic revolution would establish a particularly unique brand of state-run capitalism with very distinct Chinese characteristics. The essence of Deng's mercantilist strategy was to set up special economic zones for trading and then heavily subsidize China's exports from these zones—all the while fiercely protecting China's own domestic markets from foreign competition.

At the same time, to ensure a cheap source of labor for Chinese enterprises, Deng smashed Mao Zedong's "iron rice bowl" system. This "iron rice bowl" had been the hallmark of Chinese communism, guaranteeing jobs and housing and free health care and pensions for hundreds of millions of workers; but it was swept away in Deng's bid to make China more competitive in world markets.

The results of China's great leap forward into a mercantilist state capitalism would be nothing less than astonishing. China's economy would grow close to 10 percent annually, year after year, for more than three decades, in what would be the most impressive economic expansion of any country in history—ancient or modern.

This decades-long growth spurt has transformed China into the world's undisputed factory floor—it surpassed the United States as the largest economy in 2014.[2] China's rapid industrialization, coupled with its critical dependence on heavily subsidized exports to fuel its growth, has also made China just as heavily dependent on, and highly vulnerable to, a global supply-and-delivery chain linked by the major seas and oceans of the world.

Just consider that, as the world's largest manufacturing nation, China has also become the world's largest oil importer. Today, over 70 percent of China's petroleum imports—along with almost half of China's energy needs—must travel first from Africa or the Persian Gulf, then pass through one of the most infamous maritime choke points in the world—the Malacca Strait.

This strait, situated between the Malay Peninsula and the Indonesian island of Sumatra, is an extremely narrow and relatively shallow five-hundred-mile stretch of pirate-infested waters linking the Indian Ocean to the South China Sea. Through this narrow and perilous gateway to Asia passes not just most of China's imported oil (along with much of the oil for Japan and South Korea) but also more than sixty thousand vessels annually carrying some one-third of world trade. This volume of traffic is almost three times that of the Panama Canal and more than double that of the Suez Canal.[3]

China is, of course, keenly aware of its "Malacca Dilemma." Indeed, in November of 2003, China's president Hu Jintao accused "certain major powers" of seeking to control the strait to the disadvantage of China and called on the People's Liberation Army (PLA) to develop new strategies to insulate China from foreign coercion.[4] According to scholar Ian Storey: "Thereafter, the Chinese press devoted considerable attention to the country's 'Malacca Dilemma,' leading one newspaper to breathlessly declare: 'It is no exaggeration to say that whoever controls the Strait of Malacca will also have a stranglehold on the energy route of China.'"[5]

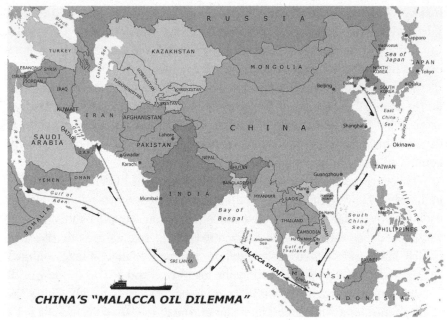

CHINA'S "MALACCA OIL DILEMMA"

Map 3.1. The Malacca Strait, through which most of China's imported oil and more than sixty thousand vessels carrying some one-third of world trade passes. Control of this strait has given rise to China's "Malacca Dilemma."

The highly congested and easily blockaded Strait of Malacca is, however, hardly China's only maritime dilemma. As the world's largest consumer of raw materials, China must likewise import vast quantities of commodities like alumina, cement, copper, lumber, nickel, and iron ore from far-flung continents like Africa and South America.

Just consider the millions of tons of copper that China imports each year from Chile—China consumes almost half of the world's annual production. This key industrial metal must travel by ship first around South America's Cape Horn, then past Africa's Cape of Good Hope, through the Indian Ocean, and finally around the southern part of Indonesia on a sixty-six-day journey traveling over fifteen thousand nautical miles.

Of course, to propel its heavily export-dependent economy—over 50 percent of its gross domestic product is trade-related—China must likewise *export* over two trillion dollars of its products annually into large markets like Europe and the United States and into smaller markets in Africa, Latin America, and across Asia. Over 80 percent of these "Made in

China" products travel by sea, and many of China's container ships must pass through other key choke points like the Panama and Suez Canals and the Strait of Gibraltar.

It is precisely this increasing vulnerability to disruptions in its trade that taps into China's deepest fear—that some type of naval blockade will be imposed by a hostile foreign power seeking to exert economic, political, or military pressure on China. As to what foreign power China believes might ever take such a step, there really is only one with the global military capability—the United States of America.

We must next ask if China's deepest fear is also a legitimate one—or simply the paranoia of an authoritarian regime famously prone to paranoia. This is a critical question for our investigation, because if Chinese Communist Party leaders truly believe a foreign power has both the capabilities *and* the intention to use a blockade strategy to bend China to its will, these leaders will, at least in their own eyes, be perfectly justified in building a military fully capable of defeating any such blockade—and by implication, defeating the United States Navy itself.

Chapter 4

AMERICA'S ONCE AND FUTURE EMBARGO?

**Question: Should China truly fear an oil embargo
by the United States and its allies?**

1. No
2. Yes

T he perhaps surprising, and even deeply unsettling, answer to this question is an unequivocal "yes." This is an assessment based on any sober analysis of past US embargo history, the current and considerable capabilities of the US Navy, and America's strategic intentions as expressed by the Pentagon in the event of a "China contingency."

From a historical perspective, the first country in modern times to impose an oil embargo was not, as many Americans assume, Saudi Arabia, which led the Arab Oil Embargo of 1973–74 against the United States. Rather, it was the United States itself in its embargo of Imperial Japan in 1941. Ironically, at least within the context of our current investigation, this decidedly American embargo was implemented as a means of forcing Japan to withdraw its occupying troops from none other than China itself.

America's embargo on oil and gasoline and other key raw materials to Japan was a harsh blow to a country dependent on the United States for fully 80 percent of its petroleum needs. This embargo, which also included the closure of the Panama Canal to Japanese shipping and a freeze on Japanese assets in the United States, is indeed a cautionary tale as it would lead to one of the most infamous preemptive first strikes in world history—Japan's surprise attack on Pearl Harbor a mere four months after the embargo was imposed.

America's embargo on Japan is, however, hardly the only one etched into the collective consciousness of Chinese Communist Party leaders. After China entered the Korean War on the side of North Korea in 1950, President Harry Truman imposed a complete trade embargo on China that would last for more than twenty years and inflict considerable damage before President Richard Nixon's "Ping-Pong diplomacy" ended the embargo in 1971.

In more recent times, the United States has also never hesitated to use the related tool of economic sanctions against a whole host of what it regards to be rogue nations. These countries—all of whom count China as a friend or ally—have included Cuba, Iran, Libya, Myanmar, North Korea, Syria, and the Sudan. Worth noting, too, are the various US sanctions slapped against Russia for its aggression in Crimea and the Ukraine.

The broader point here, detectives, is that embargoes and sanctions are an integral part of the historical DNA of the United States; and China, which to this day still is embargoed from buying weapons technologies from the United States, is well aware of this history and America's preferred *modus operandi* when it comes to exerting coercive pressure. However, it's not just what America has done in the past that so worries China. It is also America's formidable naval *capabilities*.

Indeed, since the fall of the Soviet Union in 1991, no nation on earth has had a blue-water navy capable of globally challenging that of the United States. In fact, today, the Russian Federation Navy is only about one-fourth the size of the Soviet Navy at its peak while the Russian sub fleet has shrunk from almost four hundred boats in 1985 to less than one hundred today.[1]

For the world economy, the absence of a rival blue-water navy to challenge that of the United States has been a very good thing. This nautical version of a *Pax Americana* has meant absolute freedom of movement across international shipping lanes for virtually every nation, a concomitant and dramatic increase in world trade, and resultant robust growth levels in virtually every corner of the world—and one must hasten to add here that no country has benefitted more from the American Navy protecting the ocean commons than the world's largest trader: China. That said, even a cursory view of a map of American forces around the globe certainly proves that an American sea embargo on Chinese imports and exports could be highly effective.

Consider, for example, the Persian Gulf from which much of China's oil imports originate. Here, from their headquarters in Manama, Bahrain, commanders of the US Navy's Fifth Fleet direct warships that guard not just the

Persian Gulf itself and the harrowing Strait of Hormuz but also patrol as far south as Kenya—one of many African states exporting oil to China.

America's Fifth Fleet is also responsible for protecting the southern end of the Suez Canal that exits into the Red Sea, and from the Red Sea, cargo ships on their way to China must pass through another key choke point a mere twenty miles across. This is the Bab-el-Mandeb Strait—translated literally as the "Gate of Grief"—and it is a critical strategic interface located between Yemen on the Arabian Peninsula and Djibouti and Eritrea in the Horn of Africa that helps connect the Indian Ocean and the Mediterranean Sea.

As for American command of that Mediterranean Sea, it is the US Sixth Fleet that roams from the north end of the Suez Canal all the way to the Strait of Gibraltar's gateway to the Atlantic Ocean. This passage through the Mediterranean is a particularly key journey for a large fraction of Chinese exports to Europe, Great Britain, and Scandinavia—and an equally key conduit for imported raw materials and agricultural products.

Meanwhile, in the central Indian Ocean, there is the lush, footprint-shaped seventeen-square-mile coral atoll known as Diego Garcia. This spit of land just south of the equator is one of the most strategic bases in the American matrix. It operates simultaneously as a naval base and marine base and is a key element of the American military's Global Positioning System. It also is an important landing strip for the long-range bombers that were used in both the Afghanistan and Iraq wars, and from this base, B-2 stealth bombers can easily range any major city in China.

Of course, the United States also has air force, army, naval, and marine bases that start from San Diego, leapfrog first to Hawaii and then to Guam, and move inexorably over a seven-thousand-mile journey toward American forward-operating bases in Japan and South Korea—bases far from the US mainland that are well within fighter-jet distance of the Chinese coast.[2]

As for Guam itself—a key battleground in World War II and less than two thousand miles from the Chinese mainland—it is the strategic anchor and rough midpoint of America's "Second Island Chain" of defense which stretches from the Japanese home islands through Guam to Indonesia's Papua Province and Papua New Guinea. Just thirty miles long, this fortress island is a key transient berth for the Pacific aircraft-carrier fleet. It also bristles with the best weaponry America's military branches have to offer—from B-2 stealth bombers and fifth-generation F-22 fighter jets to nuclear attack submarines and the latest drone technologies.

Map 4.1. United States military bases in the Asia-Pacific.

Of course, America's "First Island Chain" of defense is even closer to the Chinese mainland. It includes South Korea within its perimeter and runs from the Kuril Islands to Japan's home islands and then through Taiwan and Okinawa to the Philippines and Borneo. Like Guam, this First Island Chain is deeply impregnated with American naval forces and considerable firepower.

South Korea alone is home to fifteen bases and close to thirty thousand troops. Japan, which is the headquarters of the US Seventh Fleet at Sasebo and Yokosuka, houses another thirteen bases and close to forty thousand military personnel while fourteen more bases occupy almost 20 percent of the landmass of the Japanese territory of Okinawa Island.

Note, however, that these forward bases and bulwarks of the American presence in Asia are hardly the only ones China has to worry about. After being booted out in 1992, the US Navy has returned to the massive Subic Bay naval base in the Philippines—in no small part (and with no small irony) because the Philippine government increasingly fears a militarizing China. But this is not even the end of the American power-projection story.

In the South China Sea theater of operations, there is also COMLOG

WESTPAC. This is a relatively new combat-ready logistics center for the Seventh Fleet based in Singapore. It is expressly designed to "keep combatant ships and units throughout the 7th Fleet armed, fueled, fed and supported."[3] Meanwhile US marines are now being deployed "down under" in Australia at the far edges of the Asian defense perimeter as part of America's declared military "pivot" to Asia.

So what does all this global reach of the US military add up to from Beijing's perspective? Certainly a very credible threat of a highly effective American blockade of the trading routes that comprise the lifeblood of the Chinese economy. Add to this the Pentagon's frequently expressed intention to blockade China in the event of trouble—much more about Pentagon strategies later—and you have a perfectly legitimate reason for China to build up its military, particularly its global naval force, for purely *defensive* purposes.

Of course, this sobering conclusion raises the question of why the United States would ever want to impose a crippling embargo to begin with on its largest trading partner. It is a question that has all of Asia, along with the Pentagon and the White House, increasingly nervous; and it speaks directly to China's possible territorial ambitions —and possibly malign intentions.

Chapter 5

A "REVISIONIST" OR "STATUS QUO" POWER?

Question: Which description is most likely to fit a rapidly
militarizing China over the next several decades
of the twenty-first century?

1. China will be a "status quo" power interested only in
   prosperous economic engagement, a peaceful rise, and
   the opportunity to become a responsible stakeholder in
   the international world order.
2. China will behave like a "revisionist" power and use
   its growing economic and military might to expand its
   territory and hegemonic influence in Asia.

This question and clue really does cut to the heart of our "will there
be war" matter. On the one hand, if the answer is no. 1 and China
benignly seeks only prosperous engagement and a "peaceful rise" as the
rhetoric of the Chinese leadership has frequently emphasized,[1] there is a
very *low* probability of conflict.

On the other hand, if the answer is no. 2 and China does indeed intend
to use force or coercion to seize new territories in Asia and to become,
as Professor John Mearsheimer has warned, a "regional hegemon," these
revisionist and malign intentions will certainly be a recipe for military
clashes, if not all-out war.

So how might we determine whether China will act as a status quo
or revisionist power? If the past is indeed often prologue, one possible
way is to carefully analyze China's behavior since the Chinese Communist
Party seized power in 1949. In fact, even the most casual review of such a
history reveals a deep disconnect between the "peaceful rise" rhetoric of

the Chinese leadership and the reality of a long history of aggression spanning more than six decades.

This reality begins in 1950 with one of the largest imperial landgrabs
in world history: China's military conquests of Tibet and what is now
China's most northwest province, Xinjiang. Together, these two mineral-
rich spoils of war span over one million square miles and today comprise
fully 30 percent of the current Chinese land mass.

Both the invasions of these territories and the ongoing brutal treatment
of their indigenous peoples shine a very bright light on the darkest side
of Chinese authoritarianism. These invasions are also highly symptomatic
of China's historically-based territorial claims that are at sharp odds with
a body of modern international law that does not easily recognize such
"revanchist" arguments.

In 1950, China also entered the Korean War with one of the most
effective sneak attacks in modern warfare history. Under cover of dark-
ness, a full three-division army, numbering more than one hundred thousand troops, surreptitiously crossed the Yalu River into North Korea and
caught allied forces completely by surprise. The grim result: the slaughter
of thousands of US and South Korean troops.

During the early 1950s, China would likewise help the Vietnamese
drive the French colonialists out of Indochina. The defining battle at Dien
Bien Phu, planned under the watchful eyes of Chinese strategists and
prosecuted with large caches of Chinese weapons, led to a defeat no less
humiliating for the French than Napoleon's at Waterloo. After the French
withdrawal in 1954, Vietnam would be split into two nations, north and
south. This would set the stage for America's own inglorious retreat from
South Vietnam several decades later.

In 1962, China would begin the first of three surprise attacks on former
friends and allies with an invasion of India. This Sino-Indian War involved
two separate border disputes over one thousand miles apart, each with their
own unique history and each, in no small way, an extension of China's
conquests of Tibet and Xinjiang twelve years earlier.

The first border dispute, in the western theater, focused on China's
seizure of the Aksai Chin portion of the Kashmir region. The second
dispute, in the eastern theater of war, hinged around the Indian-held
Arunachal Pradesh, an area China continues to claim as "Southern Tibet."
As for the war itself, it was pure Hobbes—nasty, brutish, and short. It was

also India's most humiliating defeat—one that has left the Indian populace with a deep and abiding distrust of China.

During the 1960s, China would also play a pivotal role in America's war in Vietnam. It was not just the massive quantities of trucks, tanks, MiG jets, and artillery pieces that would help make the difference. Chinese troops numbering as many as one hundred fifty thousand also provided a very effective defense umbrella over the skies of Hanoi and Haiphong; these Chinese troops, firing both conventional antiaircraft guns and surface-to-air or "SAM" missiles, helped shoot down over one thousand American aircraft and their pilots.[2]

Ultimately, however, China's greatest contribution to the American defeat in Vietnam was its deterrence value: The most direct route to an American victory was for US ground forces to cross the demilitarized zone into North Vietnam, take Hanoi, and topple the government. America's political leaders were, however, haunted by the fear that if the United States breached the demilitarized zone, millions of Chinese troops might swarm over the border into Vietnam in much the same way they had flooded into Korea.

In the end, more than one hundred thousand Americans lost their lives or were seriously wounded in a conflict doomed to failure—in large part because of China's ability to prevent the United States from executing the strategy it needed to win. From China's perspective, this was a textbook case of implementing the principle of the ancient Chinese military strategist Sun Tzu that "the highest realization of warfare is to attack the enemy's plans."[3]

✳✳✳✳✳

The turbulent 1960s also saw an increasingly nationalistic China complain ever more stridently that Czarist Russia had unfairly annexed Chinese territory during its century of humiliation. In 1969, this rising Chinese nationalism would finally boil over into China's second surprise attack on a former ally, this time the Soviet Union.

This particular territorial dispute centered on three small river islands and about twenty thousand square miles of territory along the flanks of the "roof of the world"—the twenty-five-thousand-foot-high Pamir Mountain Range. It is an episode of violence that pointedly illustrates how a relatively small territorial dispute over several small islands can quickly climb the escalatory ladder of nationalistic furor to the brink of nuclear war. Indeed, the Soviets came ever so close to "dropping the big one" on China.[4] In light of the eerily similar nationalistic territorial claims being made by China today over islands in the East and South China Seas, this is indeed a cautionary tale.

In the 1970s, China would turn an important page in its history as a primarily land-based continental power by opening up its first major front in the maritime domain. This it did in the South China Sea in 1974 with the taking of the Paracel Islands from a then severely weakened South Vietnam.

In this particular attack—planned by Chinese premier Zhou Enlai himself—China dispatched troops supported by gunboats to occupy several of the islands claimed by South Vietnam. When Vietnamese commandos tried to retake the islands with the support of four small vessels, China responded with its own "shock and awe" armada of missile-equipped warships—along with precision bombing strikes of the islands.

At the time, the United States was neck deep in its Nixonian rapprochement with China and was desperate to extricate itself from its Vietnam morass. As a result, it refused to intervene on South Vietnam's behalf for fear of offending China, and the outgunned and outmanned South Vietnamese had no other choice but to withdraw. In this way, while the battle of the Paracels remains a very small thread in the fabric of Asian history, it offers a clear case of China using its superior firepower to outgun a weaker ally in the absence of US support.

✶✶✶✶✶

In 1979, China would complete its hat trick of surprise attacks on former allies with a blitzkrieg invasion of northern Vietnam involving hundreds of thousands of troops and hundreds more tanks. In fact, this war was the quite-predictable fruit of a centuries-old bitter enmity between the two countries set against the backdrop of an increasingly strong alliance between Vietnam and what was now China's mortal foe in the Soviet Union.

While China's Vietnam War was exceedingly short, it was grievously long on casualties. In less than one month, China may have lost more troops—some say as many as sixty thousand—than the United States lost in more than a decade in its own Vietnam War. This would not, however, be China's last armed clash with Vietnam.

In 1988, Chinese and Vietnamese forces would once again come face-to-face over another Chinese territorial grab in the South China Sea, this time in the Spratly Islands in a brutal encounter that quickly came to be known as the Johnson South Reef Massacre. Strategically located off the nearby coasts of Brunei, the Philippines, Malaysian Borneo, and Vietnam, the Spratlys are more than six hundred miles from the nearest point on the Chinese mainland.

When China sought to assert its historically based territorial claim to the Spratlys by building an observation post on Fiery Cross Reef, Vietnam responded by sending armed ships to the area. After landing on nearby Johnson South Reef, a number of lightly armed troops then raised the Vietnamese flag in protest of Chinese aggression. Chinese warships proceeded to mercilessly train their high-caliber antiaircraft guns on the protesters and slaughtered over sixty of them.[5] After this massacre, China would take control of six more of the disputed Spratly Islands, including Kennan Reef and Hughes Reef.

In 1994, China would continue its territorial expansionism in the Spratly Islands with its taking of Mischief Reef from the Philippines. In this particular gambit, when the monsoon season kept the Philippine Navy from its normal administrative patrols around Mischief Reef, Chinese naval forces surreptitiously slipped into this administrative void and erected several structures.

At that point, the Philippines could have attempted to intervene militarily to stop what its political leaders angrily denounced as a "creeping invasion."[6] However, having seen what China had violently done to Vietnamese sailors and soldiers in the Battle of the Paracels in 1974 and again in the Johnson South Reef Massacre of 1988, the out-gunned Philippine Navy refused to engage with Chinese forces. In this way, the taking of Mischief Reef quickly became a *fait accompli*.

Just one year later in 1995, China would begin an almost yearlong campaign of intimidation in an attempt to unduly influence Taiwan's first democratic election for its president. This "Third Taiwan Strait Crisis"— the first two crises occurred in the 1950s—included a series of "warning shot" missile tests fired perilously close to Taiwan's major airline routes and shipping lines. It also featured all-out war games that included some "40 naval vessels, 260 aircraft, and an estimated 150,000 troops."[7]

This particular crisis would once again bring China and the United States into direct conflict as President Bill Clinton would order not one but two carrier strike groups to the Taiwan Strait. After China backed down—an unlikely occurrence today—Taiwan's proindependence candidate won a resounding victory, in large part as a backlash against China's bullying.

Fast-forward to 2001 when Chinese and US forces would once again clash, this time about freedom of navigation and overflight in the South China Sea. In this "EP-3 incident," a Chinese fighter jet would collide with a US EP-3 reconnaissance plane, forcing the damaged plane to make a perilous emergency landing on Hainan Island. After ten days of what quickly morphed into an international crisis, the US crew of twenty-four being held hostage was released—but not before China had extracted several humiliating apologies from the United States. In addition, Chinese engineers also successfully extracted critical classified data from the plane's only partially destroyed computer hard drives.

Similar clashes occurred in 2009, 2013, and 2014 between US and Chinese naval forces and have continued to present day. Indeed, these rival naval forces now regularly stalk each other in both the East and South China Seas as well as in the Indian and Pacific Oceans.

Regrettably, relations between Chinese and Japanese military forces are even tenser. At center stage is a long-simmering dispute in the East China Sea over the Senkaku Islands, which Japan has controlled since 1895 but which China has claimed since the late 1960s after potentially large oil and natural gas reserves were discovered.

In 2010, and again in 2012, this long-simmering dispute boiled over into anti-Japanese protests that quite literally burst into flames across more than one hundred Chinese cities. Of growing concern in capitols around Asia is that some type of incident—or accident—may lead to a skirmish that, through a chain reaction, leads to a broader war that drags Japan's treaty ally, the United States, into the fray.

✶✶✶✶✶

It should be clear from this broad sweep of history that since taking power in 1949, the Chinese Communist Party has consistently engaged in repeated acts of aggression and violence over a period spanning more than six decades. When you juxtapose this Chinese history against that of

America's own exceedingly violent modern record, this is indeed a highly combustible mix.

To this point, consider this: Since the birth of the Communist Chinese nation in 1949, the United States has fought major wars in Korea, Vietnam, and Afghanistan; invaded Iraq twice; bombed Bosnia, Cambodia, Libya, Serbia, and Syria; engineered regime changes in Chile, the Dominican Republic, Guatemala, Iran, and Kosovo; conducted major drone strikes in Pakistan and Somalia; dropped combat-equipped forces into Djibouti, Eritrea, Ethiopia, Georgia, Kenya, and Yemen; and this is only a partial list of the American military's reach.

Of course, just as with China's Communist Party leaders, America's presidents and congressmen and secretaries of state and joint chiefs of staff have all sought to justify each of these demonstrations of military force on ideological, humanitarian, or national-security grounds—but the competing moralizations and rationales made by China and the United States make exactly this point. Here, we have two violent and very well-armed nuclear-tipped superpowers squaring off against each other even as an already enormous flow of economic trade between the two nations continues to increase. If you want a working definition of the word "conundrum," it certainly can be found in this relationship.

It is precisely because of this conundrum—and China's arguably malign revisionist intentions—that we must turn now in part 2 of our detective story to an examination of China's growing military capabilities.

Part 2

ASSESSING CAPABILITIES

Chapter 6

SOME SOBERING MILITARY-BUDGET MATH

Question: Who spends more on their military?

1. China
2. The United States

Given our focus on the possible dangers of China's rapid military buildup, you may, be tempted to answer "China" to this question. Please resist any such temptation. While China is swiftly expanding its military capabilities, the United States still far outspends China when it comes to two important metrics: total spending and spending as a percent of gross domestic product or GDP.

On the total spending front, while China's reported annual military expenditures are rapidly heading beyond $200 billion, the United States still spends more than three times that amount.[1] At the same time, over the last ten years, China's military spending has consumed only about 2 percent of its GDP annually while the US number is closer to 4 percent.[2]

Wow! Who is the warmonger here?

In fact, the argument that "America vastly outspends China" is frequently used to discount any possibility of an emerging China threat. It is an argument, however, that must be tempered by more than a few critical considerations.

First and foremost, any direct comparison of total military expenditures is, in and of itself, likely to be highly misleading. While the US military must project its force globally, China focuses primarily on *regional* force projection in Asia. To put this in a weapons context, American taxpayers may foot the bill for ten active aircraft carriers. However, only several of these flattops are ever on patrol in the Asian theater at any one time.

As a second consideration, one dollar of defense spending in China goes much farther than one dollar of defense in the United States. Just why is this so?

For starters, Chinese military personnel earn wages and benefits far less than their American counterparts. In addition, it is demonstrably cheaper for China's factories to churn out weapons systems—and it is not just cheap labor driving this production cost advantage. It's also the lack of any meaningful environmental controls or worker protections—yes, the air and water in China are filthy and the factories are very dangerous, but it *is* a lot cheaper to manufacture everything from autos and home appliances to missiles and submarines.[3]

As an added boost to China's cost advantage, there is also this uncomfortable truth: China does not have to spend anywhere near as much on military research and development for new weapons systems. One key reason is the vaunted ability of Chinese hackers to steal the latest weapons designs from both the Pentagon and private-sector defense contractors. Another reason is that China quite illegally reverse engineers much of the foreign technology it buys.

On this reverse-engineering front, Russia, not America, has been China's biggest victim. After Russia sold China its advanced Sukhoi Su-27 fighter, China proceeded to clone it—and then immediately began selling discounted versions of the jet on the world market, squeezing Russian sales.[4] In a laugh-out-loud moment, when they was accused of also replicating the Sukhoi Su-33 aircraft-carrier-based fighter, China's unintentionally comical defense was that its J-15 clone of the Sukhoi was actually better than the original. That's indeed true—and that's one of the problems facing opponents. China not only can steal foreign technology, it can improve upon it as well.

For all these reasons, it would be wrong to derive much comfort from the fact that Chinese military expenditures appear to fall far below that of America. This is particularly true since the spending trend lines are likely to cross in the not-too-distant future as China's GDP growth continues to significantly outpace that of the United States and as America's economy continues to perform below historical levels.

In fact, once one looks more deeply at the defense-expenditures puzzle, it should not be reassuring at all that China is using much less of its GDP each year to successfully grow its military. Indeed, the economic ease with which China's military is rapidly expanding raises this next—and quite sobering—question: Will China eventually be able to do to America what America did to Kaiser Germany in World War I, Nazi Germany and Imperial Japan in World War II, and the Soviet Union during the Cold War? That is, will China be able to use its superior manufacturing might to defeat America on the battlefield?

In thinking historically about the strategic implications of China's rise and growing size, consider this: At the start of World War II, the combined economies of Nazi Germany and Imperial Japan were only half the size of the United States.[5] If for no other reason than the sheer weight of its factories and work force, America thereby held the strategic high ground.

In fact, the statistical correspondence between economic power and military might in World War II is startling. While the United States could field over three hundred thousand military aircraft, a combined Germany and Japan had less than two hundred thousand. On the naval front, the United States had about three hundred fifty destroyers compared to Japan's sixty-three, while on the land-war front, the United States had over seventy thousand tanks compared to less than forty-five thousand for Germany.[6]

So yes, while it is true that it was brave American soldiers and sailors and flyers at the frontlines who ultimately won World War II, they were backed by heartland factories that could churn out tanks and planes and ships at rates far greater than the enemy could destroy them—definitive proof of the winning ways of what the great Prussian strategist Carl von Clausewitz once aptly referred to as "war by algebra." Today, however, many of those factories that won World War II for America have been shuttered and moved to cities with names like Chengdu, Chongqing, and Shenzhen.

As for the case of the Soviet Union, its fate as a fallen empire may be particularly apropos to the current trajectory of US-China military relations. Just consider this: Back in the Cold War days of the 1980s, President Ronald Reagan adopted a highly aggressive "star wars" strategy to vanquish the Soviet Union based on his Strategic Defense Initiative. What "the Gipper" had in mind, however, was not decisively defeating the Soviet Union on the battlefield. Rather, Reagan wanted to lure the Soviets into an expensive arms race in the hopes of breaking the "evil empire's" economic bank in the process.

As US defense expenditures (and budget deficits!) dramatically rose during the 1980s, Reagan was repeatedly criticized for his hawkish gambit.

However, "the Gipper's" strategy wound up succeeding beyond even the Reaganites' wildish dreams; looking back at the statistics on GDP growth and military expenditures during the period, we now know why.

To wit, in order to play such military spending poker with Reagan, the Soviets had to devote a far larger share of their GDP to defense—some analysts cite a figure as high as 40 percent! It was this crushing defense burden along with the collateral neglect of the other sectors of its economy that ultimately bankrupted the Soviet Union and led to its economic surrender and breakup. In comparing this Soviet fall to China's rise, Princeton professor Aaron Friedberg notes:

> China is a very different kind of military competitor than the Soviet Union was. The Soviet Union for ideological reasons cut itself off from the international trading system, cut itself off to a considerable degree from the global technological system, and tried to do everything on its own. . . . The Chinese are pursuing the inverse strategy. They are plugging themselves into the world economy and into the world technological and scientific systems as deeply as they possibly can. And that's a far smarter strategy and it's enabling them to move forward much more rapidly.[7]

Echoing this "China is not the Soviet Union" theme, Brookings scholar Michael O'Hanlon adds:

> While China's growth may slow down to a seven- or six-percent rate, it's still the fastest growing economy in the world and the number one world manufacturing economy. And that trend is not slowing in the slightest. So the idea that we could somehow just ramp up our efforts and beat the Chinese at producing war ships and fighter jets, I think, is at best a short-term partial fix. [8]

Within the context of our detective story, this sobering assessment brings to mind the advice of hockey great Wayne Gretzky to always skate to where the puck is going to be, not to where it is. To mix metaphors here, China appears to be moving on the global supremacy chessboard to a place where, if left unchecked, the United States may eventually be forced to turn over its king, at least in the Asian theater. Our next question therefore must be: Just what might China's strategy look like over the next several decades to achieve its goals?

Chapter 7

THE GHOST OF ADMIRAL LIU HUAQING HAUNTING ASIA

Question: Does China seek to drive US military forces
 out of Asia?

1. No
2. Yes

I n many ways, this question brings us back to our discussion with Professor John Mearsheimer at the beginning of this book. Recall that he insists that over time, because of the dynamics of great-power politics, China must inevitably seek to be the regional hegemon in Asia as a matter of both self-defense and survival.

If Mearsheimer is right, the answer to the above question must inevitably be *yes*. That is, China can never be the hegemon of Asia as long as the United States remains the dominant power in the region.

The question, of course, about this particular question is whether there is any real evidence beyond the speculation of a mere political scientist to support the provocative assertion that China seeks to drive the US military out of Asia. Perhaps the best place to start looking for such evidence is in the actions, thoughts, and writings of one of the great military folk heroes of China—Admiral Liu Huaqing.

Vietnam best knows Admiral Liu as the commander who ordered the slaughter of Vietnamese sailors and soldiers during China's taking of the Paracel Islands in 1974. In a similarly dark vein, Chinese dissidents first think of Admiral Liu as the commander of the troops responsible for the Tiananmen Square massacre in 1989. These dark-prince clouds on his record notwithstanding, Admiral Liu will likely be best remembered as the father of the modern Chinese navy who once famously quipped that he would "die with his eyes wide open" if China did not have its own aircraft carrier before he passed away.[1]

Fig. 7.1. Admiral Liu Huaqing, the "father" of the modern Chinese navy and architect of the strategy to drive the US out of the Asia-Pacific, meets with Admiral James A. Lyons Jr., commander in chief of the US Pacific Fleet, in 1986 during a ceremony celebrating the first visit by US Navy ships to China in forty years. (Photograph by the Department of Defense, November 1, 1986, from the National Archives and Records Administration.)

For a figure as important as Liu, he is surprisingly obscure outside of China. However, during the 1980s, when Deng Xiaoping was famously converting China into a mercantilist global trader, it was Liu, as Deng's right-hand man, commanding China's navy.

At this propitious time of Deng's economic revolution, China was still primarily a continental power with little perceived need for the global projection of naval power. However, even as Deng was busily opening China to global trade, Admiral Liu was having a "parallel vision."[2] In this vision, Liu could see very clearly that it would eventually fall upon his own navy to protect the global trading routes Deng was busily building; Liu began working in earnest to forge a navy to rise to that globalized China occasion.

In this sense, Liu was very much what Professors James Holmes and Toshi Yoshihara of the US Naval War College have called a "Mahanian" figure. In the nineteenth century, it was Alfred Thayer Mahan—second president of the college and himself the forefather of the modern American navy—who pioneered the concept of global naval force projection as being critical to the economic prosperity of a nation.

In Mahan's world, it was only through the command of the seas that such prosperity could be assured. Such command, in turn, depended on two key parameters: (1) the industrial capacity of a nation to produce sufficient merchant ships and naval fleets to access vital trading routes, and (2) a system of forward bases that could service both merchant and military vessels.

According to Holmes and Yoshihara, while Liu staunchly denied being a follower of the Western imperialist Mahan, his actions have belied his Mahanian intentions.[3] Indeed, it was Liu who first articulated the three-step Mahanian strategy that China appears to be closely following to this day.

In Liu's vision, the critical first step was for China to break out of what he called the "near seas" and the "First Island Chain." As has been noted, this First Island Chain runs from the northern tip of the Kuril Islands, down through the home islands of Japan, all the way to the southern tip of Japan's Okinawan territories. As the centerpiece and rough center point of the First Island Chain, the line defining this chain next passes through Taiwan and then across the Luzon Strait to the Philippines and down to Malaysian Borneo.

Of course, the "First Island Chain" metaphor is just that; there are no real chains strung across the waters of the East and South China Seas. Imaginary though the island chain may be, it is a metaphor that nonetheless weighed heavily on the mind of Admiral Liu, and it continues to be an obsession with Chinese strategists to this day.

In fact, China's focus on breaking out of the First Island Chain is entirely appropriate because of the very real constraints this chain poses for China's navy. One clear problem is that Liu's "near seas" are riddled with choke points; another is that China's surface ships are easily ranged by missiles or fighter jets from American forward bases in countries like Japan, the Philippines, and South Korea.

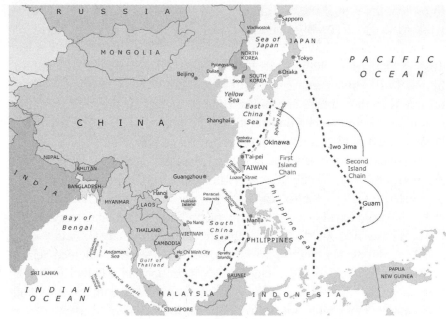

Map 7.1. Map of the First and Second Island Chains.

To Admiral Liu, therefore, it was painfully obvious that the first step to achieving global naval supremacy was to break the bonds of the First Island Chain. As to how that might be done, that will be the topic of our next chapter. For now, know that the second step in Admiral's Liu's recipe for Mahanian supremacy was breaking out of the "Second Island Chain."

This Second Island Chain starts at the midpoint of the Japanese home islands. It then swings out into the Pacific over to the Northern Mariana Islands, which include most notably Saipan. The line of the Second Island Chain next travels to its rough midpoint at Guam. and from there it moves over to Palau, finally ending at Indonesia's Papua Province and Papua, New Guinea.

What each of these Pacific Island links in the Second Island Chain have in common is their strategic importance as "stepping stones" that were used by the US Navy to fight its way back from a bloodied and battered Hawaii through the Pacific to eventually be in a position to bomb the Japanese home islands, and thereby force the Japanese to surrender. This is a history that was certainly not lost on Admiral Liu. Today, Guam—once the site of one of the costliest battles of World War II—looms particularly large as a strategic American base, anchoring the Second Island Chain in much the same way that Taiwan anchors the First Island Chain.

For Admiral Liu, the goal was to break out of this Second Island Chain by the year 2020, and the now-aircraft-carrier-equipped Chinese navy appears well on its way to hitting this target. Liu, no doubt, is lying in his grave both with his eyes firmly shut and a smile on his face.

As for the third step in Admiral Liu's strategy was for China to achieve *global* naval supremacy by the year 2050. In fact, the scope of Admiral Liu's vision was absolutely breathtaking given that he articulated this vision back in an era when the Chinese navy was more akin to a coast guard than a global fighting fleet.

Today, there is considerable evidence both from Chinese military documents and from Western military analysts that China's strategic path is closely following Admiral Liu's three-step blueprint.[4] Unfortunately for the cause of peace, this is a blueprint that by definition is a zero-sum game. Indeed, if China succeeds in breaking out of the First and Second Island Chains and commanding global waters, it will only be able to do so through the defeat—or acquiescence—of the US Navy.

Chapter 8

THE GAME-CHANGING AIRCRAFT-CARRIER KILLER

Question: Just how hard is it to hit an aircraft carrier traveling at 30 knots in open water with a missile launched from a thousand miles away?

1. Hard
2. Very Hard
3. Almost Impossible

This form of missile attack is in fact so difficult that only one nation in the world has (maybe) been able to figure out how to do it—China. Like the advent of the English Longbow and trebuchet in medieval times, frame-torpedo mines in the American Civil War, machine guns and tanks in World War I, and combat aircraft and aircraft carriers in World War II, the arrival of China's "antiship ballistic missile" onto the world's weapons stage is a truly game-changing event that now threatens to upset the entire balance of power in Asia.[1]

At present, this increasingly tenuous balance of power between a rising China and much of the rest of Asia rests on the presence of American aircraft-carrier strike groups and US forward bases in the region. However, if China's antiship ballistic missile can indeed destroy American carriers—there remains at least some conjecture about this—the entire foundation of America's projection of power into the Asian theater would be destroyed as well. In the process, China would finally realize the strategic dream of Admiral Liu Huaqing to break out of the First and Second Island Chains within which, at least from China's view, China is now contained by a hegemonic American sea power.

To better understand the game-changing significance of China's antiship ballistic missile, let's first do a little *Missiles 101*. As a general rule, there are two types of missiles that can carry either conventional or nuclear warheads.

Cruise missiles are typically propelled throughout their flight not by rockets but by small jet engines. Such cruise missiles never leave the earth's atmosphere. They must be powered by their engines throughout their flight, and they often fly very low to the ground, following the earth's contours to avoid detection.

In contrast, *ballistic* missiles are initially rocket powered in the first stage of their journey, and they are typically launched into a high suborbital spaceflight above the earth's atmosphere. In this rarefied air, ballistic missiles can then travel in free-space flight without substantial need of fuel, often for considerable distances; this is their great advantage over typically much less expensive cruise missiles. When a ballistic missile is ready to acquire its target, it goes into free fall in its reentry stage into the earth's atmosphere, gaining great and deadly speed in the process.

The engineering feat China's antiship ballistic missile accomplishes is this: Once the missile falls back toward Earth, it can quickly lock on to a relatively small target in a very big sea—like an aircraft carrier or destroyer—and even take evasive action on the way to destroying that target with great precision. It's not for nothing that China's civilian and military leaders alike openly call this game-changing new weapon their "carrier killer."[2]

In truth, China's antiship ballistic missile is just one of a broader class of "asymmetric weapons," like cruise missiles, relatively inexpensive diesel-electric submarines, mines, and even small, missile-equipped high-speed catamarans. These weapons are "asymmetric" in the sense they cost very little relative to the high-value targets they seek to destroy.

For example, an antiship ballistic missile launched from the Chinese mainland or a conventional cruise missile fired from a fast-moving catamaran may cost China a few million dollars, but each has the firepower to destroy a $10 billion US aircraft carrier.[3] And let's not forget the five thousand American souls that would perish with a direct hit.

On this point, Georgetown University lecturer and former Pentagon insider Phillip Karber observes:

> We have the world's strongest navy. Our navy today could probably take on all the other navies in the world and win in a conventional war,

including against the Chinese and Russians. But, the Chinese have been playing [it] smart. They have been developing what's called asymmetric weapons like the anti-ship ballistic missile which may be able to hold our naval fleet hostage. And that means we will have less and less ability to bring that naval power to bear locally.[4]

Fig. 8.1. Taking dead aim at a US carrier at sea is a launcher for China's "carrier killer" missile—the DF-21. (Photograph from informationdissemination.net.)

It is precisely the asymmetric nature of China's expanding military arsenal—coupled with its growing technological capabilities to pull off feats like hitting an aircraft carrier at sea—that is causing so much consternation within both the Pentagon and the many countries of Asia that depend on the United States aircraft-carrier fleet to defend their interests. In fact, China's almost obsessive focus on neutralizing America's aircraft-carrier strike groups aptly highlights a great cultural and geopolitical divide between two nuclear-tipped military superpowers now aggressively jockeying for strategic position—with both superpowers increasingly uncomfortable in each other's midst.

On one side of this divide is a China forged in the crucible of a century of humiliation at the hands of foreign powers. From this vantage point, China sees its growing arsenal of asymmetric weapons as a purely *defensive* military buildup designed to execute what it calls a "counterintervention" strategy, the goal of which is simply to protect the Chinese mainland, and particularly the vast wealth along the Chinese coast.[5]

Of course, the United States sees China's counterintervention from an entirely different perspective—and even refers to it by a different name. To US military analysts, China is practicing a strategy of "anti-access, area denial" that is primarily offensive, rather than defensive, in nature.[6]

This strategy is also highly escalatory in that it both seeks to drive US forces out of Asian waters (the area-denial component) and then ensures those forces don't come back (the anti-access piece).

To an American nation founded on the principle of freedom of the seas—and to a country that relies heavily on trade for its prosperity—China's "anti-access, area denial" gambit is simply unacceptable. Inevitably, red lines in the sand and seas are going to be drawn and crossed—and the prospect of war will likely rise.

It must be said very clearly at this point, however, that the likely goal of China in developing its suite of asymmetric weapons is not necessarily to sink American ships. Rather, in the spirit of Sun Tzu's *Art of War* maxim that the highest goal is to "win without fighting," China is simply seeking to make America believe it *can* sink its carriers *if* it needs to.

In this way, China is not trying to put up what US Naval War College professor James Holmes calls a "hard shield" to "keep the US Navy completely out of theater."[7] Rather, it is simply raising the perceived costs and risks of American ships operating in Asian waters—and it is thereby making the bet that an already war-weary America will ultimately cut and run without a fight.

We can see, then, that by pursuing its counterintervention strategy, China is not just taking its cue from the East and Sun Tzu. The strategy also epitomizes the thoroughly Western thinking of Carl von Clausewitz's "war by algebra." In the spirit of this renowned Prussian military theorist, China is presenting the United States with a classic problem in cost-benefit analysis that forces US policymakers and military commanders to ask this uncomfortable question: Are the economic and national-security benefits of being in Asia worth the now significantly increasing risks and attendant costs to American naval forces and American forward bases? In a strictly Clausewitzian "war by algebra" world, as China's power grows, America must increasingly answer "no" to this critical question—or so the Chinese thinking goes.

Here, US Naval War College professor Toshi Yoshihara explains how Sun Tzu's East may one day meet Clausewitz's West in the contested waters and skies of the Asia-Pacific. Says Yoshihara:

> [China's] goal is not to inflict a massive military defeat on US naval forces. Rather, it is to change the strategic political calculus inside the White House so that the perceptions of the increased costs and risks of intervening in Asia induces decision-makers to hesitate, hem and haw, and delay decision-making to such an extent that it creates enough time for China to resolve any conflict in its favor. This will create new reality on the ground such that it becomes irreversible; and therefore, this fulfills what the Chinese are hoping to do, which is to win without fighting, essentially, to create this "no-go zone" such that no shot is fired in anger in the first place.[8]

It is precisely because of the possibility of such a grim outcome—and because China's new antiship ballistic missile is acting as the escalatory tip of the Chinese spear—that the United States, with the assistance of allies like Japan and Australia, is introducing far more advanced missile-defense systems into the region. Of course, the importation of these AMD systems into the theater is, in and of itself, likewise escalatory because China's likely response will be to simply build more missiles in an attempt to "swarm" and thereby overwhelm any such systems—a classic case of a "security dilemma" arms race playing out before our eyes.

Note, however, that the introduction of American advanced missile-defense systems in response to China's growing missile threat is not just escalatory. It is also highly destabilizing. This is because a US missile shield may not just neutralize China's conventional missile arsenal, it also, inevitably, and perhaps quite unintentionally, will threaten China's nuclear "second strike" capability. This is highly destabilizing because it is just such a second-strike nuclear capability that is the foundation of nuclear "mutually assured destruction" deterrence, that is, "if I can second strike you back with deadly nuclear missiles, you won't strike me first."

Fig. 8.2. Chinese mobile missile launchers—for taking dead aim at American aircraft carriers with the DF-21 "carrier killer" missile—on parade in Tiananmen Square. (Photograph from Naval Open Source INTelligence.)

In fact, this observation on nuclear deterrence is a perfect segue to our next chapter on one of the most vexing and destabilizing nuclear-tipped elements of the Chinese military landscape—its feared "Underground Great Wall."

Chapter 9

THE UNDERGROUND GREAT WALL OF CHINA

Question: How many nuclear warheads does China have
stockpiled beneath its "Underground Great Wall"?

1. 30
2. 300
3. 3,000

The truly scary part here is that it is difficult to know the answer to this question. However, if the rumors and conjectures about China's vaunted "Underground Great Wall" are even remotely true, China will likely win this nuclear warhead contest hands down—if not today, then certainly in the coming decades. As the *Bulletin of the Atomic Scientists* warns: "Today, China is the only one of five original nuclear weapons states that is increasing its nuclear arsenal."[1]

To understand the breadth, depth, and significance of China's emerging nuclear-warhead threat, it is useful to return to a little *Missiles 101*. In a nutshell, there are three main classes of missiles by range and reach for the world to worry about.

First and most forebodingly, there are the *strategic* missiles. These are the long-range intercontinental ballistic missiles or "ICBMs" that form the backbone of a country's nuclear strike and deterrence capabilities. With a range of between three thousand and ten thousand miles,[2] the most sophisticated ICBMs are capable of reaching any point on the planet from any other point—say, from Szechuan Province to Los Angeles, or from Minot, North Dakota, to Beijing.

In contrast, *tactical missiles* have a range of usually less than two hundred miles and are designed primarily for short-range battlefield applications. As their big advantages, tactical missiles can provide deeper strikes than conventional artillery while being very difficult to defend against. Tactical missiles are also relatively cheap and can deliver anything from conventional high-explosive warheads or nuclear warheads to chemical or biological payloads—the undear-departed Saddam Hussein's "Scuds" are a prime example.

Finally, *theater missiles* fill in the distance gap between strategic and tactical weapons. They range from around two hundred miles to more than two thousand miles, and they are designed to hit targets literally "in theater"—meaning within the region of a country like China. For example, China would use its theater missiles to strike targets in Guam, India, Japan, the Philippines, South Korea, or Vietnam.

Besides the distinction of missiles by distance, it is also useful to think about how such missiles can be launched. In the old days of the Cold War, both the Soviet Union and the United States set their nuclear-tipped ICBMs into fixed-point silos "hardened" with tons of cement and steel. However, as technology has improved, fixed silos have become much easier to pinpoint from space with the Global Positioning System while silo-seeking missiles have become so accurate they can literally blow the doors off a fixed silo. As a result, countries like Russia and China—the United States still lags far behind—have moved to a "whack-a-mole" system of mobile launch sites that makes it far more difficult for an enemy to take out their nuclear arsenals.

Finally, there is an important distinction between how the rockets that propel the missiles are fueled. In the old days, this was strictly a liquid-fuel game. The problem with liquid-fueled rockets, however, is that they take a relatively long time to prepare for launch, and during that time, they are highly vulnerable to being detected and destroyed on the ground. Solid-fuel rockets, on the other hand, solve this problem as they can be launched much faster than liquid-fueled rockets—within seconds or mere minutes—and they are also much safer and easier to store.

✶✶✶✶✶

Given this *Missiles 101* checklist, let's get back to our question of how China stacks up when it comes to its nuclear-warhead capabilities. But of course this question also gets us back to the problem of a lack of transparency in China's nuclear-weapons program. Such a lack of transparency is in sharp contrast to both the United States and Russia, which have worked hard to use the arms-control treaty process to reduce the prospects of nuclear war.

That process began in earnest in 1991 when the United States and Russia's predecessor, the Soviet Union, signed the first Strategic Arms Reduction Treaty known as "START." This treaty limited each country's nuclear arsenal to six thousand warheads deliverable by no more than a total of 1,600 ICBMs and bombers. By 2001, this treaty had "resulted in the removal of about 80 percent of all strategic nuclear weapons then in existence"[3]—by any measure, an astonishing success.

After the first START agreement expired in 2009, the United States and Russia entered into a New START agreement in 2011 that further reduced the nuclear arsenals of both countries. This even more stringent new treaty set aggregate limits on the numbers of deployed intercontinental ballistic missiles to seven hundred, slashed the number of nuclear warheads on deployed ICBMs to 1,550, and halved the combined number of launchers and heavy bombers allowed to eight hundred.[4]

While the START process has gone a long way toward reducing the nuclear stockpiles of the two former cold warriors, China has steadfastly refused to meaningfully participate in any form of arms reduction. Instead, China has used the occasion—and cover—of these treaties to develop its own missile and warhead capabilities across a broad spectrum without any apparent constraint. As former Pentagon advisor and Georgetown University lecturer Phillip Karber notes:

> The Chinese today have the largest range of nuclear-capable missiles of any country in the world. And what I mean by that is they can go from very short range to intercontinental. We and the Russians, under the Intermediate Nuclear Forces Treaty abolished an entire class of medium and theater missiles. . . . So the Chinese are unique, they have the entire spectrum of these missiles.[5]

At the center of China's development of long-range precision-strike nuclear missiles is the Second Artillery Corps, with its vaunted Underground Great Wall. The Second Artillery Corps itself begins with its own bit of deception and misdirection. It was established as the "second" rather than "first" corps by Premier Zhou Enlai back in 1966 as a means of concealing its importance to the outside world; its true mission was only revealed publicly in 1984. That mission is to run China's complete missile arsenal—both ballistic and cruise as well as conventional and nuclear.

The centerpiece of the Second Artillery Corps' missile strategy is indeed its Underground Great Wall. Construction on what essentially is a maze of underground tunnels wide and high enough to accommodate large trucks commenced back in the late 1960s as China first began to develop its nuclear weapons program. Today, this network features over three thousand miles of truck and rail routes crisscrossing the country, and these routes are fully capable of transporting mobile missiles and launchers at speeds of up to sixty miles an hour. As Professor Karber, America's foremost Underground Great Wall expert, notes: "China's trucks and trains can get to a spot and have their missiles ready to fire in about fifteen minutes. They feel pretty safe with that because by the time our satellites might detect that activity, they have already launched."[6]

Nor is the existence of this Underground Great Wall a matter of speculation. Rather, this stunning facility was revealed with great fanfare on Chinese national television as far back as 2006.

What is a matter of speculation is the number of nuclear warheads China may be hiding within this vast and opaque web of nuclear-strike capabilities. At the conservative end of the spectrum, the Pentagon has consistently estimated that China has no more than 240 to 400 nuclear warheads.[7] However, Karber issued a report in 2013 raising the possibility that China may have as many as three thousand nuclear warheads stored within its Underground Great Wall. If true, China's total number of warheads would be roughly equal to the *combined* American and Russian arsenals allowed under the new START agreement.[8]

While Karber's study was roundly criticized in some quarters for exaggeration—one representative from the Union of Concerned Scientists called it "ridiculous" and "lazy"[9]—such criticism misses the broader point that China's nuclear-warhead development is proceeding apace in total secrecy and without limits. Such criticism also ignores the fact that China is perfecting a land-based delivery system that is virtually impregnable. Moreover, the incredible mobility of China's strike force in moving nuclear weapons at high speeds underground to different launch sites adds further to the "whack-a-mole" difficulty of neutralizing such a strike force. In comparison, America's land-based nuclear weapons are almost exclusively housed in fixed silos with locations widely publicized on internet sites like Google.

There is one other important consideration for our detective story when it comes to China's Underground Great Wall: Because no one knows just how many missiles China has hidden, this lack of transparency has become a potent tool of coercive Chinese power. Indeed, when news of the existence of China's missile-tunnels program broke, many countries throughout Asia expressed both fear and alarm.

At the same time, because no one outside of China really does know how many nuclear missiles and warheads actually exist, China can dismiss any claims of large stockpiles as greatly exaggerated. In this way, China can have it both ways—stockpile what it may want but plausibly deny any large stockpiles.

Chapter 10

THE MISSILES "R" US
OF THE WORLD

Question: Which country has the largest, and most diverse,
conventional-missile arsenal in the world?

1. China
2. Russia
3. The United States

While there is considerable speculation as to the size of China's strategic-nuclear-missile arsenal, there is far more agreement on this fact: China has become, in the colorful words of journalist Bill Gertz, the "Missiles "R" Us" of the world.[1]

In fact, the buildup of China's nonnuclear conventional missiles has followed logically from its strategic commitment to a relatively inexpensive asymmetric-weapons strategy as well as historically from Chairman Mao Zedong's tactical preference for "swarming" or overwhelming an enemy.

China's missile focus has also followed inevitably from its assessment of the Asia-Pacific chessboard. Notes the *Economist* magazine on this point in describing missiles as "the pillar of China's military modernization":

After awesome demonstrations of American firepower, in Operation Desert Storm in the first Gulf war, and then in 1996, when the United States sailed two carrier strike groups close to Taiwan to deter Chinese aggression, China felt that it could no longer depend on sheer manpower for its defense. So it has invested heavily in the strength and technical sophistication of its missiles.[2]

As for the nature of the Chinese missile threat itself, journalists these days have tended to become fixated on China's new carrier-killing antiship ballistic missile, while experts like Professors Bernard Cole of America's National Defense University and Lyle Goldstein of the US Naval War College believe that the cruise missile, which has been around for a very long time, may ultimately be even more dangerous.

To Cole, the emerging and "very challenging" China cruise-missile threat comes not from China's ability to produce vast numbers of increasingly faster and more sophisticated missiles. Rather, this threat ultimately comes from China's development of "space-based assets and other sorts of radars" that allow China to far more accurately detect and track its targets.[3]

Here, Professor Goldstein drills down on some of the dangers of one particular type of Chinese cruise missile—the antiship cruise missile. Says Goldstein:

> [S]ome of the latest versions of Chinese antiship cruise missiles are superior in range and speed to American systems like the Harpoon missile, which is not as capable. So this is an area where they're ahead of us, and that's very disturbing. But another aspect that's disturbing is just how many different ways China can deploy its cruise missiles, whether it be through missile catamarans, very capable surface ships, and also submarines.[4]

As for the numbers themselves, Taiwan alone is reported to be in the crosshairs of over 1,500 Chinese missiles[5]—a likely overkill if there ever were one but more likely simply a coercive tool to deter Taiwan from ever declaring its independence. On this point, Mark Stokes of the International Assessment and Strategy Center laconically notes:

> As early as 1993, all the way up until the present day, whoever sits in the presidential office within Taiwan, in essence, is within seven minutes of destruction. And so that puts a certain psychological pressure upon the population.[6]

Taiwan, however, is hardly the only Chinese target with a Maoist swarm of missiles pointed at it. Consider, for example, the plight of Japan, which is now locked in an increasingly contentious territorial dispute over the Senkaku/Diaoyu Islands in the East China Sea.[7] As Professor Goldstein describes the potential battlefield:

When we look at the breakdown of how different capabilities would alter the strategic balance in, say, the East China Sea, to me, the Japanese navy faces a very grave threat from land-based [missile] systems. For example, the anti-ship cruise missiles based on [China's] shore could range Japanese naval units in the vicinity of the Senkaku/Diaoyu Islands and could, I think, probably decisively defeat them. So the cruise missile threat is huge; and one concern I have is that the focus purely on anti-ship ballistic missiles probably may, in effect, take our eye off the ball, which is the cruise missile threat.[8]

Beyond Taiwan, there is also the increasing vulnerability of America's forward bases stretched along the First and Second Island Chains. While America's reasonably mobile aircraft carriers have at least a fighting chance of evading China's antiship missiles, America's fixed forward bases are, in effect, sitting ducks for GPS precision-guided pounding Chinese salvos. They are also likely very dead ducks if America's missile-defense systems fail because virtually—and perhaps inexplicably—none of America's forward bases are "hardened" with sufficient amounts of concrete and steel to any significant degree against missile attack.

This threat is becoming all the more dire because China is not just churning out more and more missiles from its factory floor. It is also constantly on the march to develop new and ever–more-deadly missiles. One case in point is China's hypersonic glide vehicle, first tested in 2014. This missile is capable of reaching speeds of up to Mach 10—that's ten times the speed of sound or 7,700 miles per hour. [9]

It's not just the speed of this missile that makes it so dangerous. As *Aviation Week* grimly explains: A hypersonic glide missile can also "execute a pull-up maneuver after entering the atmosphere and approach its target in a relatively flat glide. It will therefore be detected later than a ballistic warhead [so] there is less time to react." Furthermore, "because the hypersonic glide missile can maneuver aerodynamically, it is [also] much harder to hit."[10]

As an equally alarming case in point, there is also the new DF-31B, a road-mobile, intercontinental ballistic-missile system, specifically designed for traversing through and hiding within China's rough and remote mountainous region. As Bill Gertz notes: "Mobile missiles are considered a greater strategic threat because tracking their location and targeting them in a conflict is very difficult."[11]

✱✱✱✱✱

With respect to our core "will there be war" question, it is hard to deny that China's growing missile capabilities are becoming both highly destabilizing and highly escalatory. Perhaps the biggest problem here is that a Chinese mainland bristling with missiles threatens to undermine, if not outright destroy, the twin pillars of American force projection in Asia—aircraft-carrier strike groups and forward bases.

China's growing missile threat thereby leads to one of the most perplexing questions now confronting America's Pentagon and White House: What should be the US response if China uses its conventional-missile arsenal to launch a first strike attack from the Chinese mainland against American aircraft carriers or forward bases? Should America strike the mainland back with conventional weapons at the risk of sparking an escalatory spiral that might lead to a nuclear exchange? Or is there an alternative response that might preserve America's forward position in Asia without triggering nuclear war?

This question is at the core of a growing debate between two competing schools of strategic thought. One "Air-Sea Battle" school does indeed sanction retaliatory strikes on the mainland. A second school goes by varying names such as "Offshore Control" and "War-at-Sea," and it seeks to counter Chinese aggression through a naval blockade and economic strangulation.

We will drill down into the wisdom—or perhaps lack thereof—of each of these possible responses to Chinese aggression in later chapters. For now, let's continue with our inventorying of Chinese capabilities, beginning with mine warfare.

Chapter 11

ANY SHIP CAN BE A
MINESWEEPER—ONCE

Question: What percent of American naval ships sunk or
seriously damaged since the end of World War II
were struck by mines?

1. 0%
2. 20%
3. 40%
4. 80%

The *US Naval War College Review* is not exactly known for its comedy,
but in a seminal article, analyst Scott Truver managed several intro-
ductory quips that perfectly capture the acute danger that mine warfare
poses. To wit: "A mine is a terrible thing that waits," and "any ship can be
a minesweeper—once."[1]

As to our lead question above, since the end of World War II, a total
of nineteen American naval ships have been sunk or seriously damaged by
hostile forces. While missiles, torpedoes, small aircraft, and smaller boats
all had their day in that sinking sun, mines accounted for fully fifteen of the
mission kills—just about 80 percent.

It's not really the sinking of ships *per se* that makes the mine such a
powerful weapon. Rather, it is the psychological impact mines have on the
battlefield and their collateral ability to terrorize, and thereby paralyze, an
opposing navy.

To understand this impact, imagine you own a sprawling five-thou-
sand-acre ranch; then further imagine that you know that just a single land
mine capable of blowing off your legs has been planted somewhere on your
property. How inclined would you be to hike your acreage? And just how

much time and money would it take to "sweep" for that needle-in-a-hay-stack mine before you found it and resumed your unrestricted activities?

In fact, the primary purpose of mine warfare is to deny access to an area through a combination of psychological terror and the lengthy time it takes to effectively sweep mines. In this way, mines represent the epitome of an asymmetric weapon designed to execute an area-denial strategy—and mines thereby fit like hand in glove into China's emerging war-fighting capabilities.

The ability of mine warfare to terrorize and paralyze is readily apparent in a long history that Chinese strategists themselves have meticulously studied. In fact, America—both as a mine perpetrator and as a mine victim—has taught China much of what it is now operationalizing on the battlefield today.

On the "America as perpetrator" front, one of the most effective strategies used by the United States in the Vietnam War was the mining of Haiphong Harbor. On May 8th, 1972, during Operation Pocket Money, American planes from the aircraft carrier *Coral Sea* dropped what would be the first of over eleven thousand mines into the waters of North Vietnam's most important seaport.[2] By paralyzing shipping lanes, this mine gambit effectively cut off over 80 percent of imports into North Vietnam—and this economic blow had a good bit to do with getting North Vietnam back to the Paris bargaining table.

Chinese strategists likewise have closely studied the important contribution that mine warfare played in forcing Japan's unconditional surrender at the end of World War II. Here, while the atomic bombs dropped on Hiroshima and Nagasaki typically take all the credit for Japan's surrender, the aerial laying of more than twelve thousand mines by B-29 bombers around Japan's home islands also played an important supporting role.

In noting the effectiveness of what was accurately dubbed Operation Starvation, Rear Admiral Kenneth Veth calculates that "the total tonnage of Japanese shipping sunk or damaged by mines in the last six months of the war"—over a million tons —was "greater than that which can be attributed to all other agents combined, including submarines, ships' gunfire, and Allied bombing."[3] Veth goes on to point out that based on interviews with Japanese civilians and military leaders, it is clear that this mine warfare campaign did indeed play a significant role in Japan's surrender.

This kind of "paralysis by mines" echoes an earlier era when, during the Korean War, North Korea deployed more than three thousand mines and thereby "utterly frustrated an October 1950 assault on Wonsan by a 250-ship United Nations amphibious task force."[4] Rear Admiral Allen Smith perfectly captured the frustration of the moment when he grimly quipped: "We have lost control of the seas to a nation without a navy, using pre-World War weapons, laid by vessels that were utilized at the time of the birth of Christ."[5]

As for Scott Truver's minesweeper joke leading off this chapter, it may be useful to add here that during the attempt to sweep the North Korean mines, three minesweepers were sunk, five destroyers were severely damaged, and over a hundred sailors were killed or wounded.

What has perhaps been most informative to Chinese strategists about these American experiences is just how effective extremely low-cost mines can be at destroying very high-cost capital ships. Mines truly are the weapon of choice for a "poor man's navy"—and the epitome of asymmetric warfare.

On this point, consider that during the First Gulf War in 1991, one single Italian-made Iraqi mine costing a mere $25,000 scored a mission kill on the billion-dollar USS *Princeton*. This vessel is one of the most sophisticated of America's Aegis cruisers,[6] and the irony of its crippling is that while the *Princeton* was scanning the horizon and the skies above for Iraqi Scud missiles, it was felled by a lowly mine with no Iraqi naval vessel within fifty miles of it.

While mines may be the ultimate weapon for a poor man's navy like that of Iraq or Iran, put in the hands of a rising superpower like China, mines can be truly devastating. This is not just because China can afford to stockpile vast quantities of them—it claims to have over fifty thousand mines and the world's largest inventory;[7] China has also brought to bear its increasing technological prowess to develop and deploy a whole range of new and innovative smart mines. By China's own admission, this arsenal consists of over thirty varieties of contact, magnetic, acoustic, water-pressure, remote-control, mobile, and rocket-rising mines.[8]

Just consider the rocket-rising mine: Hidden in waters as deep as six thousand feet, this deadly spear lies in wait for its computer to recognize any one of a number of signatures of a passing military ship—acoustic, electric, magnetic, or pressure. After ten large cargo ships might go by, along with four more civilian oil tankers and hundreds of fishing boats, a Japanese destroyer or a US nuclear-powered submarine comes within range and presto, the rising mine is lifted by rocket to close to its target through the water at speeds of over 175 miles per hour.[9]

Fig. 11.1. The PLA Navy practices laying down mines in the busiest global trading route in the world. (Photograph courtesy of China Defense Forum.)

✳✳✳✳✳

Beyond the matter of China's rapidly expanding mine-warfare capabilities, there is this disturbing—and highly destabilizing—aspect of China's area-denial mine strategy. To wit: Rather than rely solely on military planes, ships, and submarines to seed its mines, China is actively recruiting its vast, putatively "non-combatant" civilian fishing fleet to the effort. As US Naval War College professors Andrew Erickson, Lyle Goldstein, and William Murray note: "Chinese writings frequently mention the incorporation of civilian shipping into naval service for such functions as mine warfare."[10]

In this vein, Chinese military analyst Hai Lin offers this sobering math: "China currently has 30,000 iron-hulled mechanized fishing trawlers" and "each vessel can carry 10 mines." In addition, "there are another 50,000 sail-fishing craft," and "each can carry two to five sea mines." Similarly, Chinese scholar Ying Nan extols the virtues of using civilian vessels because they "offer sufficient numbers, 'small targets,' reasonable mobility, and unsuspicious profiles." Of course, such a blurring of the line between civilian and military ships runs totally contrary to international norms.[11]

As to just exactly what China wants to achieve strategically with its arsenal of mines, there are numerous possibilities. For example, as Professors Erickson, Goldstein, and Murray write: "In a conflict over the Spratly Islands [in the South China Sea], Beijing could choose to reinforce its claims to specific islands with carefully limited minefields as an alternative to a prolonged, expensive, and potentially more provocative surface warship presence."[12]

Similarly, mines would no doubt play a lead role in any attempt to take Taiwan by force. The likely targets "would be Taiwan's ports, most of which are highly susceptible to mining, given the shallow waters that surround most of Taiwan."[13] In fact, with its large mine arsenal, the Chinese navy "is already fully capable of blockading Taiwan and other crucial sea lines of communication in the Western Pacific area."[14]

As we shall see in the next chapter, however, China's rapidly growing mine-warfare capabilities are hardly the only undersea threats raising the temperature of Asian waters.

Chapter 12

NUKES AT SEA AND SLEEPLESS IN SEATTLE

Question: Are Chinese ballistic-missile submarines now capable of striking American cities like Seattle, Chicago, and New York with nuclear warheads?

1. No
2. Yes

As every World War II–movie buff knows, one of the purposes of submarines is to attack and sink enemy ships. However, a second and arguably far more important role for the sub in this modern age is to serve as a critical component of a nation's nuclear-strike capabilities and therefore its nuclear deterrence.

As we briefly discussed in an earlier chapter, the concept of nuclear deterrence rests, first and foremost, on the reliability of a country's "second strike" capabilities. To wit: If I can strike your major cities back with a devastating salvo of nuclear missiles after you strike my cities first, you will be far less inclined to launch that first strike to begin with.

In fact, China and the United States have historically been characterized by starkly different levels of second-strike capabilities—with America the clear leader on this critical front. However, as American bard Bob Dylan's song says, "the times, they are a-changin'."

Consider first, then, the American side of the deterrence ledger. Its second-strike capability certainly includes both land-based intercontinental ballistic missiles and long-range bombers. However, it is America's nuclear-powered ballistic-missile submarines—known as SSBNs (Ship, Submersible, Ballistic, Nuclear)—that arguably provide the most assured destruction in America's deterrent triad. Just why is this so?

Well, as previously noted, in today's high-tech Global-Positioning-System world, America's land-based missiles can now be far more easily destroyed in their fixed silos by precision strikes. At the same time, America's aging bomber fleet has become more and more vulnerable to the increasingly sophisticated air-defense systems of potential nuclear rivals like China and Russia.

In contrast, America's nuclear-powered submarine fleet suffers from no such vulnerabilities. With their supreme stealth capabilities and concomitant ability to travel ultra-long distances without surfacing, US subs are able to lurk in deep waters quite literally out in the middle of the ocean—but well within range of any country that may think about sending a first nuclear strike in America's direction. In this way, the fourteen vessels in the US fleet of ballistic-missile nuclear submarines have been America's best sentry dating back many decades to the earliest days of the Cold War.

Fig. 12.1. A Chinese Jin-class ballistic-missile nuclear submarine armed with Julang-2 missiles capable of hitting any city in America with nuclear warheads. (Photograph used with permission from REUTERS/ Guang Niu/Pool.)

Of course, this "second strike at sea" situation has been quite the opposite for China, which historically has been unable to field a modern nuclear-submarine fleet. However, this particular strategic calculus radically changed in 2014 when China finally reached critical mass in the development and deployment of its new Jin-class ballistic-missile submarine. Longer than a football field, this Type 094 sub is capable of launching up to sixteen Julang-2 missiles with a range of up to 7,500 miles.

And here's some sobering math: China may have as many as five Jin-class submarines operational; and if each of their sixteen JL-2 missiles can indeed deliver up to four warheads each, as some analysts suggest, this would give China a combined ability to fire over three hundred nuclear warheads toward American soil[1]—thus giving the phrase "sleepless in Seattle" a whole new twist.

Fig. 12.2 China's "James Bond" underground base hiding ballistic-missile nuclear submarines that can hit Seattle and Los Angeles with nuclear warheads. (Photograph by DigitalGlobe/Scapeware3d. Used with permission from Getty Images.)

As for the actual threat China's new ballistic-missile nuclear subs may pose, some critics have sharply questioned their stealth capabilities. For example, George Washington University professor Amitai Etzioni dismisses China's naval arsenal in general as "junk" and discounts their submarines as "very loud."[2] In a similar, but more clinical fashion, researcher Christian Conroy claims that the Jin-class boats create "a detectable sonar signature,"[3] while Professor T. X. Hammes of America's National Defense University just calls them "pretty noisy."[4]

Note, however, a newer and quieter Type 096 Tang-class model is already in development—so China's newfound ability to field a credible second-strike capability should therefore not be underestimated. Seth Cropsey of the Hudson Institute has framed the need for caution:

> Although their submarines are not as good as ours, they're inventive, imaginative, ingenious and excellent at copying; and I expect that they will turn out better and better boats in the future.[5]

It should also be noted that China's new ballistic-missile submarines can only function properly as a deterrent if they can freely and secretly roam from their Hainan Island base into the deeper waters of the Pacific—and thereby range much closer to American shores. However, to reach the relative safety of the Pacific, China's nuclear subs must first squeeze through any one of a number of choke points along the boundaries of the First Island Chain. During this run for deep waters, China's subs are therefore just as vulnerable to interdiction by American attack subs as America's ICBM fixed silos may now be to Chinese long-range precision-missile strikes. In contrast, American nuclear subs have no such choke-point worries because ports like Newport News and San Diego offer almost immediate deepwater access.

It is precisely because China believes it must break the bonds of the First Island Chain that China is building its relatively small fleet of ballistic missile nuclear submarines. However, to this end, China is also rapidly accumulating the largest, and most lethal, fleet of conventional diesel-electric submarines in the world. As we shall see in the next chapter, these diesel-electric boats may well pose an even greater danger to America and its allies than China's nascent nuclear-submarine fleet.

Chapter 13

CHINESE SUBS LAY IN WAIT— WITH EUROPE'S COMPLICITY

Question: Which countries have helped China deploy a conventional diesel-electric submarine fleet increasingly capable of destroying American, Japanese, and Vietnamese naval vessels?

1. France
2. Germany
3. Russia
4. All of the above

The diesel-electric sub first came to deadly prominence during the U-boat reign of terror in World War II, and it may rightfully be called one of the world's first hybrid vehicles. Diesel engines not only provide propulsion; they also run generators to charge a companion bank of electric motors. These much-quieter electric motors can then provide far-stealthier (albeit much slower) propulsion once the submarine is submerged.

Until recently, the primary rap against the diesel-electric sub has been that it has to surface (or at least "snorkel") every few days to exchange stale air for fresh air and to use its diesel engines to recharge its batteries. The big problem here is that diesel engines are highly "air dependent." That is, they both consume large amounts of air and generate significant amounts of exhaust gas in the combustion process. In these ways, a sub's diesel engines can quickly deplete the sub's air supply.

The fact that traditional conventional diesel-electric subs have to surface or snorkel frequently is no small security matter. During such recharging and oxygenating periods, diesel-electric subs are highly vulnerable to detection; here, nuclear subs have the clear advantage as their engines use no oxygen at all, and they can stay submerged for months.[1]

Today, however, technological change in the form of the development of "air-independent propulsion systems" has radically altered the diesel-electric submarine seascape. Such systems can solve the diesel sub's air-dependency problem in a variety of ways.

For example, Swedish-made systems burn diesel fuel with liquid oxygen from cryogenic tanks while the Germans have come up with a way to use hydrogen fuel cells. In these ways, air-independent propulsion systems allow diesel-electric subs to remain submerged for far-longer periods—up to two weeks or more—and thereby greatly improve their stealth capabilities.

This quantum leap in diesel-sub stealth technology is highly relevant to our story because China has jumped hard onto the air-independent propulsion bandwagon. While it cannot yet manufacture these systems by itself, China is buying the requisite technology literally by the boatload from foreign countries. And these new systems can be used for more than just newly constructed submarines; they can also be retrofitted to older boats in China's fleet.

Here, then, is the ultimate relevance of this technological development to our detective story: If you had to invent a naval weapon tailored for the waters of the East and South China Seas, it would be hard to do better than a diesel-electric submarine powered by an air-independent propulsion system. Indeed, these conventional diesel subs are the ultimate "passive aggressive" anti-access, area-denial weapons. All they need do is lie in wait virtually undetectable for an enemy vessel to come within range of either their long-range torpedoes or their cruise missiles, and that targeted vessel—whether it be a Japanese destroyer or a US aircraft carrier or a Vietnamese submarine—is likely to wind up as a mission kill.

For China, this particular anti-access, area-denial weapon is all the more potent because of the high numbers of submarines that China is both building on its own and buying from the Russians. Consider that since the 1990s when it began its massive submarine buildup, China has swelled its fleet to over sixty hulls; and it currently has plans to build fifteen more of the latest Yuan-class boats with German propulsion. On top of this, China has ordered four Russian Lada-class submarines[2] that feature sound absorbing tiles on their exteriors and ultra-quiet skewed propellers; and these Russian boats may be even quieter than those with air-independent propulsion.

Fig. 13.1. A gaggle of submarines and warships celebrating the sixtieth anniversary of the founding of the People's Liberation Army Navy. Built with German and Russian technology, the ultraquiet subs can lay in wait for US, Japanese, and Vietnamese warships. (Photograph used with permission from REUTERS/Guang Niu/Pool.)

And here's the big picture: By aggressively populating the relatively close confines of the East and South China Seas with large numbers of these submerged "passive aggressive" weapons, China's conventional diesel-electric subs will be working synergistically with the other anti-access, area-denial weapons we have already discussed—weapons ranging from antiship ballistic missiles to rocket-rising mines. All of these systems will work in concert to significantly raise the costs and risks of US naval forces operating in the region—with the diesel-electric sub playing the pivotal undersea role.

✷✷✷✷✷

This lethality of China's conventional diesel-sub fleet not only underscores the importance of China's anti-access, area-denial strategy and the danger it poses to the American fleet, it also provides a vivid example of how putative American allies are quite wittingly—and profitably—helping China develop capabilities that increasingly threaten American military personnel when big bucks are to be had.

In fact, the top-of-the-line German diesel engines that are now running so many of China's submarines (and other ships, like frigates) should not really be available to China at all. This is because there continues to be both a European and US ban on the export of military equipment to China.

While this ban was imposed on human-rights grounds after China's Tiananmen Square massacre in 1989, it has in recent years become a ban in name only, at least for the Europeans.[3]

That's because countries like Germany and France are readily selling "dual use" technologies like diesel engines under the guise that they will be used for civilian rather than military purposes. In this "dual use" shell game, European companies brazenly exploit this "civilian use" loophole to sell China state-of-the-art equipment to best prepare a Chinese sub to intimidate a Philippine or Vietnamese Coast Guard vessel or sink an American or Japanese ship.[4]

That Europe's ban on selling military equipment to China is simply a cruel corporate inside joke is reflected in statistics compiled by the Stockholm International Peace Research Institute. These data indicate that France, Britain, and Germany alone account for almost 20 percent of Chinese military imports.[5]

As Andrei Chang of the *Kanwa Asian Defense Review* succinctly put it: "Without European technology, the Chinese navy would not be able to move."[6] This observation suggests this new variation on an old Leninist dictum: "The allies of a capitalist will readily sell the rope to hang that capitalist."[7]

Chapter 14

DOWN TO THE SEA IN SURFACE SHIPS

Question: Which statement most accurately describes
China's aircraft carrier, the *Liaoning*?

1. It is an important symbol of national pride to Chinese citizens.
2. It is a small training carrier that poses little or no threat to US–carrier strike groups in the Pacific.
3. The *Liaoning* can exert strong coercive pressure on other countries in the region like the Philippines and Vietnam.
4. All of the above.

There is no question China's aircraft carrier, the *Liaoning*, poses no direct danger to the United States. It is a relatively small carrier with little in the way of advanced electronics or weaponry, and, because of its short flight deck, it is launching under-equipped planes.

That said, many experts who have dismissed the carrier as nothing more than a symbol of national pride to the Chinese may be significantly underestimating its training value as China constructs several much-larger and quite-modern carriers.[1]

These same experts may also be missing the role of the *Liaoning* as a coercive tool as China seeks to resolve many outstanding territorial disputes in the East and South China Seas in its favor.

In fact, the story of the *Liaoning* reveals as much about Chinese deception as it does about China's global military intentions. It is a long and twisting tale that begins on December 4, 1988—the day the Soviet Union launched a brand-new aircraft carrier called the *Riga*.

Exactly a decade later, and seven years after the fall of the Soviet

Union, that aircraft carrier, by then renamed the *Varyag*, sat as a rusting hull, stripped of its engine and rudder, wasting away in a Ukrainian shipyard. That's when a group of Chinese entrepreneurs purchased the carrier for the alleged purpose of turning it into a floating casino berthed in Macao.

Of course, this casino ruse hardly fooled the US State Department and the Pentagon—particularly because the shell company behind the deal was run by former Chinese-military officers. Moreover, the United States had seen this type of ruse before. After a similar Chinese front company purchased the Australian carrier HMS *Melbourne* allegedly for scrap in 1985, "the flight deck of the Melbourne was kept intact and used for pilot training in carrier takeoffs and landings."[2]

Fig. 14.1. A Chinese Shenyang J-15 Flying Shark launches off the "ski jump" deck of China's first aircraft carrier, the *Liaoning*. It was bought "used" from the Ukraine under the ruse that it would become a floating casino in Macao. (Photograph from USNI News.)

To stop China from getting what could become its first operational aircraft carrier back to a Chinese shipyard for renovation, US officials quietly pressured Turkey to block the towing of the carrier through the Bosporus Strait. This pressure worked for over a year as the towed hull circled the Black Sea like Godot waiting for spiritual enlightenment. Eventually, however, a cash-strapped Turkey succumbed to the lure of Chinese inducements, and the ship was freed.[3]

After a perilous journey back to China—at one point the towed ship broke free in high winds and heavy seas—the carrier was refurbished and refitted in a Dalian, China, shipyard; it would complete its sea trials in January of 2014.[4]

Today, the *Liaoning* is indeed a great source of pride to the Chinese people. Its picture is everywhere, and everyone from little children to senior citizens love to mimic the iconic deckhand or "shooter" pose that signals each plane's takeoff.[5]

This is light years away from the 1970s when one Chinese official famously remarked: "China will never build an aircraft carrier. Aircraft carriers are tools of imperialism, and they're like sitting ducks waiting to be shot."[6]

Today, the *Liaoning* has also come to be a great source of fear to nations like the Philippines and Vietnam—both of which are involved in contentious maritime disputes with China. As Heritage Foundation scholar Dean Cheng has noted:

> When you look at the South China Sea and when you look at where various countries have their airfields and their air forces, what you can very quickly see is that much of the South China Sea is very far from land. So, as a result, if you put even a small aircraft carrier there, what you can create is something like an air defense bubble; and one of the lessons the Chinese have taken away from the wars of the past twenty years—Desert Shield, Desert Storm, the Balkans, Afghanistan—is that air superiority is essential to winning modern wars. You may not win with air superiority, but you will certainly lose without it; and so the ability to deploy an aircraft carrier, even if it is just to keep three or four modern aircraft overhead, is a huge advantage when everybody else in the area really can't put any aircraft overhead for any sustained period of time.[7]

As for the *Liaoning*'s broader strategic value, it is true that the carrier lacks the sophisticated avionics and flight-control software of an American carrier. In addition, because it is a full football field in length shorter than American carriers, the planes that take off from its deck also cannot carry the full complement of weapons that American planes can.

That said, China looks to be playing the long game when it comes to establishing hegemony. That's because as a training carrier, the *Liaoning* fits in quite well with Admiral Liu Huaqing's original vision of global force projection by the Chinese navy by 2050.

At least based on the current frenetic activity in Chinese shipyards, it does indeed look like China will soon be fielding numerous modern carriers—along with the critically needed "picket ships" like cruisers and destroyers that make up an aircraft-carrier strike group and protect the carrier from all external threats.

To better understand the concept and role of "picket ships," consider the typical American-carrier strike group. Besides the centerpiece aircraft carrier, it includes a multimission Ticonderoga-class guided-missile cruiser tasked with the full complement of antisubmarine, antisurface ship, and antiaircraft warfare. To assist in this multimission purpose, the carrier strike group also includes two slightly smaller Arleigh Burke–class destroyers as well as the vaunted Aegis Combat System—an integrated naval weapons system designed to simultaneously track literally hundreds of incoming threats at any given time.

Now here's the broader point: If China had no intention of projecting its naval power globally, it would have little need for any of the very expensive capital ships that make up a carrier strike group. In fact, just the opposite is true as China is now building these capital ships at an alarming rate in shipyards up and down the coast of China.[8]

Of course, once China is able to field its own carrier strike groups, the possibility of conflict between China and the United States will likely increase—perhaps exponentially. This will be particularly true if China seeks to use its enhanced naval power to impose its will on lesser-equipped nations as it is already seeking to do with much success in the East and South China Seas.

✶✶✶✶✶

Before leaving the topic of surface ships, it may be useful to move from big ships like destroyers and carriers to one of the smallest but most potent vessels in China's growing anti-access arsenal—its missile-carrying stealth catamarans. These Type 022 Houbei-class boats are barely fifty yards long, but they each carry two cruise missiles, travel at speeds close to 40 knots, and truly pack an out-sized punch.

In fact, China is churning these boats out in record numbers, and they fit quite well into Mao Zedong's aforementioned trademark strategy of "swarming." For example, in an attack on an American-carrier strike group, a hundred of these catamarans moving at high speed toward the strike group might unleash their missiles in "salvo attacks" as the carrier group simultaneously comes under fire from antiship ballistic missiles, shore-based cruise missiles, and torpedoes and missiles fired by attack subs. No matter how good the American Aegis system is—and it has never really been tested by the types of swarming attacks China is rapidly developing the capabilities to mount—Aegis is likely to be overwhelmed by sheer numbers. This type of scenario once again recalls Josef Stalin's adage that "quantity has a quality of its own."

What is perhaps ultimately most disturbing about China's missile catamarans is how China got the design in the first place. In fact, as with China's "Made in Europe" diesel-electric submarine fleet, the "dual use" technology for China's missile catamarans was likewise supplied by a putative friend and ally.

In this case, the Australian company AMD first sold a number of its catamarans to China strictly for civilian river, seaport, and ferry purposes.[9] However, once these business ties were established, China coaxed AMD into a joint venture with a company in Guangzhou; it was this joint venture—Sea Bus International—that adapted the basic AMD design for military use. And so now we face the prospect of an Australian-designed Chinese catamaran powered by French diesel engines firing Russian-bought missiles at American, Japanese, or Vietnamese ships.[10] Sometimes you just gotta *not* love the forces of globalization.

Chapter 15

THE BEST AIR FORCE
SPIES CAN STEAL

Question: The Third Taiwan Strait Crisis of 1995–1996 illustrates
the strategic importance of:

1. Air superiority
2. Naval superiority
3. Both 1 and 2

As epiphanies go, it would be hard to top the one China's top military brass had about the need for both air and naval superiority from the 1995–1996 Taiwan Strait Crisis. This third crisis over Taiwan in four decades was triggered by, of all bizarre things, a simple announcement by Taiwan presidential candidate Lee Teng-hui that he would speak on "Taiwan's democratization experience" at his American alma mater, Cornell University.

Fearful that Lee might formally voice his support for Taiwan independence, Beijing quite literally fired a series of "warning shot" missile tests less than forty miles off Taiwan's bow in July of 1995. This provocation was followed over the next several months by a second wave of missiles, live ammunition exercises, and finally a "mock Taiwan invasion" in November.

In December, the United States finally responded by sending the USS *Nimitz* aircraft-carrier strike group toward the Taiwan Strait. This was the first time American ships had patrolled the strait since 1976, and several months of quiet followed the strike group's arrival. However, as the March 1996 presidential election in Taiwan approached—this would be Taiwan's first direct election of a president—China once again ratcheted up its pressure.

That pressure began in early March when China launched its third, and then fourth, set of ballistic-missile warning shots. Over this five-day period, China also conducted all-out war games with the participation of some "40 naval vessels, 260 aircraft, and an estimated 150,000 troops."[1]

While China's first and second missile tests had been comfortably out of the range of Taiwan's major airline routes and shipping lanes, these third and fourth missile salvos were far too close and effectively constituted a Chinese Communist blockade of the Taiwan Strait. In response, President Bill Clinton moved the USS *Independence* aircraft-carrier strike group, already stationed in the Pacific, to waters much closer to Taiwan and then summoned the USS *Nimitz* from the Persian Gulf, ordering it to proceed at high speed.

To the chagrin of Beijing's leadership, its brute-force attempts to intimidate Taiwan's electorate totally backfired. Indeed, the crisis wound up boosting Lee Teng-hui's poll numbers from a plurality to a majority; he won with 54 percent of the vote as the first directly elected president in Taiwan history.

Of course, once America's carrier strike groups steamed into the area, the People's Liberation Army realized it had absolutely no answer for a force that could command both the seas and skies above. In this way, the Third Taiwan Strait Crisis was simultaneously an "ahah" epiphany and a "never again" moment for Beijing. For if China were to ever take Taiwan, it would have to neutralize the US Navy—and the only way to do that was to also deny the United States the ability to dominate the skies above.

Since China's Taiwan epiphany, it has sought to develop a world-class navy—along with its anti-access strategy designed to keep America's carriers away from Taiwan. China has also steadily transformed its air force from a motley collection of aging aircraft into a modern armada capable of going toe to missile toe with any rival in the region.

✱✱✱✱✱

In pursuing its air-force modernization program, China has followed a two-pronged strategy. One prong involves retiring and replacing its old, vintage second- and third-generation aircraft from the 1950s and 60s with at least fourth-generation technology.

The second prong has involved a Manhattan Project urgency—and no small amount of espionage. It has focused on developing the latest fifth-generation fighter jets to match those of the premier "Joint Strike Fighters" of the United States as embodied in America's F-22 and F-35 jets.

To understand the importance of fifth-generation fighter jets to China—and how their development is likely to be highly escalatory—it is first necessary to understand the basic US strategy for victory in every conflict it has fought since the day after that "day of infamy" when Imperial Japan seized the skies above Hawaii and bombed Pearl Harbor halfway to oblivion. That strategy is to always first clear the skies and command enemy airspaces with "air superiority" fighters like the fifth-generation F-22.

Once air dominance is thus established, other fighter jets like the F-35, working in tandem with long-range bombers like the B-2 and B-52, can then have their way with enemy ships at sea or enemy assets on the ground such as tanks, artillery, and personnel. Through such air dominance, the United States can control any battlefield and thereby maximize its chance of victory—as China learned firsthand during the Third Taiwan Strait Crisis and as a keen third-party observer over the ensuing decades in analyzing American campaigns in places such as Afghanistan, Iraq, and Serbia.

Of course, the ability of America to dominate the air spaces and therefore the battlefield depends critically on it maintaining a technological edge over its opponents in its fighter jet technology. A case in point is the aforementioned F-22.

The Lockheed Martin F-22 Raptor is arguably the most potent fighter jet on the planet. It combines fourth-generation stealth with fifth-generation super-agility. It is also capable of "supercruise," which allows the fighter to exceed speeds of almost twice the speed of sound over long ranges without afterburners.

Finally, and most importantly, F-22s are blessed with a quality called "sensor fusion" that distills millions of bits of real-time data into "a single, simple picture of the battle space."[2] As Lockheed Martin's chief test pilot Paul Metz futuristically describes it: "This de-coupling of the pilot from the role of sensor operator and data analyst is the most profound change in cockpit design since the advent of fighters. It frees up tremendous human RAM [random access memory] to use for intuition, insight, innovation and inference—the attributes that make a human being so dangerous and a fighter pilot so lethal.[3]

As for the F-35, its mission is both air defense and ground attack along with reconnaissance, and it comes in three launching flavors—conventional, short takeoff from aircraft carriers, and vertical. To former marine fighter pilot and Pentagon administrator Ed Timperlake:

> The F-35 is a game changer. It combines stealth and a cockpit fusion engine that gives each pilot uniform knowledge of the rest of the air battle fleet along with the ability to make situational decisions based on real world combat information—a capability heretofore unknown for information in a cockpit.[4]

In terms of our "will there be war" central question, there are at least three observations to be made about America's F-22 and F-35 programs. The first is that America built less than two hundred of the F-22s before Congress—in the face of a weak economy, high cost overruns, and soaring budget deficits—cancelled further construction of the planes. This is an excellent example of how the lack of American economic might (coupled with no small dose of Pentagon incompetence) can quickly affect the ability to field sufficient military forces. Here, the current inventory of F-22s is generally regarded to be insufficient to fulfill America's air-superiority function on a global basis.

Second, and in sharp contrast to the sinking US fighter-jet sun, China is moving forward at breakneck speed seeking to field its own mutant versions of the F-22 and F-35. For example, the Chengdu J-20 "Mighty Dragon" appears to be a multirole fighter combining elements of both America's F-22 and F-35 while China's Chengdu J-31 "Gyrfalcon," possibly designed for aircraft-carrier use, offers a more compact design evocative of the F-35.[5]

What is perhaps most interesting about the Chengdu J-20 from a political perspective is the infamous "in your face" public debut it made in 2011. This debut took place "just hours before US Defense Secretary Robert Gates sat down with Chinese President Hu Jintao," ironically "to mend frayed relations." [6] As for Gates himself, he would later shrug off the embarrassing incident by saying he was assured by President Hu that it was a mere coincidence. However, taken at face value, this explanation means either the top Chinese civilian leader was lying to Gate's face or the Chinese military has far more autonomy than the world has been led to believe.[7] As the conservative *Wall Street Journal* editorialized: "If the military deliberately kept Mr. Hu in the dark, that would reinforce concerns that hawkish elements in the military are increasingly driving China's foreign policy—including ties with the United States."[8]Whether it was a civilian president's lie or the actions of a rogue military, the news is decidedly not good for the prospects of peace.

Fig. 15.1. Top: The Chengdu "Mighty Dragon" fifth-generation fighter built with F-22 blueprints and data stolen from the American Pentagon and its defense contractors. Bottom: The American Lockheed-Martin F-22 Raptor. (Photograph used with permission from Reuters.)

The third observation that pertains to our "will there be war" question is perhaps the most disturbing. It speaks directly to how China has used a combination of old-fashioned spycraft and modern cyberwarfare to steal America's blueprints for its most advanced weapons.

Consider, for example, the aforementioned Chengdu J-20. Its stealth technology was first acquired back in 1999 when an American F-117 Nighthawk fighter was shot down by a vintage Soviet SA-3 missile over the skies of Serbia. This was the first time one of America's putatively invisible fighters had ever been hit, and while the Pentagon racked it up to a lucky shot, the wreckage that was strewn over the Serbian countryside was systematically swept up by Chinese agents. These spies literally went door to door offering Serbian farmers and civilians lucrative payments to surrender the plane's parts—some of which were "the size of small cars."[9] These parts were then transported back to China and assembled in a way that revealed much about America's vaunted stealth capabilities.

Of course, stealth is just one of the many components of a fifth-generation fighter. As to how China got the rest of the technology for the Chengdu J-20, this came down to one of the most comprehensive and effective "hack jobs" thus far in computer espionage history.

As early as 2007, Chinese cybersoldiers effectively penetrated not just the Pentagon to make off with much of the classified information on the Joint Strike Fighter project, but also Britain's largest defense contractor, BAE—one of the copartner companies helping to build the F-35. Taken from these unsuspecting Brits were critical data on fifth-generation design, electronic systems, and performance.[10]

In these old and new ways of spycraft, China has been able to steal classified information and intellectual property that cost American taxpayers hundreds of billions of dollars to research and develop. As a further turn of the research-and-development screw, China is now using the fruits of its espionage to build weapons that, over time, may turn out to be even more effective than America's.

✶✶✶✶✶

Viewed once again through the lens of our "will there be war" question," it should finally be noted that China's ability to steal the latest American fifth-generation technology may be highly escalatory as well. As Senior Fellow Richard Fisher of the International Assessment and Strategy Center laments, the only way the United States can maintain its domination of the skies once China reaches fifth-generation parity will be for the United States to develop sixth-generation fighters—and Fisher is urging American policymakers to do just that.[11]

Of course, spending hundreds of billions of dollars more to stay ahead of a rival with an economy every bit its equal will be a significant additional drain on American taxpayers. At the same time, such an arms race will divert resources from higher-productivity private-sector investments and further strain an already struggling American economy. It is for these reasons alone that American citizens and taxpayers may be both rightfully incensed by China's espionage and perhaps fearful for the future.

Chapter 16

DENY, DEGRADE, DECEIVE, DISRUPT, AND DESTROY IN SPACE

Question: From China's perspective, America's preeminence
in space-based command, control, communications,
intelligence, surveillance, and reconnaissance or
"C4ISR" is:

1. America's greatest military strength
2. America's most glaring military weakness
3. Both 1 and 2

W hile the Third Taiwan Strait Crisis offered China an epiphany about its need to develop air and naval superiority, it was America's "shock and awe" campaign in the First Gulf War in Iraq in 1991 that put an exclamation point to the power of space-based warfare. In that humiliation of Saddam Hussein and his "feet of clay" Republican Guard, America's ability to see the battlefield from the ultimate high ground of space and its "information dominance" were the keys to a swift victory that produced few American casualties—less than three hundred—while killing or wounding over one hundred thousand Iraqi troops.[1]

Since that 1991 Gulf War—arguably China's own "Sputnik moment"—China has been aggressively seeking to develop its own space-based capabilities. And it has been equally hard at work producing a whole range of what the West refers to as "silver" or "magic bullets" and what China refers to as "assassin's maces." The goal of China's assassin's maces, as the Pentagon has described it, is to "deny, degrade, deceive, disrupt, or destroy" America's eyes and ears in space.[2]

In seeking to knock America off its ultimate strategic high-ground perch, the Chinese military's underlying presumption is this: While America's space-based capabilities have made its military the most powerful and effective in the world, an overreliance on its satellite network to provide situational awareness on the battlefield is now making America highly vulnerable to attack.

✶✶✶✶✶

Before describing China's growing space-based capabilities—and their escalatory implications—it may be useful to first reflect briefly on the importance of the "strategic high ground" in warfare. It's an importance that dates back centuries to military strategists like China's Sun Tzu who once advised to always "observe on the high ground."[3] The brilliant Prussian strategist Clausewitz likewise notes that "an elevation gives a better command of view" and gives a "better chance of hitting."[4]

Over time, the military's search for the strategic high ground has evolved from simple treetop perches in the Stone Age to observation balloons in World War I, reconnaissance planes in World War II, high-altitude spy planes in the 1960s, and finally the complex US satellite network that now rings the earth today.

Unfortunately for the cause of peace, America's highly effective militarization of space now has the potential to cause far more instability than was ever observed even during the chilliest days of the Cold War. In that war, the United States and the Soviet Union never wavered from their strong tacit agreement to leave each other's satellite systems alone. This is because each side very clearly understood the critical role that space reconnaissance and surveillance plays in nuclear deterrence. Indeed, it was precisely the ability of each side to constantly see what the other was doing with its intercontinental ballistic missiles that provided *both* sides with the assurance that neither was attempting to launch a first strike against the other.

Today, however, China wants no part of any such tacit understanding with the United States.[5] Instead, its strategists see space simply as the next frontier and battlefield of "informationalized warfare" rather than any peaceful sanctuary or extraterrestrial commons. Nor, given the evolution of warfare since the end of the Cold War, is China's willingness—indeed its growing eagerness—to weaponize space an unreasonable position.

Here's the very clear problem: China has had a front row seat to a series of offensive military campaigns waged by a potential rival in countries like Afghanistan, Iraq, Kosovo, Serbia, and Syria. In each case, these American campaigns were run (if not always won) quite effectively from the strategic high ground of space—and often with the goal of "regime change" in mind. Thus, while space was primarily an instrument of peace and deterrence during the Cold War, it has now morphed into a very effective ultimate weapon—and both China and the United States now very clearly understand that whichever side holds that strategic high ground is far more likely to prevail against the other should actual shots be fired.

Because such battle lines have now been drawn—ironically between the world's two largest economies and trading partners—China has embarked on an extremely aggressive campaign to develop both its offensive and defensive space capabilities. With one fist, it wants to possess the same kind of space networking that will allow it to run its own military campaigns as effectively as the Americans. With its other fist, China seeks to develop its assassin's maces to neutralize or destroy America's advantage in space.

CHINA'S GROWING SATELLITE NETWORK

China is well on its way to reaching its goal of emulating America's space network. While the American space program has been effectively grounded, China is moving ahead with ambitious plans to go to the moon, Mars, and beyond. In addition, having been left out in the International Space Station cold by Russia and the United States, China is also rapidly constructing its own outer space headquarters—and possible Star Wars fortress.

As for anyone who thinks China's reach for the stars is the silly fantasy of a country that can only make cheap electronics and poisonous pet food, think again. In fact, the foundation of China's space program rests on its global leadership in launching heavy payloads at the lowest price in the global launch market.

Over the decades, China has developed its cost-effective launch capability—the *sine qua non* of any space program—primarily by servicing the world market in commercial satellites. This is a role that first dropped into China's lap in the wake of America's 1986 space shuttle *Challenger* disaster.

Prior to *Challenger*, the United States had planned to launch the bulk of its commercial and military satellites from the bays of its space shuttle.[6] However, after the tragedy, the shuttle program was sharply curtailed, and US companies began taking their satellite business to China.

This quantum leap in US launch demand provided a big rocket boost to the Chinese space program in three ways. First, it allowed China to significantly expand its launch facilities. Today, China has four very active launch pads spread across the country.[7]

As a second benefit, the arrival of often very naïve US commercial-satellite customers allowed the Chinese to steal sensitive satellite technology prior to the launches. Of course, the Chinese were only supposed to launch the satellites, not go over them with a fine reverse-engineering comb; but this was an intellectual-property theft opportunity too good to miss, and today, stolen satellite technology has given China a big boost in the building of its own network.[8]

Third, and hardly inconsequential, because China continues to serve the global commercial-satellite market, it can spread its fixed-launch-site costs between that market and its own domestic military needs. This, in and of itself, provides a huge cost advantage over the United States and other rivals. In economic terms, China now has a strong comparative advantage in an activity once dominated by the United States.

As to just what China seeks to accomplish with its ambitious space program, one can think of this in two distinct military dimensions. First, China wants an American-style information network to provide situational awareness for any battlefield—maritime or terrestrial. Second, it seeks to deploy both conventional and nuclear weapons in space for use both as instruments of coercion and deterrence as well as actual weapons of war.

To fulfill the information function, China is building its own complex reconnaissance, surveillance, and weather-satellite network. A critical piece of this network is its BeiDou Navigation Satellite System, named after the Big Dipper constellation. It will cover the world with thirty satellites in geostationary or nongeostationary orbit, and BeiDou is aiming for GPS accuracy within fifty centimeters.[9]

China's acute lack of transparency comes into escalatory play on the deployment-of-weapons front. The problem for the rest of the world is that it simply does not know just what China is sending up into space in its payloads—or what weapons it might eventually deploy on its space station.

This uncertainty raises inevitable questions, such as this seemingly paranoid query: Is China preparing to deploy a deadly string of nuclear-warhead pearls above the globe, ready to be dropped should war break out?

As for whether such a query is truly paranoia, it certainly is not—at least if one takes the Chinese strategic literature at face value. In fact, this literature is riddled with detailed discussions of the use of advanced space weapons to defeat an enemy that is often *explicitly* identified as the United States.

A case in literary point is *Space War* by Colonel Li Daguang. Li advocates "destroying or temporarily incapacitating all enemy space vehicles that fly in space above our sovereign territory" even as he calls for the use of both "land-based anti-satellite weapons" and "anti-satellite satellites" to "deal a crippling blow to the enemy."[10]

As for removing any doubt that the "enemy" in question is America, consider this shot across the bow from the *Qiushi Journal*, an official publication of the Central Committee of the Chinese Communist Party:

> China should make efforts to develop space weapons as soon as possible, as this is the most effective military means of attacking the United States. If we can eventually fire missiles from a satellite, the United States will find that it has nowhere to hide; it will find itself entirely exposed to the attack radius of Chinese weaponry.[11]

Ultimately, however, it may not be China's development of its own weaponized satellite network that proves to be so destabilizing in the coming decades. Rather, it may well be China's aggressive plans to take down America's own satellite network—a network one must hasten to add that is not only a key component of US military strategy but also the lifeblood of America's increasingly informationalized economy.

As to just how China plans to knock out America's satellite network, it seems to have even more ways to do so than Paul Simon had to leave his lover in his famous song. Broadly speaking, this myriad of Chinese antisatellite weapons falls into two broad categories—"hard kill" and "soft kill."

For the poster child of "hard kill," we need only look to China's infamous 2007 antisatellite weapons test. On January 11th of that year, China launched a direct-ascent antisatellite interceptor riding a multistage rocket shot from the Xichang Satellite Launch Center. The intended target was one of China's own obsolete weather satellites traveling more than five hundred miles above the earth in polar orbit. The test resulted in a direct hit—no small feat. [12]

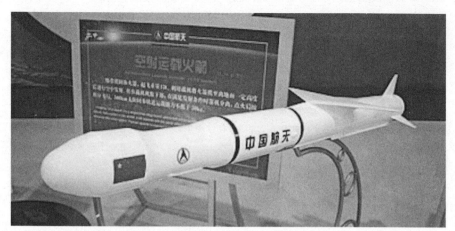

Fig. 16.1 A Chinese antisatellite "hard kill" missile like this one created the largest single mass of space debris in history during a test. Such missiles are designed to knock out the American satellite network. (Photograph from the Chinese Internet via International Assessment and Strategy Center.)

Beyond such "kinetic hard kills," there are also "soft kill" techniques. These range from jamming satellite communications to using high-energy lasers to "dazzle" or temporarily blind satellites. In fact, China tested just such a dazzling technique on a US satellite way back in 2006.[13]

Of course, China's increasing antisatellite weapons capabilities threaten not only America's command of the strategic high ground along with its economy, but also one of the key pillars of nuclear deterrence. Indeed, the moment that China shoots down, blinds, or otherwise disables an American military satellite, America might well presume as a matter of national security that China is in the process of launching a first nuclear strike against it—a strike that will no longer be visible to the satellite eye. At such a point, a US president may see no other alternative but to strike first. And so at least one variation on the end of the world might result from a war with China.

Chapter 17

THE INTERNET MEETS
MEPHISTOPHELES

Question: Which of the following activities represent applications
of cyberwarfare?

1. Stealing intellectual property from private businesses
   to strengthen one's own economy and military while
   weakening the economy and military of a rival
2. Destroying or disabling critical infrastructure such as
   an enemy's air-traffic-control network, electricity grid,
   banking and financial systems, or subways
3. Stealing military defense secrets during peacetime to
   maintain weapons parity with a rival
4. Destroying, disabling, or redirecting an enemy's aircraft,
   missiles, ships, or tanks during wartime
5. Gaining strategic or tactical advantage on the battlefield
   through deception and misdirection
6. Monitoring, or interfering with, military communications
7. All of the above

I think you get the "all of the above" picture here, and looking back on
the emergence of the Internet in the 1990s, it may well turn out to be the
biggest Mephistophelian bargain of all time. For counterbalancing all of
the wonderful gifts the Internet brings us—from GPS and iTunes to online
education and video conferencing—is the emergence of a new and silent
but supremely powerful weapon of both selective and mass destruction.

Unfortunately for the cause of peace, no country has been more
aggressive in seeking to develop its cyberwarfare capabilities than China.
Nor has any country so actively deployed at least some of those capabilities during what is supposed to be a time of peace and robust global trade.

China's aggressiveness on the cyberbattlefield is further compounded by the rapid increase in cyberespionage by the United States since the Al Qaeda terrorist attacks on the World Trade Center in New York City and the Pentagon in Washington, DC, in 2001. While the United States has sought to justify its actions on the basis of national security, the court of world opinion does not appear to be buying into this "American exceptionalism" argument. One unfortunate byproduct of America's fall from the moral high ground has been far less global condemnation of China's cyberwarfare activities than the level of those activities likely warrant.[1]

To understand this particular threat vector, it may be useful to start with the disturbing fact that computer hacking in China is anything but illegal. Instead, it has become a very attractive career path for a whole new generation of Chinese youth raised on an electric blend of ultranationalism and Internet connectivity.

To pursue this career path, some Chinese youth will attend one of the many private schools set up across China to teach various techniques. These relatively low-level Chinese hacker "trade schools" are big business; they operate out in the sunshine with full government sanction and generate tens of millions of dollars in revenue a year.[2]

Still other Chinese hackers-in-training will take the higher-education path to master the engineering and mathematical intricacies of cyberespionage, attending prestigious universities like China's Harbin Institute of Technology.[3] However, the preferred route for many would-be elite hackers is to attend a foreign university, preferably in the United States. Not only is the education often better; such study abroad also allows the hacker to carefully study the host country and its infrastructure for possible later targeting.

As for the hacking done directly by the government, China's cybercommand is under the full control of the People's Liberation Army. It consists of over one hundred thousand cyberwarriors and is stretched across "12 bureaus and three research institutes."[4]

Perhaps the most notorious of China's cybercommand operations is an advanced persistent-threat military unit housed in a twelve-story building in the Pudong district of Shanghai, where an "advanced persistent threat" is a computer-network attack of long duration. As documented in a watershed report by the Mandiant consulting firm, the Chinese military's elite band of Shanghai hackers alone is reportedly responsible for compromising over 140 foreign companies "spanning 20 major industries."[5]

Fig. 17.1. A platoon of China's more than one hundred thousand cyberwarriors. From digital sweatshops like these, China infiltrates the computers of the Pentagon and American industry with computer viruses, Trojans, and worms. (Photograph from the Drum.)

On this industrial front, China's hackers seek not just to steal the obligatory blueprints, research and development, and proprietary manufacturing processes of foreign businesses large and small. They will also vacuum up everything from emails, contact lists, and test results to pricing information and partnership agreements.

Such economic hacking by groups like PT1 also highlights the unique collaborative arrangement that China's state-owned enterprises have with the People's Liberation Army. In many cases, a key hacking goal is to improve the position of a Chinese company relative to a foreign competitor.

As a second putatively peacetime front in China's cyberwarfare, there is also the ongoing massive theft of US weapons systems. We have already discussed this problem within the context of compromised elite weapons such as the F-22 and F-35 fifth-generation fighters, but a more complete list includes "more than two dozen major weapons systems . . . critical to US missile defenses and combat aircraft and ships."[6]

According to the *Washington Post*, this list features "the advanced

Patriot missile system known as PAC-3; an Army system for shooting down ballistic missiles known as the Terminal High Altitude Area Defense or THAAD; and the Navy's Aegis ballistic-missile defense system. In addition, there are vital combat aircraft and ships, including the F/A-18 fighter jet, the V-22 Osprey, the Black Hawk helicopter and the Navy's new Littoral Combat Ship, which is designed to patrol waters close to shore."[7] As defense analyst Richard Fisher has opined on this systematic extraction of America's most important defense secrets, "it's truly frightening."[8]

Still a third major cyberwarfare front involves attacking critical infrastructure such as an enemy's electricity grid, water-purification plants, air-traffic control, subway systems, and telecommunications. The twin goals here are to sow chaos among the populace as well as to bring the enemy's economy to its knees.

Consider, for example, China's successful hack of Telvent—a software company that "keeps detailed blueprints on more than half of all the oil and gas pipelines in North and South America and has access to their systems."[9] Said one analyst of the stunning implications of China's hack:

> [I]f someone hired me and told me they wanted to have the offensive capability to take out as many critical systems as possible, I would . . . do things like what happened to Telvent. . . . It's the holy grail."[10]

It is precisely these kinds of cyberattacks that were featured in a seminal work entitled *Unrestricted Warfare* published in 1999 by two top colonels in the People's Liberation Army.[11] This volume provides yet another example of how a careful reading of the Chinese strategic literature is quite effective at unmasking China's true military intentions—no one can say the world was not warned.

Moving still further up the cyberwarfare gradient from peacetime hacks to all-out war scenarios, we next have to consider China's possible attempts to implant "Trojans" and other malware into the computer and electronic circuitry of America's weapons and logistics systems. The ultimate goal here is to mobilize this malware to destroy, disable, misdirect, or otherwise neutralize US capabilities during times of conflict or war.

To understand just one of the possible dangers, consider this "Manchurian Candidate" scenario:

A Chinese engineer at a factory in Chengdu designs a "kill switch" into a complex, custom computer chip. China then exports these secretly embedded "Manchurian" chips to the United States where they become embedded in America's defense systems. Meanwhile, just as in the classic film "The Manchurian Candidate," these chips await some kind of signal from Chinese hackers that activates them—just imagine an aircraft carrier-based American F-35 jet fighter scrambling to assist Taiwan or Japan in the event of a Chinese attack and seeing its engines shut off or its electronic systems go dead in mid-flight.[12]

In fact, planting such Manchurian chips is remarkably easy to do since China has become the world's *de facto* factory floor. Modern software programs have millions of lines of code within which to bury a virus or Trojan while microchips for our computers and phones contain hundreds of millions of logic gates within which to hide a malicious digital payload. As to whether this prospect is some paranoid fantasy, such chips have *already* been discovered in the American defense system.

For example, one University of Cambridge researcher found a backdoor in a military-grade chip that was supposed to be one of the "most impenetrable"[13] in the American arsenal. The chip in question, commonly known as the PA3, is used not just in weapons but also in civilian applications like nuclear power plants and public transport.[14]As *Aviation Week* notes: "The potential for specialized microchips from China to find their way into US computers and networks, or even into conventional Western weapons systems, isn't just a frightening prospect—it is a chilling reality."[15]

Of course, the Chinese government continues to vehemently insist it is not involved in any kind of organized cyberwarfare. However, if we are to "seek truth from facts" as Chinese leader Deng Xiaoping once famously urged, the facts strongly prove otherwise.

As to how China's cyberwarfare capabilities ultimately relate to our "will there be war" core question, this may well be another case in which a new and very different kind of war between China and the United States is already well underway. Here, American Enterprise Institute scholar Michael Auslin has the last word on this sore and sorry subject:

> We don't take cybersecurity seriously, and we don't take defense secrets seriously. The Chinese stole reams and reams of data on our missiles

back in the 1990s under the Clinton administration. All of a sudden they had intercontinental ballistic missiles that could effectively reach the United States. During the Bush years they stole information on the F-35 and other things. During the Obama years, they've stolen information on our drones. I mean we just think we're so big and we're so sophisticated and we're so technologically advanced that whatever we build is going to beat the other guy; and they've been robbing us blind and robbing the American taxpayer blind of billions of dollars of development and research money for decades.[16]

Chapter 18

THE DARK STRATEGIC BEAUTY OF THE NONKINETIC THREE WARFARES

Question: Which war-fighting capabilities have been more effective at advancing China's territorial ambitions in the twenty-first century?

1. "Kinetic" weapons like destroyers, fighter jets, and ballistic missiles
2. "Nonkinetic" weapons like psychological warfare, media warfare, and legal warfare

Here, just as the pen can often be far mightier than the sword, it may well turn out that China's "three warfares" will prove to be far more effective at expanding China's maritime and land boundaries than any arsenal of ballistic and cruise missiles or any fleet of Chinese aircraft carriers. Because this is true—and because in their own ways, the three warfares are highly escalatory—it is important for our detective story that we gain a more sophisticated understanding of what these three warfares entail.

The three warfares were first officially recognized as an important war-fighting capability in 2003. That's when China's Central Military Commission, in conjunction with the Chinese Communist Party, officially approved the strategy.

The definitive work on the implications of the three warfares for Chinese force projection has been authored by University of Cambridge professor and former White House advisor Stefan Halper. In a report to the Pentagon, Halper describes the three warfares as "a dynamic three-dimensional warfighting process that constitutes war by other means."[1]

To Halper, the three warfares represent a particularly potent nonkinetic form of attack in a modern era in which it is increasingly difficult to use kinetic military force to advance territorial goals. Indeed, as Russia's adventurism in the Ukraine has demonstrated, any such unlawful display of kinetic force is likely to draw immediate condemnation—along with economic or other sanctions from one's trading partners.

So just what are the three warfares? The first is "psychological warfare," the goal of which is to deter, demoralize, or otherwise shock an opponent nation and its civilian population and thereby discourage the opponent from fighting back. As Halper describes the scope of China's psychological warfare: "It employs diplomatic pressure, rumor, false narratives, and harassment to express displeasure, assert hegemony and convey threats."[2] Halper notes further that "China's economy is utilized to particular effect."[3]

Thus, for example, when China imposes an economic boycott on Japan for rare earths or bans Chinese tourism, it hopes to coerce a Japanese populace that is hungry for prosperity and struggling with economic stagnation into acquiescing to China's territorial demands regarding the Senkaku Islands. In a similar vein, when China sends large flotillas of civilian ships to surround a contested area like Scarborough Shoal or Second Thomas Shoal, its "cabbage strategy" goal is to intimidate the Philippines and force its military to back off in the face of overwhelming numbers.[4]

The second of the three warfares is "media warfare." Its goal is to shape public opinion both domestically and internationally in a way that leads unwary media consumers to accept China's version of events. Its use follows Stefan Halper's maxim that "it is not the best weapons that win today's wars but rather the best narrative."[5]

Heritage Foundation scholar Dean Cheng describes such media warfare as a "constant, on-going activity aimed at long-term influence of perceptions and attitudes."[6] As Halper puts it: The goals are to "preserve friendly morale; generate public support at home and abroad; weaken an enemy's will to fight; and alter an enemy's situational assessment."

While China engages in media warfare across the spectrum—books, movies, magazines, the Internet—it has invested particularly heavily into turning its Chinese Central Television Network (CCTV) into a global propaganda force. In fact, in the same year Chinese military and political leaders first embraced the three warfares in 2003, CCTV inaugurated a *faux* twenty-four-hour news channel designed to directly compete with the likes of the BBC and CNN for the hearts and minds of the world.

In 2011, China substantially upped the media-warfare ante when it set up a major studio in Washington, DC, replete with non-Chinese "white face" and "black face" American anchors and reporters. The beauty of such a faux-CNN news model is that CCTV can shrink-wrap its propaganda around healthy doses of pure news while reaching over forty million Americans—along with hundreds of millions more viewers in the rest of the world.

Thus, when yet another incident breaks out between China and the Philippines involving the dispute over Scarborough Shoal or Second Thomas Shoal, CCTV is there to quickly advance China's narrative—often before the Western media are even on to the story. In a similar vein, when tensions mount over the Senkaku Islands, CCTV will quickly launch a strong offensive blaming "right-wing nationalists" in Japan for any incident or escalation.

The last of the three warfares is "legal warfare," also known as "lawfare." China's strategy here is to operate within the existing legal framework to effectively bend—or perhaps rewrite—the rules of the international order in China's favor.

Consider, for example, China's insistence that it be able to restrict freedom of navigation within its two-hundred-mile exclusive economic zone as defined by the United Nations Law of the Sea Treaty. In fact, this claim has *no* legal basis within the context of the actual Law of the Sea Treaty language—the treaty is quite clear on this point. Yet China repeatedly and falsely asserts the opposite—in the spirit of the oft-repeated axiom that "if you say it enough, they will believe it."

Still another example of China's aggressive lawfare is the use of bogus maps to support its territorial claims—a tactic at least one commentator has dubbed "mapfare."[7] For example, in 2012, China outraged many of its Asian neighbors by including a map inside of new Chinese passports depicting many of the disputed areas in the South China Sea as sovereign Chinese territory. In this way, China sought to use such clever cartography to both bolster and mark its territorial claims. And so the three warfares go.

✶✶✶✶✶

Here, then, is the broader point. If we are to believe scholars like Stefan Halper and Dean Cheng, China's use of legal, media, and psychological warfare is a new form of aggression that China is using to advance its expansionist and revisionist goals. From this perspective, the beauty of the three warfares in today's modern age is that they offer a new form of nonkinetic weaponry to achieve goals that in earlier times could only be realized through kinetic force. Moreover, the three warfares combine in a highly synergistic way.

Fig. 18.1. White-hulled paramilitary ships like the China Marine Surveillance vessel in the foreground are at the tip of the Chinese spear in the East and South China Seas. This boat tussles with a Japanese Coast Guard vessel in Japan's territorial waters near the Senkaku/Diaoyu Islands. (Photograph by the Asahi Shimbun. Used with permission from Getty Images.)

For example, in many of its territorial disputes with its neighbors in the East and South China Seas, China first asserts false territorial claims based on vague history—that's the legal warfare. It next projects nonkinetic force in the forms of everything from white-hulled civilian fleets to economic boycotts—that's the psychological warfare. Finally, it seeks to win the media battle by controlling the narrative—in this case, portraying a "peaceful China" as a victim of foreign-power domination during its century of humiliation that is only trying to right a historic wrong.

Viewed through this lens, China's deployment of the three warfares in pursuit of its expansionist ambitions is revealed for what it is—a new type of warfare not yet recognized as such by China's opponents. However, it is clearly aimed at achieving expansionist and revisionist goals that were previously only achievable through the use of kinetic military force.

If this interpretation of China's behavior is indeed correct, our "will there be war" question is in some sense definitively answered. To wit: China is *already* waging war against America and its allies on the new nonkinetic battlefields of the three warfares in much the same way Chinese cyberwarriors are prosecuting their undeclared war in cyberspace.

Given this reality, it may well be long past time that institutions like the Pentagon in America and other defense ministries in Asia expand the scope of their national security missions to include the development of strategies to directly combat the three warfares.

Chapter 19

THE SUM OF ALL
CHINESE CAPABILITIES

**Question: Do China's emerging war-fighting strategies and
capabilities constitute a rising threat to peace and
stability in Asia?**

1. No
2. Yes

As we end part 2 of our detective story, it is perhaps time for a
brief progress report. So let's review how all of the various clues
regarding China's intentions, strategies, and new capabilities are currently
stacking up relative to our central "will there be war" question.

Regarding China's military *intentions*, there appears to be a strong,
and at times very confusing, convergence between China's legitimate
desire to defend its homeland and protect its global trade routes and its
far-more controversial and offensive-minded expansionist quest to control
additional territories, air spaces, maritime features, and sea lines of communication in Asia.

As an example of this convergence, consider that China's successful
control of the East and South China Seas would materially improve China's
ability to defend both its homeland and its trading routes. However, such
defensive benefits can only be achieved through *offensive* actions against
weaker neighbors like Japan, the Philippines, and Vietnam.

In a similar vein, the successful *offensive* taking of disputed land features like the Senkaku Islands in the East China Sea and Second Thomas
Shoal in the South China Sea would allow China to improve its *defense*
through the construction of additional military facilities like garrisons, airstrips, and radar installations. Such takings would also provide China with

greater access to oil and natural-gas reserves and thereby help China solve its "Malacca Dilemma" by reducing its dependence on Persian Gulf oil. But again, such defensive enhancements can only occur through aggressive revisionist actions.

This convergence of economic, expansionist, and national-security motives together with the blurring of lines between defense and offense leaves us with at least one reasonable interpretation of the present situation: What may have begun as a purely defensive military buildup by China to defend its homeland and economic interests has now dangerously morphed into the development of an increasingly modern, offensive-minded military force that, over time, will be increasingly capable of globally projecting power.

Turning to China's *capabilities*, we have seen that they include not just the obligatory traditional weapons of war—from mines and missiles to aircraft-carrier strike groups and fighter jets. They also encompass a series of highly disruptive military technologies that threaten to radically alter the balance of power in Asia.

These disruptive weapons technologies range from China's "carrier killing" antiship ballistic missile and its diverse arsenal of antisatellite weaponry to computer malware capable of knocking fighter jets like the F-35 down from the skies—or knocking out civilian targets deep within an enemy's homeland like air-traffic control, bank networks, and subway systems.

The obvious conclusion to draw from this picture is that as the military capabilities of an arguably revisionist China continue to grow, so, too, will the potential for conflict. In other words, the most likely answer to the question leading off this chapter is that China's emerging war-fighting strategies and capabilities do indeed constitute a rising threat to peace and stability in Asia.

Our next question, therefore, necessarily must be: What might be the likely triggers, trip wires, or flash points for any such conflict? More specifically, what is the set of circumstances that might lead to shots being fired between China and any one of a number of countries—from Japan, India, and the Philippines, to Vietnam, South Korea, the United States, and, of course, Taiwan?

It is to these possible circumstances and their attendant scenarios that our detective story must now inevitably turn—but not first without these words of caution from chess grand master Garry Kasparov:

Many politicians and pundits in the Free World seem to think that refusing to acknowledge you are in a fight means you can avoid losing it. But ignoring the reality of a conflict puts more innocents . . . instead of trained soldiers . . . on the front lines.[1]

Part 3

TRIGGERS, TRIP WIRES, AND FLASH POINTS

Chapter 20

THE (ALMOST) UNSINKABLE AIRCRAFT CARRIER OF TAIWAN

Question: Which of these factors are likely to play the most important role in triggering a war between China and the United States over Taiwan?

1. Nationalism
2. Geostrategy
3. Ideology
4. Morality

I t is axiomatic that the probability of war between two countries rises with the size of the stakes. At least on the basis of this particular axiom, Taiwan must stand at the head of the class when it comes to possible triggers for a war between China and the United States. To understand why this is so—and why all four elements of our lead question may well come into play—it is important to view Taiwan through the different perspectives and prisms of Beijing and Washington.

US Naval War College professor Toshi Yoshihara may have best summarized the nationalist stakes for Beijing when he observed that:

China considers Taiwan to be the last lost piece of territory during the Century of Humiliation [and that it] is a sacred imperative on the part of the Chinese to retake Taiwan and bring Taiwan back into the embrace of the motherland.[1]

Because this is so, Yoshihara warns that:

[A] great power war between China and the United States is possible because the Chinese have stated repeatedly over decades that Taiwan is something the Chinese are prepared to fight over."[2]

It would be wrong to conclude, however, that China's quest to retake Taiwan is rooted only in the passions of nationalism and the "never again" pride caused by their century of humiliation. Indeed, there are at least two additional, highly compelling reasons why Beijing believes it is imperative to bring the "renegade province" of Taiwan back into the mainland's authoritarian fold—one geostrategic, the other ideological.

The geostrategic reason is rooted in the first three rules of real estate: location, location, location. The abiding fact here is that Taiwan is located at almost the exact midpoint of the First Island Chain. Says Chinese Major Generals Peng Guangqian and Yao Youzhi of the geostrategic implications: "If Taiwan should be alienated from the mainland . . . China will forever be locked to the west side of the first chain of islands in the West Pacific." In that case, "the essential strategic space for China's rejuvenation will be lost."[3]

As for the ideological dimensions to the taking of Taiwan, Beijing's very big problem across the Strait is the very big success of liberal democracy as it is being practiced almost to perfection by its pesky renegade province. To be historically clear here, the Nationalist government of Generalissimo Chiang Kai-shek and his heavily armed Kuomintang followers did *not* import the institution of democracy into Taiwan when they arrived in 1949. Instead, for decades, the Generalissimo ran a government that, in its own authoritarian way, was every bit as brutal and harsh as that being commanded by Chairman Mao on the mainland.

The quite remarkable story of Taiwan, however, is that it has morphed into a vibrant and well-functioning democracy ever since its president was first democratically elected in 1996. Indeed, on Taiwan, it is a rough-and-tumble world of open debate and ideas, extremely high voter-participation rates, and peaceful transitions of power that offer a textbook case of how political freedoms can successfully evolve along with the growth and increasing openness of a national economy.

In candid fact here, Taiwan's democracy deeply frightens Beijing's authoritarians precisely because it offers proof positive to the people of China and the rest of the world that one of Beijing's most oft-repeated lines is a big, fat lie: That somehow, because of their culture and character, the Chinese people need a strong authoritarian government for their economy to prosper and their Confucian society to properly function.

For all these reasons—nationalism, geostrategy, and ideology—Beijing needs to bring Taiwan back under mainland control. Of all China's avowed "core interests" that it has proclaimed that it will be willing to fight for, Taiwan is the *sine qua non*.

✭✭✭✭✭

On the other side of this complex equation, there is, of course, the United States. The perennial question asked both in Beijing and Washington—as well as in Taipei—is whether America remains prepared to fight for the defense of Taiwan in a battle where it seemingly has far less stakes. In fact, US presidents over the decades have given Beijing considerable reason to believe that America may be willing to sacrifice Taiwan on some altar of political accommodation or economic pragmatism.

Recall, for example, that President Richard Nixon and his secretary of state Henry Kissinger treated Taiwan as a mere pawn to offset the power of the Soviet Union and engineer an expedient exit from the Vietnam War. To those ends, Nixon and Kissinger paved the way for Taiwan's removal from the United Nations and its replacement by the People's Republic of China in 1971.

Fast forward now to the 2000s. After pledging to do "whatever it takes" to protect Taiwan, President George W. Bush went on to publicly rebuke Taiwan's president in 2003 for "comments and actions" that indicate "he may be willing to make decisions unilaterally to change the status quo, which we [in the United States] oppose."[4] Democratic president Barack Obama soon followed in Bush's fence-straddling footsteps when, like his predecessor, he refused to sell advanced weapons systems to Taiwan for its defense. [5]

Of course, in charting a prudent policy course on Taiwan, Washington's political leaders always face this perennial problem: The US economy is heavily dependent on trade with China so there is great reluctance to rock that boat. As a further political twist, many of Washington's elected officials are just as heavily dependent on massive campaign contributions from American multinational corporations that have a strong vested interest in the growing China trade. Thus, both the politics and economics of trade dictate restraint when it comes to US support of Taiwan.

To experts like Professor Yoshihara, however, such American "restraint"—along with a growing history of presidential vacillations—spell increasing danger. This is because these signals of American indecision and meekness may one day embolden a rapidly militarizing China to make its final invasion push. To Yoshihara, that would be a gross Chinese miscalculation of the actual firmest of America's resolve on the Taiwan question.[6]

Here, it is not just that the United States has significant moral and ideological stakes in Taiwan's survival as a thriving democracy committed to free and peaceful trade. There is also this cold geostrategic reality described by Heritage Foundation scholar Dean Cheng:

Taiwan is perhaps the single most developed piece of the First Island Chain once you leave Japan and Okinawa. So to walk away from Taiwan would, in a sense, be to open the gates for China's navy to be able to access the central Pacific with very little in the way of other obstacles.[7]

To this, Professor Yoshihara adds:

If China were to ever take Taiwan either peacefully or by force, China gets to cut that First Island Chain in half, essentially cutting in half the US forward posture in the Asia-Pacific region. This would be unprecedented in the history of US military posture in the Asia-Pacific since the end of World War II.[8]

This is a "US military posture" that quite clearly depends on an indispensable triad of America's treaty alliances with nations along the First Island Chain, its forward military bases on many of those islands, and the defense of Taiwan as the anchor and centerpiece of that First Island Chain. It is a posture that is a logical extension of the Japanese attack on Pearl Harbor—a "day in infamy" that taught America what can happen when isolationism rules and the ships and troops are pulled back from the Asia-Pacific.

It is also a military posture that is at least in part derived from another bloody event in World War II. To wit: During General Douglas MacArthur's humiliating retreat from the Philippines following the Pearl Harbor massacre, it would be squadron after squadron of Japanese planes taking off from Taiwan that would utterly destroy MacArthur's bombers and fighter planes both in the air and on the cratered and smoldering landing strips of the Philippine archipelago. No wonder MacArthur coined the famous "unsinkable aircraft carrier" phrase to describe Taiwan.[9]

Chapter 21

THE WILD CHILD AND WILD CARD OF NORTH KOREA

Question: Which of these "wild card" scenarios is most likely to trigger a possible war between China and the United States?

1. An internal collapse of the North Korean regime due to famine, an internal power struggle, or social unrest
2. A North Korean provocation of South Korea such as the shelling of one of its islands, an attack on one of its commercial airliners, or the sinking of one of its ships
3. An American preemptive strike on North Korea's nuclear-weapons facilities to prevent further development of North Korea's nuclear-bomb capabilities
4. Deployment of a state-of-the-art ballistic-missile defense shield by the United States and its Asian allies to defend against a North Korean missile attack
5. A major invasion of South Korea by North Korean troops
6. A nuclear-missile strike by North Korea against Japan, South Korea, or the United States

If you were an intelligent speculator betting on any one of the above possibilities, you'd probably assign the highest probabilities to the "internal collapse" and "provocation" scenarios—at least based on past history. At the same time, you'd likely assign the lowest probability to the "nuclear-missile strike" scenario—which would be tantamount to nuclear suicide by North Korea.

Here, however is the very big problem: Any truly intelligent speculator must assume rationality to properly handicap outcomes; but once you cross the 38th parallel into the hermitic and Stalinist kingdom of North

Korea, all rationality bets are off on a police state run by a young, erratic megalomaniac with the backing of one of the world's largest armies.

As a practical matter, this absence of rationality means that all of the above scenarios *are* on the table. Therefore, the task before us, dear detectives, is to come to better understand the complex chain of events that might bring China and the United States into direct conflict should any of these scenarios unfold. Let's start, then, as it is so often useful to do, with a little history and background.

Since the Korean War armistice in 1953, North Korea has been almost perfectly sealed off from the rest of the world as a matter of leadership choice. It is a choice founded on an ideology known as *Juche*, which was first introduced in 1955 by North Korea's original "great leader," Kim Il-sung.

Literally translated, Juche means "self-reliance." By following Juche's autarkic path for more than six decades, North Korea's succession of Kim-family dictators has led the country's perpetually starving masses straight down the path to a proverbial "nasty, brutish, and short" Hobbesian existence. (On the "short" part, Hobbes didn't quite have this in mind, but chronic malnutrition has left a new generation of North Koreans an average of several inches shorter than their South Korean counterparts.)[1]

Today, after more than sixty years of Juche autarky, the North Korean economy is generally considered to be a basket case by many experts. However, it is not just the absence of a robust global trade that has held growth back.

In the hopes of feeding its starving masses, North Korea has remained primarily an agrarian economy. However, relatively poor soil, a shortage of arable land due to its mountainous terrain, communist-style production methods, and repeated cycles of floods and droughts (and the lack of adequate infrastructure for flood control) have resulted in a string of famines that have literally starved to death more than 10 percent of North Korea's population of about twenty-five million.[2]

As for what little manufacturing capacity North Korea has, it is devoted primarily to weapons production. Indeed, its ballistic-missile program alone siphons off more than one billion dollars a year from the economy[3]—this for a country with an annual gross domestic product of only around $15 billion a year (as compared to South Korea's more-than-one-*trillion*-dollar economy).[4]

In a related "guns versus butter" vein, North Korea maintains the fourth largest army in the world behind only that of China, the United States, and

India. This it does with a population base of roughly 8 percent that of America's and a mere 2 percent of China's. On top of all this, the Kim-family dynasty has been notorious for squandering government revenues on their own personal consumption of luxury goods ranging from "cosmetics, handbags, leather products, [and]watches" to "electronics, cars and top-shelf alcohol."[5]

It's not for nothing then that North Korea's economy is in a perpetual state of crisis, and the only real reason it has yet to collapse as the Soviet Union finally did under the weight of corruption and communist inefficiency is because of China. The abiding fact here is that China provides North Korea with as much as 90 percent of its energy imports and 45 percent of its food.[6] Take that Chinese lifeline away, and North Korea would likely quickly implode.

The question, of course, is: Why does China continue to prop up a regime that increasingly threatens to drag China itself into the vortex of war—and very possibly nuclear war? While at least some Chinese leaders are increasingly asking that very question, Beijing's clear fear is that in the event of a North Korean collapse—or even a rapprochement between North and South Korea in the tradition of West Germany's effective absorption of East Germany—a unified Korea would side with the American-South Korean democratic alliance rather than with an authoritarian China.

Economically, China has also found North Korea to be a very pliable colony to exploit for the resources it needs for its own factory floor. As noted by the Council on Foreign Relations: "growing numbers of Chinese firms are investing in North Korea," and "these companies have made major investments aimed at developing mineral resources in North Korea's northern region."[7]

At the political level, over the last several decades, North Korea likewise has served as a very important, albeit darkly cynical, "bargaining chip" for China. For every time North Korea exhibits some new form of outrageous behavior—a missile shot here, a nuclear-bomb test there—a perennially naïve America turns to China in the hopes it will help control its "wild child." The problem for the United States, however, as Professor Aaron Friedberg has aptly described it, is that while China has been "effective at setting the table, it has never served the meal."[8]

As a final, and not inconsequential, reason for Beijing's continued backing of an increasingly unstable and erratic regime, there are the close ties between the armies of North Korea and China that date back to the Korean War. During this conflict, over a million soldiers on the North

Korea-China side lost their lives at the hands of the "American imperialists." While this war was over sixty years ago, these military roots nonetheless still run deep, and it has been very difficult for China's civilian leadership to develop a harder line on North Korea because of these ties.

Fig. 21.1. The wild child and wild card of North Korea Kim Jong-un (center front) presides over his loyal troops. (Photograph used with permission from Reuters.)

✳✳✳✳✳

For all of these geostrategic, economic, political, and familial reasons, the fortunes of China and North Korea remain tightly intertwined. As to how these ties that bind might lead to war, let's first consider the "internal collapse" scenario."

Suppose, then, that despite massive Chinese aid, the North Korean economy finally does fall of its own weight and chaos reigns in the capital of Pyongyang and throughout the country. In the wake of this collapse, millions of North Korean refugees stream into South Korea or north across the Yalu River into China.

At this point, with the North Korean army suddenly in a rogue, and perhaps fugue, state and North Korea's nuclear weapons in the hands of God knows who, South Korea and the United States decide it is in the best interests of peace to send troops into North Korea to secure its nuclear weapons and bring about a rapprochement between the two countries. Of course, China will likely send in troops as well; and the only question becomes: What happens when Chinese, North Korean, South Korean, and American troops meet? It is far too easy to see how things might quickly escalate.

Now, what about the "provocation" scenario? One need only look to the past to see that history might easily repeat itself. Consider just this partial list of incidents in which:

- North Korean MIGS shot down a US Navy reconnaissance plane, killing thirty-one Americans;[9]
- North Korean agents felled a South Korean airliner with a planted bomb, killing all 115 passengers and crew aboard;
- a North Korean submarine landed commandos on South Korean soil, provoking battles that killed sixteen South Korean soldiers and civilians;
- another North Korean sub sank a South Korean naval vessel, killing forty-six sailors;[10] and
- the North Korean army lobbed about 170 artillery shells and rockets at Yeonpyeong Island, causing significant damage and killing two South Korean marines and two civilians.[11]

Further contributing to the possibility of an escalating conflict in the wake of any new such provocation is the political hard line Seoul has adopted since the election in 2012 of South Korea's first female president, Park Geun-hye. This steely-eyed daughter of former South Korean dictator Park Chung-hee is certainly no stranger to North Korean aggression— her mother was shot and killed by a North Korean assassin with a bullet intended for her father.

After defeating a far more liberal opponent in 2012, Park vowed in 2013 to respond to any new North Korean provocation "swiftly and decisively" *and* without any regard for "political considerations."[12] She also promised that North Korea would be "erased from the earth" if it ever launched a nuclear attack.[13]

Now what about the "preemptive strike" scenario? Might the United

States decide to preemptively bomb North Korea's nuclear facilities as a means of denying it the capability to produce additional nuclear weapons?

Given that the United States and Israel have had this very same debate over whether to preemptively bomb Iran's nuclear centrifuges, this scenario is hardly far-fetched. Indeed, an additional fear here besides North Korea itself using the bomb is that North Korea might sell fissionable material to some of the most dangerous actors on the world stage such as Iran or Pakistan or terrorist organizations like Al Qaeda.

In fact, the only reason this "preemptive strike" scenario may be improbable is that North Korea's nuclear genie is already out of the bottle. The reason: In 2003, while President George Bush's national-security team was preparing to invade Iraq, North Korea used this distraction to clandestinely move from its civilian nuclear-reactor facility more than eight thousand spent fuel rods that it had hitherto agreed to keep under wraps.[14] By reprocessing these spent fuel rods, North Korea was then able to extract sufficient quantities of weapons-grade plutonium and spirit this deadly fissionable material away to hidden locations immune from any preemptive strikes.

Since that time, North Korea has conducted a series of underground nuclear tests; and these bombs have progressively increased in megatonnage and sophistication. On the basis of these tests, most experts now believe that North Korea has essentially reached "critical mass" as a legitimate nuclear power.

This observation leads us to the "nuclear attack" scenario. In this scenario, if North Korea were to launch one or more nuclear-tipped missiles aimed at South Korea, Japan, or the United States, one likely US response might be a retaliatory nuclear strike that would fulfill President Park's promise of "erasing" at least Pyongyang from the face of the earth.

While it would be difficult for China to disagree with the righteousness of such an American response, there is still the matter of US nuclear-tipped missiles being launched at least in the direction of China. If China were to fear some of those missiles might be coming its way, it's fair to say that anything might happen.

Note, however, that it's not just the possibility of a nuclear strike by North Korea that is so escalatory. There is also the matter of how the United States and its allies in Asia are *already* responding to this perceived threat. In fact, this response brings us to our next possible catalyst for war, the "ballistic-missile defense" scenario.

Through US eyes, it seems perfectly rational for America to introduce a far more sophisticated missile defense system into the Asian theater[15] in response to North Korea's repeated threats of "all-out nuclear war."[16] China, however, has responded with sharp criticisms of any such ballistic-missile shield, claiming this shield is aimed not just at North Korea but also at China itself.[17]

Stripped of Beijing's rhetoric, this is just one more variation of the "security dilemma" we have previously discussed as an escalatory factor. China's fear—really quite legitimate—is that a state-of-the-art American missile-defense system in Asia may also allow the United States to block China's "second strike" capability. This would, in turn, open the door to a preemptive first strike by US forces against China—so China must inevitably respond by producing much higher quantities of missiles and warheads in the hopes of swarming, and ultimately overwhelming, the new missile-defense system. And so the "security dilemma" dance of escalation goes.

As for our remaining "the North invades the South" scenario, its most unsettling aspect is the "tyranny of proximity."[18] While the capital of North Korea, Pyongyang, is almost one hundred miles from the 38th parallel dividing North and South, the South Korean capital of Seoul is a mere thirty miles from advancing North Korean troops and tanks. If nothing else, this strategic advantage provides a perennial enticement to a North Korean military perhaps eager for a fight.

Of course, it is unlikely that the United States would ever allow itself to be drawn into another land war in Korea. Instead, it would likely use its air and naval power to help the South Koreans repel any invasion. Former Marine fighter pilot and Pentagon insider Ed Timperlake bluntly describes what must be done:

> First and foremost, you have to kill and cripple the command structure of the dear leader because he can press a button and launch a nuke. He's proven he has them. So you have to attack immediately. It's going to be horrible. There are twenty thousand artillery tubes that will kill a lot of people. But if you resort to a symmetric fight, a ground fight, with North Korea, you've lost the battle before you've begun. You have to take him out and take him out brutally and quickly.[19]

But again, once North and South Korea engage "brutally and quickly" with America in the mix—either on land or in the skies—China would be hard-pressed to remain on the sidelines.

Chapter 22

ON THE ROCKS IN THE EAST CHINA SEA

Question: In the coming decades, which strategic path is Japan
likely to follow in response to a rising China and
different possible perceptions of its American defense-
treaty ally?

1. After concluding that a weak or vacillating America is
   likely to abandon it, a "Hiroshima be damned" Japan
   develops its own nuclear weapons and charts an
   independent course.
2. After concluding that a weak or vacillating America is
   likely to abandon it, a "bandwagoning" Japan accedes
   to China's hegemony and becomes part of an Asian
   economic condominium led by China.
3. Firm in its belief that America will honor its treaty
   obligations and continue to provide Japan with its nuclear
   umbrella, a "staunch ally" Japan expands its economic
   ties with the United States and other allies in the region
   while bolstering its conventional military and missile-
   defense capabilities.

How Japan responds to the challenge of a rising China—and possibly a declining America—will no doubt have a significant impact
on the future of war and peace in Asia. A "Hiroshima be damned" Japan
armed with atomic bombs arguably raises the risks of actual nuclear war in
Asia. A "bandwagoning" Japan allied with China against the United States
conjures up a replay of Imperial Japan's "Greater East Asia Co-Prosperity
Sphere" and World War II—perhaps with a very different victor and ending.

Even a "staunch ally" scenario is no guarantee the bullets won't fly as it would certainly spur China, in the spirit of our by now well-known "security dilemma," to produce more and more bullets. So what's the only country to suffer a nuclear holocaust likely to do—caught as it is between an inglorious imperial past, a pacifist present, and a highly uncertain future?

In choosing exactly which of Yogi Berra's proverbial forks in the road to take, the first troubling truth Tokyo must grapple with is this: It has cast its *economic* lot in with a rising Chinese power harboring a citizenry that seemingly has little but hate and disdain for Japan. Nor should this enmity be any surprise as China's new generations have been fed a steady diet of hateful and fearful messaging in everything from history books that highlight Imperial Japan's atrocities to the roughly two hundred movies a year that inevitably cast Japan as the villain.[1]

The equally troubling truth here is that Tokyo has also cast its *national security* lot in with an America that is in the midst of one of its all-too-periodic flirtations with neoisolationism. Nor is this any surprise as the problem America now faces in fulfilling its defense-treaty obligations to staunch allies like Japan is both an economic and political one—and the two are ineluctably intertwined.

On the economic front, chronic US budget deficits are being resolved in no small way by dramatic cuts in defense spending. In fact, these defense-budget cuts have found little opposition amongst an American public profoundly and deeply war-weary after dutifully funding two of the longest wars in American history, those in Afghanistan and Iraq.

On the political front, perhaps if those wars had ended better, American taxpayers might be more willing to finance an American military "pivot" to Asia. However, with Iraq literally in burning pieces and a resurgent Taliban in Afghanistan, many Americans—particularly those struggling on the economic front—are simply fed up.

It follows that, at least from a Japanese perspective, the United States looks increasingly like it has an economy no longer strong enough to sustain its military commitments, a populace that is losing its political will, and a political system in gridlock no longer wise enough to establish its defense spending priorities. Not surprisingly, then, even when American presidents or secretaries of state or chairmen of the joint chiefs of staff profess their strong commitment to Asian allies like Japan, their counterparts in Tokyo or Seoul or Manila are dutifully and rightfully skeptical.

What, then, is a twenty-first century Japan supposed to do in the face of this increased uncertainty over the commitment of its most important ally and protector? This is a particularly crucial question since Japan has increasingly found itself at the tip of China's coercive spear.

Indeed, it has become almost a daily occurrence for some element of the Chinese military to challenge Japan's defense forces. Whether it is a fleet of Chinese warships steaming uncomfortably close to Japan's territorial waters, Chinese fighter jets or reconnaissance planes encroaching on Japan's air space, an armada of civilian and paramilitary Chinese vessels executing a "cabbage strategy" around Japan's Senkaku Islands, or the Chinese press waging relentless media warfare against an allegedly ultranationalist Japan, it is a continuous Beijing drumbeat that has ratcheted up tensions in the region.

It is precisely because of this mounting pressure that Japan's ultimate choice of its strategic path cannot be separated from the question of whether the United States will fulfill its defense-treaty obligations in the event of a Chinese attack. In thinking this choice through, however, it is critical to understand the scope of what America's treaty obligations really are.

The very real "will there be war" problem here is that these obligations are not just a matter of whether the United States would send ships and troops to help Japan should China be so imprudent as to invade the Senkaku Islands or shoot down a Japanese plane for entering disputed airspace. America's treaty obligations also speak directly to the question as to whether the United States will truly provide the nuclear umbrella it has promised to hold over Japan for more than sixty years if conflict does indeed erupt. Here, a little more history may well be in order.

✺✺✺✺✺

When the United States and Japan entered into their mutual defense pact in 1952, this seemed to be a good deal for both countries. From the US perspective, America got to maintain forward bases on Japanese soil to protect its interests in Asia and because Japan committed to a small, defense-oriented military, American citizens would not have to worry about another Pearl Harbor.

From Japan's perspective, this was a fine deal as well. With American taxpayers effectively footing the bill for its defense, Japan could devote its considerable economic resources to peaceful development and trade.

For more than six decades, as part of the longest mutual defense treaty in modern history, neither Tokyo nor Washington ever imagined this treaty might be invoked because of an attack on Japanese soil. As Senior Fellow Sheila Smith of the Council on Foreign Relations has noted:

In the early years, the US-Japan alliance was first and foremost a Cold War arrangement that allowed the forward deployment of American forces in the region. If there were ever going to be a conflict in Asia, it wasn't going to happen on Japanese territory. Instead, it would be all about the Korean Peninsula or perhaps a Taiwan Strait contingency.[2]

Today, however, both Tokyo and Washington must worry about the direct engagement of Japanese and Chinese forces and the probability, however low it may seem in the abstract, that China might respond during a conflict with a nuclear strike or threat of a nuclear strike. It is in contemplating any such nuclear-strike scenario that Tokyo must rightfully begin to wonder whether the United States will offer its nuclear arsenal in defense of Japan in a new age of Chinese nuclear capabilities that bring counterstrikes on Los Angeles or Chicago or New York onto the chess board.

Put simply, this is Japan's "will the United States be willing to trade Los Angeles to save Tokyo?" dilemma. In truth, asking an ally to expose its major cities to nuclear obliteration is certainly a lot to ask—and both Tokyo and Washington are increasingly aware of this subtext in their treaty alliance. This is all the more true in Washington because of the attendant problem of so-called moral hazard. To wit: America's commitment to defend Japan and its territories raises the possibility that Japan may engage in behavior that is more bold—and possibly more reckless—than it otherwise would be.

Of course, here is the nub of the matter: As soon as Tokyo begins to doubt the certainty of America's promised nuclear umbrella, Japan must contemplate at least two alternatives to the "staunch ally" scenario.

The first, the "bandwagon" scenario, is the classic "turn over the king and admit defeat" move in a chess match. In this scenario, Japan sees China as the ultimate winner in the struggle for Asian hegemony—so a kowtowing Japan simply switches sides and throws its lot in with a new Imperial China.

The obvious downside for Japan is that any "bandwagon" scenario would necessarily involve the surrender of Japanese claims to the Senkaku Islands. A vassal Japan would also likely have to accept China's definition of its maritime rights—and thereby lose its fishing and oil and gas rights in much of the East China Sea. Moreover, should an Imperial China really want to flex its revanchist muscles, Japan might even have to surrender its Okinawan territories and allow them to be restored as the Ryukyu Islands in a Chinese empire.

On the economic front, Japan might fare a bit better as it would likely enter into a "condominium" arrangement with China. This arrangement would in all probability include a protectionist trade zone between the two countries—with America as the odd trading partner out—as well as the adoption of the Chinese renminbi as a reserve currency replacement for the US dollar.

In fact, there is at least some logic to this "bandwagon" scenario given the high degree of economic interdependence that already exists between China and Japan As for the potential of this scenario as a trigger or trip wire for war, it stems largely from the profound negative impacts a Chinese-run economic condominium likely would have on both the economic prosperity and national security of the United States.

Economically, America runs the risk of being forced to trade on unfavorable terms with China's condominium, with an attendant reduction in both trade and US GDP growth. Militarily, there is also this strategic hat trick to consider: The United States loses its forward bases, America's missile-defense shield in Asia is lowered, and, as China projects its power further and further into the Pacific, US cities from Seattle to Washington, DC, become more and more vulnerable to nuclear strikes or blackmail. For these reasons alone, such a "bandwagon" scenario might lead to greater conflict between China and the United States over time.

Now what about the "Hiroshima be damned" scenario? Here Japan's extreme aversion to developing its nuclear-weapons arsenal because of the bombs dropped on Hiroshima and Nagasaki is only matched by Japan's almost certain ability to quickly build and deploy highly sophisticated nuclear weapons.

The abiding fact here is that Japan's more than sixty years of experience using nuclear reactors to generate electricity for the home islands has given it both the expertise and the fissionable material to rapidly develop a nuclear bomb. Wed that expertise and material with Japan's vaunted manufacturing prowess and, unlike countries like Iran and North Korea, which are slowly developing relatively small bombs, Japan could have a bevy of the biggest ones almost overnight.

This stark possibility does indeed shine a bright light on one of the most important functions of US force projection in Asia, namely, to keep the nuclear peace. Here, most experts believe that the likelihood of nuclear war in Asia is far lower if countries like Japan and South Korea remain without nuclear weapons themselves and simply rely on the United States for deterrence. However, once the reliability of that American nuclear umbrella comes into question, all bets—and the brakes on nuclear proliferation in Asia—are off.

Given that the "Hiroshima be damned" scenario is likely to be even more destabilizing than the "bandwagon" scenario, the question must be asked as to whether the "staunch ally" scenario would fare any better at keeping the peace. The answer here inevitably hinges on how China responds to a growing economic and military alliance between America and Japan.

On the one hand, if China is simply and pragmatically probing the limits of Japanese and US resolve with its current trajectory of aggression, then a "staunch ally" scenario should enhance the peace. As Pentagon analyst Michael Pillsbury has framed this "peace through strength" principle, if China probes and finds weakness, it will proceed. However, if it strikes and finds steel, it will retreat.[3]

On the other hand, if China becomes more and more vulnerable to its own internal nationalistic pressures—or if its leaders believe that a military buildup by a US-backed Japan is likely to lead to another foreign humiliation—China will dutifully follow the "security dilemma" script and redouble its efforts to arm itself. Of course, at that point, war becomes more and more likely.

From this stark assessment, you should see how important it is that the leaders of China, Japan, and the United States have frank discussions about both their capabilities and intentions as they seek to find a durable and lasting peace. However, as we shall discuss in a later chapter, one of the biggest obstacles to peace in Asia is China's extreme aversion to negotiation and transparency. And so Japan as a trigger or trip wire for war will loom large in the decades ahead—and much of what happens will be driven by the degree of US commitment and resolve in the region.

Chapter 23

A PARACEL ISLANDS PRELUDE
TO THE NEXT VIETNAM WAR

Question: Which of these statements about the
Chinese-Vietnamese relationship is *not* true?

1. China and Vietnam are both ruled by Communist Party
   governments.
2. Buddhism and Confucianism are important parts of the
   historical cultures of both China and Vietnam.
3. China played a pivotal role in helping Vietnam expel both
   French and American military forces.
4. China and Vietnam remain close friends and strong allies.

In fact, the correct answer here is no. 4: China and Vietnam remain any-thing but close friends and strong allies despite their numerous similarities; there are ample historical reasons for this. In ancient times—going back to 100 BCE—China invaded Vietnam and ruled it for a thousand years before the Vietnamese people rose up and expelled their conquerors. As we have already noted, as late as 1979, China similarly invaded Vietnam as "punishment" for its alliance with the Soviet Union—although it was primarily China that was truly punished as its army suffered extremely heavy casualties.

This invasion history notwithstanding, the primary source of enmity between the two countries today is China's repeated bullying of Vietnam in the waters of the South China Sea. While the South China Sea is often referred to as a "marginal sea"—meaning that it is partially enclosed by islands—there is nothing "marginal" about a body of water that is the largest in the world after the five oceans.[1] Indeed, through the South China Sea's more than one million square miles fully one-third of all global shipping now transits.

It's not just this modern day "silk and spice" trade that makes the

South China Sea so important. Its waters are also home to some of the most fertile fishing grounds in the world in a region where fish is a key source of protein. In addition, beneath its seabed may lay oil and natural-gas reserves comparable to that of the Persian Gulf.

Most broadly, and strategically, it may also be accurately said that whoever controls this gateway to the Indian Ocean also controls Southeast Asia itself—and perhaps East Asia as well given that much of the oil that lights the lamps of Japan and South Korea must first pass through the South China Sea.

Given these high economic and national security stakes, it should come as no surprise that the South China Sea is also a center of intense conflict. As for possible war triggers, trip wires, and flash points involving China, there are at least two sets.

The first, examined in this chapter, involves Vietnam and is centered on the Paracel Islands group in the northern part of the South China Sea. The second, examined in the next chapter, revolves primarily around the Philippines and land features such as the Spratly Islands group to the south.

Let's begin then with a tour of the Paracel Islands—arguably ground zero in any potential war between China and Vietnam. These islands are located a little over three hundred miles from Hainan Island in China and a little under two hundred miles from Da Nang, Vietnam. They consist of just thirty small islets, sand banks, and reefs with a total surface area of a mere 1.3 square miles.

Small in land mass though they may be, these land features are, however, spread out over 5,800 square miles of ocean. As such, they convey very expansive resource rights under the United Nations Law of the Sea Treaty.

In particular, and as we have discussed previously, under the Law of the Sea Treaty, nations are granted two-hundred-mile Exclusive Economic Zones radiating out from their coastlines. Within these so-called EEZs, these nations are entitled to all of the natural-resource rights both within the waters themselves—think fish here—and beneath the seabed—think oil and natural gas.

Now here's the key "will there be war" point: It is not just the large coastlines of countries like China from which EEZs can be delineated. If an island is habitable, no matter how small it may be, it gets a two-hundred-mile EEZ as well—one that radiates in a full 360-degree sweep.

In fact, this is a key point often lost on analysts and journalists who routinely devalue disputes over the Paracel and Spratly Islands as meaningless squabbles over worthless "rocks in the sea." This is, however, an extremely myopic view. As MIT professor Richard Samuels has duly noted, because of the expansive maritime rights that the Law of the Sea Treaty conveys even to seeming "rocks," the seas no longer contain the islands but rather the islands contain the seas.[2]

The broader implication of this point for our "will there be war" question is one aptly noted by former White House advisor Stefan Halper: A continental power like China can significantly extend its maritime rights in "concentric circles" and in "leapfrog effect" simply by taking control of even very small islands in the South China Sea.[3] Indeed, by seizing the Paracels from Vietnam, China has effectively extended its EEZ from two hundred miles to over three hundred miles from mainland China. In similar leapfrog fashion, with its successful Spratly Island grabs, China can now claim an EEZ that reaches out over five hundred miles.

Of course, through this revanchist process, China's EEZ has begun to significantly overlap with the Exclusive Economic Zones of other countries in the region, and how these overlapping resource rights should be resolved has become a matter of fierce contention. It is precisely when a bullying China resorts to coercion or outright military force to settle these disputes in its favor that the waters of the South China Sea at least figuratively begin to boil.

Today, in the case of a simmering and often seething Vietnam, such Chinese bullying takes many different forms. For example, Chinese fishing vessels, often accompanied by Chinese coast-guard ships, continue to push Vietnamese fishermen further and further out from waters that Vietnam has fished for centuries. While these contested waters are often clearly within Vietnam's own Exclusive Economic Zone, they are also caught within the Paracel Islands overlap claimed by China—a claim all the more noxious to Vietnam given that China seized the Paracels from it to begin with.

In similar coercive fashion, China's ships have cut the cables of Vietnamese oil exploration rigs and otherwise are deterring Vietnam from developing oil and gas reserves clearly within its EEZ via swarming displays of military and paramilitary force. On top of this, China has deployed its own fleet of massive floating oil exploration rigs that have made regular, and often well-publicized, incursions into waters claimed by Vietnam.[4]

In response to such Chinese bullying, Vietnam has embarked on its own very rapid military buildup; and to be clear: There is absolutely no "security dilemma" involved here where two countries are innocently *misreading* what might in reality only be the *defensive* military buildups of the other. Rather, this is an old-fashioned and highly dangerous *offensive* arms race—Vietnam knows a rapidly militarizing China wants its natural resources, and it is responding to this undisguised aggression with its own quite-significant military buildup to protect itself.

For example, to counteract Chinese naval power, Vietnam is acquiring a potent fleet of Russian Kilo-class submarines while Russia has already "provided enough Yakhont antiship missiles to the Vietnamese navy to equip a battalion."[5] As a very effective strategic complement to Vietnam's submarine fleet, these missiles have sufficient range so as to be "considered a considerable threat to Chinese vessels operating in the disputed waters."[6]

Nor is it just Vietnam's navy muscling up. Its air force is adding twelve more supermaneuverable Russian Su-30 jet fighters to an already substantial arsenal, and "taking off from Bien Hoa" near Ho Chi Minh City in the north, these fighters have a combat radius that "covers the entire South China Sea."[7] Meanwhile, from the Phu Cat Air Force Base along the southern coast of Vietnam—a former US base during the Vietnam War—Vietnamese fighter jets and bombers are within easy reach of China's military installations on Hainan Island.[8]

As a still further complication to this "will there be war" equation, there are the cautious overtures now being made to the United States by a Vietnam perhaps hoping to tuck itself beneath the same kind of security umbrella now enjoyed by other US allies in Asia such as Japan and the Philippines. There is, of course, no small irony here given that the two countries fought a bitter war for more than a decade.

That said, having defeated the United States, Vietnam is not afraid of it, and in its strategic calculation, it would rather have a superpower friend physically located over seven thousand miles away than a superpower foe on its borders with a long history of invading Vietnamese territory. To analysts like Naval War College professor Lyle Goldstein, however, any such new formal defense-treaty alliance between Vietnam and the United States might actually become itself a trigger or trip wire for war.

As Goldstein sees it, if the United States were to establish forward bases in Vietnam, this might constitute a "red line" for China. The more subtle underlying point here is that while China understands the historic relationship between the United States and the Philippines and can tolerate a renewed US naval presence at the Philippine's Subic Bay facility, Vietnam has been a historic rival for centuries, and any substantial US military presence in Vietnam would constitute both a significant escalation and a provocation.[9]

At the end of the day, then, the China-Vietnam trigger is one fraught with dangerous possibilities and no shortage of strategic conundrums. Whether this trigger is ultimately pulled will depend not just on how aggressively China continues to press its claims but also on how diplomacy in the region dances around any emerging American-Vietnamese alliance.

Unfortunately, this is not the only trigger the world must worry about in the South China Sea. The other, which we will discuss in the next chapter, involves the southern part of the South China Sea, principally the Spratly Islands but also other key land and maritime features such as Macclesfield Bank and Scarborough Shoal.

Chapter 24

A HUNGRY COW'S TONGUE IN THE SOUTH CHINA SEA

Question: Which of these countries laying claims to the Spratly
Islands in the South China Sea is farthest in distance
from those islands?

1. Brunei
2. China
3. Malaysia
4. The Philippines
5. Vietnam

Strategically located off the nearby coasts of Brunei, Malaysian
Borneo, the Philippines, and Vietnam, the Spratly Islands consist of
roughly 750 reefs, islets, atolls, cays, and islands. Spread out as they are
over more than 164,000 square miles of blue water, the nearest of these land
features are still more than six hundred miles from the Chinese mainland.[1]

While the Spratlys are far more numerous in land features than the
Paracels to the north, these two island groups anchoring the South China
Sea nonetheless share at least three things in common. First, the Spratlys
stand guard over several critical sea lines of communication that provide
access to the Indian Ocean. Second, as with the Paracels, the Spratlys are
also home to incredibly fertile fishing grounds, and third—perhaps most
important as a possible trigger or trip wire for war—at least some estimates
of the potential oil and gas reserves of the Spratly Islands put them on par
with those of the Persian Gulf.

Because of both their strategic significance and economic value, over
forty of the Spratly land features are occupied by military forces from fully
five different countries, including not just China but also the aforementioned
Malaysia, the Philippines, Taiwan, and Vietnam.[2] In fact, territorial rivalries

are so high within the Spratlys that many of the small land features look like cartoonish caricatures of armed camps—picture here Yosemite Sam with guns and missiles blazing. Indeed, in some of the most beautiful and pastoral waters of the world, fortress islets bristle with heliports, airstrips, docks, harbors, and fortified platforms erected on the tiniest of footprints.

A poster child for this phenomenon is China's Mischief Reef, taken by force from the Philippines in 1994. As China's easternmost occupied outpost in the South China Sea, Mischief Reef has steadily morphed into a full-fledged military garrison featuring a five-story fortified cement bunker and three octagonal buildings sitting on stilts.[3]Protected as they are by a battery of antiaircraft guns, these structures now house valuable communications and radar systems for monitoring aircraft and ships in the area as well as for guiding ballistic and cruise missiles in a war-fighting scenario.[4]

THE COW'S TONGUE NINE-DASH LINE

So just how is it that a country like China, so far from the Spratlys relative to much closer claimants like Malaysia and the Philippines, can insist on sovereignty over *all* of the islands in the Spratly chain? The answer to this question is central to our detective story because it involves a particularly pernicious conflict incubator known formally as China's "nine-dash line"—and known often derisively as China's hungry "cow's tongue."

This *U*-shaped territorial line first appeared in 1947 in a location map published by the Nationalist Chinese government, and it does indeed take the peculiar shape of a cow's tongue. After the fall of the Nationalists and with their retreat to Taiwan, this cow's tongue line was quickly embraced in 1949 by a new Communist government not wishing to appear weaker than its predecessor.[5]

As to why China's nine-dash line is so controversial, one need only glance quickly at a map to understand the line's expansive, expansionist, and revisionist implications. So picture now this nine-dash line in your mind's eye:

It begins in the Luzon Strait at the northeast edge of the South China Sea above the northern tip of the Philippines. It then runs to the south and west parallel to the coastlines of the Philippines and Brunei, effectively tracing the lower boundary of the South China Sea. After reaching Malaysian Borneo just below Brunei, the nine-dash line next curves across the

South China Sea toward the southern tip of Vietnam. It finally turns north, passing the coastline of Vietnam and ending in the Gulf of Tonkin off the coast of China's Hainan Island.

Map 24.1. China's *U*-shaped territorial "nine-dash line" aka "cow's tongue."

In this way, China's expansive cow's tongue encompasses almost 90 percent of the South China Sea. Indeed, if China's claim were forced upon the region, it would effectively transform the South China Sea into a "China lake."

To understand just how expansive China's nine-dash line really is, consider the East Natuna natural-gas field in Indonesia's Natuna Island group. This field, discovered in the 1970s, remains one of the largest untapped reserves in the world, with proven gas reserves estimated at forty-six trillion cubic feet.[6]

While the East Natuna field is clearly within Indonesia's Exclusive Economic Zone—and almost one thousand miles from China—the field is also within the boundaries of China's nine-dash line. This is a "mapfare" point made emphatically by China in 1993 with the publishing of a map that included East Natuna. Since that time, a nervous Indonesia has, without success, repeatedly sought to clarify whether China has really staked out a historical claim and will one day attempt to enforce it.

As to just how China is now pressing its cow's tongue claims—and how this might be a trigger or trip wire for war—China has come a long way from its Maoist days where it simply seized islands in the South China Sea at the point of a gun. In fact, China's taking of Mischief Reef in 1994 without actually having to fire a shot marked the new beginning of a subtle evolution in Chinese strategy that critics today refer to as "salami slicing." As Professor T. X. Hammes of America's National Defense University explains: "Salami slicing is a strategic concept where China doesn't ever put on enough pressure to get a military push back but uses just enough pressure to seize territory."[7]

Today, the centerpiece of China's salami slicing is the clever use of large fleets of white-hulled boats like fishing vessels and maritime surveillance ships to advance China's territorial claims in very small increments, ergo the "salami slicing" metaphor. Of course, always waiting over the coercive horizon are China's gray-hulled warships should they be needed.

To see how China's salami slicing now works—and how it could well drag the United States into a conflict—we need look no farther than China's successful taking of Scarborough Shoal in 2012 from the Philippines.

✶✶✶✶✶

Scarborough Shoal is a triangular-shaped chain of reefs, rocks, and small islands about 115 nautical miles off the Philippines' Zambales Province on the western side of Luzon Island and well within the Philippines' Exclusive Economic Zone. Barely thirty-four miles in circumference, the shoal covers an area of about sixty square miles while only one of its land features, South Rock, is above water at high tide.

China's taking of Scarborough Shoal, which is more than six hundred miles from the Chinese mainland, began in April of 2012 with an incursion into the shoal by a flotilla of white-hulled Chinese fishing vessels. When a gray-hulled Philippines naval ship was dispatched to investigate, it found the Chinese vessels laden with an assortment of endangered species along with large amounts of contraband in the form of coral and live sharks. When Philippine officials attempted to arrest the fishermen, they were blocked by several vessels of China's white-hulled China Marine Surveillance fleet, and a tense standoff ensued.

During the course of this standoff, a series of violent protests erupted in both China and the Philippines. At the same time, Chinese hackers launched a series of cyberattacks against key Philippine government agencies.

To further boost its coercive soft power, China even rolled out a boycott of Philippine exports to China and a *de facto* ban on Chinese tourism. These economic weapons were particularly harmful to the Philippines' economy given its heavy trade dependence on China.

In June of 2012, US diplomats thought they had successfully mediated a resolution that required both China and the Philippines to withdraw from the area and negotiate a peaceful settlement. However, while the Philippines kept its end of the deal, China never left—a treachery that Philippines president Benigno Aquino would compare, albeit with some hyperbole, to Nazi Germany's annexation of Czechoslovakia.[8]

The following month, China further escalated the crisis by blockading a portion of the shoal where Filipinos have fished for generations. It then proceeded to issue a fifteen-mile fishing ban around the area in question.

Throughout this salami-slicing crisis, China effectively used what one of its own generals proudly described as a "cabbage strategy." As previously noted, this strategy involves surrounding the contested zone with so many different types of civilian and paramilitary vessels that the area is wrapped layer by layer like a cabbage.[9]

At the center of this cabbage strategy, and at the tip of China's coercive spear, is the aforementioned white-hulled China Marine Surveillance force—China's equivalent of the American Coast Guard. According to the former commander of the US Pacific Fleet James Fanell (Fanell was fired by the Pentagon for blunt statements such as this[10]): "Unlike US coast guard cutters, China Marine Surveillance cutters have no other mission but to harass other nations into submitting to China's expansive claims."[11]

And here is what is perhaps most clever and interesting about China's use of white-hulled "peace ships" rather than gray-hulled warships to advance its territorial claims: By using such putatively nonkinetic force, China appears far less threatening in the media. Moreover, if the Philippines or Japan or the United States responds with gray-hulled warships, they immediately become the "bad guys" in the media narrative. Never mind that China's gray-hulled ships are always waiting over the horizon to intervene should its civilian vanguard get into trouble.

In fact, this white-hulled, salami-slicing strategy is taking place within the context of the much larger "three warfares" strategy we discussed in an earlier chapter. Just remember Stefan Halper's three-warfares maxim that it is not necessarily the best weapons that win today's wars but rather the best narrative. Remember, too, that one of the goals of the nonkinetic three warfares is to advance territorial ambitions that in earlier times might have only been realized through kinetic force.

For its part, saddled with a ragtag navy no match for China's, the Philippines has tried to fight China's salami-slicing might with legal right using a bit of lawfare of its own. In particular, and in the face of angry Chinese denunciations, the Philippines filed a request for arbitration before the International Tribunal for the Law of the Sea for the express purpose of legally discrediting China's "nine-dash line" and its derivative claims on land features such as Mischief Reef and Scarborough Shoal.

In a rare strategic misstep, China refused to participate in the arbitration. By doing so, it not only lost the opportunity to have a representative present, it ironically also speeded up the process.

Should China lose the case—it is still being deliberated but the ruling is not subject to appeal—the effective international legal death of the cow's tongue would send shock waves throughout the South China Sea. Of course, should China defy a losing ruling, this might provoke a military response by a Philippines now morally emboldened by its legal success.

One clear danger here is that the United States might be dragged into any conflict between China and the Philippines by virtue of America's mutual defense treaty with its long-time ally. Possible flash points include not just Scarborough Shoal but also other disputed areas that include Second Thomas Shoal now occupied by the Philippines but under Chinese siege and Macclesfield Bank already forcibly taken by China.

Note, however, that from an American perspective, its mutual defense pact with the Philippines creates the potential for yet another dangerous variation of "moral hazard." Specifically, this defense treaty might encourage the Philippines to engage in stronger actions against China than it otherwise would. The result may be to drag America into a war it did not seek and would desperately like to avoid.

As we have already seen, this is exactly the same kind of moral-hazard dilemma the United States faces as China seeks to have its way with American-ally Japan in the adjacent East China Sea. More broadly, as the United

States tightens its alliances in Asia with other countries increasingly wary of China—including Indonesia, Malaysia, Singapore, and Vietnam—the moral hazard possibility that one or more of these countries will act more boldly toward China than they otherwise would without American support will grow along with the possibility of war, thereby making the South China Sea a simmering cauldron indeed.[12]

Chapter 25

CHINA'S NEW
MONROE DOCTRINE FOR ASIA

Question: Which statement most closely corresponds to
international law?

1. All nations have the right to both freedom of navigation
   and overflight in the seas and airspaces beyond the
   twelve-mile territorial limits of other countries.
2. Any nation has the right to restrict both freedom of
   navigation and overflight within the two-hundred-mile limit
   of its Exclusive Economic Zone.

As lead questions go in our detective story, this may well be the most arcane. However, it is also one of the most critical because China is not just engaged in numerous *territorial* disputes that now constitute war triggers and trip wires. China is also waging an increasingly escalatory *jurisdictional* battle with the United States over America's right to conduct normal military operations within Asian waters.

Of course, the underlying question about this contentious battle is whether China is trying to implement its own version of the Monroe Doctrine. As University of Chicago professor John Mearsheimer notes:

> From China's point of view, it would be ideal if they could duplicate in Asia the feat that the United States has accomplished in the Western Hemisphere—dominate all its neighbors and push the United States far away, just the way the United States pushed all the European great powers far away in the 19th century via the Monroe Doctrine.[1]

Of course, the best way for China to peacefully implement a Monroe Doctrine with Chinese characteristics is to use a combination of "lawfare" and coercion to close the seas to US military vessels. And therein lies the tale of this chapter.

In fact, the question of whether the seas should be open or closed is an age-old one that dates back to the days in which the Roman Empire effectively sealed off the Mediterranean Sea. Perhaps the most important historical marker in this debate is the year 1609 when Hugo Grotius, a jurist of the Dutch Republic, argued in a work entitled *The Free Sea* for the principle of *mare liberum* (Latin for "open sea").[2]

At the time, the Dutch Republic was fiercely challenging England for primacy in world maritime trade, and England, through the pen and person of John Selden, fired back at Grotius in a 1635 book not surprisingly entitled *Mare Clausum* or "closed sea." While Selden argued that the seas could be "blue territory" controlled by a sovereign just like any other territory, Grotius insisted that they should be international waters open to all nations for trade.

In 1702, this "open versus closed sea" debate was effectively settled when another Dutch jurist, Cornelis van Bijnkershoek, came up with a brilliantly practical way to apply Grotius's theory. He argued that a country's effective control of its coastline should only extend as far as the range of its weapons. Thus was born the "cannon-shot rule." It established the limit of a country's territorial seas to three miles—roughly the range of the most advanced cannon of the time—and it was only within one nation's three-mile limit that freedom of navigation by other nations could be restricted.[3]

It was this three-mile limit that became the most universally accepted definition of the boundaries of international waters, and it would hold until passage of the 1982 United Nations Law of the Sea Treaty. This treaty not only increased the territorial waters limit to twelve miles, but far more profoundly, and as we have previously discussed, it also defined a two-hundred-mile Exclusive Economic Zone extending out from each nation's coastline.

While the Law of the Sea Treaty has helped foster peace and stability in much of the rest of the world by establishing seemingly clear rules for a nation's maritime rights, it has had the completely opposite effect in the East and South China Seas. One key reason: China has taken the novel position that both freedom of navigation and overflight are *also* restricted within a nation's EEZ. today, China is using this legal claim to justify its ongoing harassment of US military ships and planes in the region.

To be abundantly clear here, *nothing* in the actual treaty supports China's position. Rather, China's EEZ gambit—truly tantamount to a new

Monroe Doctrine for China in Asia—simply represents yet another highly innovative "three warfares" attempt to control new territory not by kinetic military force but rather through nonkinetic means.

Indeed, if China's "closed seas" doctrine were accepted within the tight confines of the East and South China Seas, this revisionist legal rule would effectively give China control over two of the most lucrative trade routes in the world. At the same time, such a closed-seas rule would effectively bar US military vessels not just from much of Asia but also from freely operating in "roughly one-third of the world's oceans that are now EEZs."[4]

It is for these stark economic and national-security reasons that the United States fiercely opposes any such change in the international rules—and any return to John Selden's seventeenth century "closed seas." In the examples that follow—starting with a spectacular 2001 collision of both metal and principles in the skies near China's Hainan Island—we shall see that this jurisdictional clash has already led to numerous military confrontations between China and the United States.

FREEDOM OF OVERFLIGHT TAKES A DIRECT HIT

You may recall from our earlier chapter on China's submarine capabilities that touristy Hainan Island also plays host to one of China's most important and diverse military installations. This island not only houses a large squadron of highly maneuverable, missile-equipped Russian-built fighter jets; it is also home to a very sophisticated signals-intelligence facility that monitors the communications of US and other military forces operating in the region.

Perhaps most impressively, Hainan Island's vast underground caverns within the confines of the Yulin Naval Base ably hide China's growing fleet of Jin-class ballistic-missile submarines. This is a fleet now fully capable of delivering nuclear warheads as far away as San Francisco, St. Louis, and Boston. It's not for nothing the US military wants to keep close tabs on Hainan Island.

As for what transpired in the skies near Hainan Island on April 1, 2001, a US Navy EP-3 reconnaissance plane was conducting normal operations when two Chinese J-8 fighters intercepted it. In fact, one of the Chinese pilots, Lieutenant Commander Wang Wei, was well known by his American counterparts for his top gun antics—Wang had, on several previous occasions, made very dangerous passes at US planes.[5]

On this day, as the US EP-3 flew a straight line on autopilot, top gun Wang would have his own very deadly "Icarus moment" when the tail fin of his fighter accidentally struck the EP-3's left aileron. As the J-8 fighter was cut into two pieces and Wang ejected from his plane—never to be seen again—the impact sent the US plane into a steep dive. With twenty-four American crew members on board, the plane would drop eight thousand feet in thirty seconds and another six thousand feet before the pilot, Lieutenant Shane Osborn, got the wings back to level and the nose up.

At this perilous point, Lt. Osborn made a fateful decision: he chose to make an emergency landing at Lingshui Airfield on Hainan Island where, upon landing, he and his crew were promptly arrested and detained. This was despite the fact that international law permits such emergency landings.

In the ensuing diplomatic furor, China repeatedly asserted its right to prohibit military flights within its two-hundred-mile Exclusive Economic Zone, all the while extracting several humiliating apologies from the American side. Finally, after ten days, the US crew was released—but not before China had successfully mined critical classified data from the plane's computer hard drives.

What is perhaps most remarkable about this 2001 EP-3 collision given the international incident that ensued is the fact that even today, Chinese planes and cowboy pilots routinely harass US reconnaissance planes using highly dangerous maneuvers. A particularly over-the-top case in point is offered by the more recent "in your face" moves of a Chinese jet jock. According to the Pentagon, the Chinese pilot's intimidation included a barrel roll over a Navy Poseidon-8 aircraft, a 90-degree pass across the P-8's nose with weapons bared, and a "fly-along" within twenty feet of the P-8's wingtips.[6]

Of course, it's not just freedom of overflight in the skies of Asia that Chinese forces are contesting. There have also been numerous clashes on the high seas over freedom of navigation.

A classic case in point is the "Impeccable Incident." The USS *Impeccable* is a relatively small and unarmed catamaran-type ocean-surveillance ship tasked with monitoring submarine activity using a state-of-the-art "towed array" sonar system that is literally towed behind and beneath the ship.[7]

In an incident now infamous in US Navy circles, the *Impeccable* was operating well beyond China's territorial limits but within China's Exclusive Economic Zone when a Chinese war frigate defiantly crossed the *Impeccable*'s bow at a range of about one hundred yards—perilously close by naval standards. This bullying maneuver was immediately followed by another bow crossing along with a series of no less than eleven flyovers by a Chinese Y-12 marine-surveillance plane—with the plane buzzing as close as six hundred feet to the *Impeccable*'s bridge.

Two days later, a white-hulled China Marine Surveillance vessel upped the intimidation ante by contacting the *Impeccable* over bridge-to-bridge radio, declaring her operations illegal, and warning the ship to leave or "suffer the consequences." Those consequences would come with a vengeance a day later as the gray-hulled *Impeccable* was stalked by five Chinese civilian white-hulled ships, including two fishing trawlers that came within a mere fifty feet of the *Impeccable*.

Most provocatively, when the *Impeccable* tried to leave the area, the fishing trawlers blocked its path and attempted to snag the towed sonar array with grappling hooks. Finally—in a graphic illustration of how small clashes can indeed lead to escalatory responses—America's commander in chief, President Barack Obama, ordered the guided-missile destroyer USS *Chung-Hoon* to protect the *Impeccable*.

✳✳✳✳✳

It is precisely these types of jurisdictional battles between an "open seas" America and a "closed seas" China that are becoming far too numerous to count. The clear danger is that one of these incidents may result in an exchange of fire that ignites a war.

It is also far too easy to see how this might happen. In one likely scenario, planes collide and pilots are killed. This provokes extreme nationalist responses on both sides, and it's a quick race up the escalatory ladder.

Such scenarios notwithstanding, the biggest war trigger may not be an accident at all. Instead, as China's military might grows, it may quite deliberately attempt to enforce its own "closed seas" view of the world in an attempt to bar the US military from the waters and airspaces of Asia.

Of course, no US president is likely to tolerate such an action as it would deal a heavy blow to both the national security and economic prosperity of the American nation. Thus, while Taiwan independence may well be a red line for China that the United States and Taiwan dare not cross, freedom of navigation and overflight may well be America's red line in Asia.

Chapter 26

BYE, BYE TO HINDI-CHINI BHAI-BHAI

Question: Which source of friction between China and India is the most likely trigger or trip wire for war between these two most populous countries in the world?

1. A territorial dispute involving Aksai Chin or Arunachal Pradesh
2. China's supply of nuclear and conventional weapons to India's archenemy Pakistan
3. India's harboring of the Dalai Lama and other issues related to China's authoritarian grip on Tibet
4. China's diversion of key sources of India's water supply
5. Any or all of the above

This is a very difficult question to answer because at the present time, the best answer is likely to be no. 1, a territorial dispute, or no. 2, the ever-simmering Pakistan conundrum. However, the Tibet question embedded in answer no. 3 remains a perennial thorn in the side of China-India relations, while the China-India "water wars" signaled by answer no. 4 may well vault to the top of the list in the decades ahead as water becomes more and more scarce in these two already severely water-constrained nations. For these reasons, the best answer of all to our lead question may well turn out to be no. 5, any or all of the above.

Let's look, then, first at the territorial disputes involving Aksai Chin and Arunachal Pradesh. In fact, it was these two prime pieces of strategic real estate more than 1,200 miles apart that served as the original battlefields in the bloody 1962 Sino-Indian War.

Aksai Chin is about the size of Switzerland, and this Chinese-controlled but India-contested territory sits on the easternmost portion of the autonomous Indian state of Jammu and Kashmir. For China, this virtually uninhabited high desert provides an essential north-south transportation and logistics link between its two most western territories—Xinjiang Province and Tibet.

This essential link—officially known as Chinese National Highway 219—runs for more than one thousand miles from Yecheng in Xinjiang to Lhatse in Tibet and passes right through Aksai Chin. In fact, it was the construction of this critical road segment in the mid-1950s—and no small amount of deception by China—that first inflamed Indian passions and set the stage for the 1962 war.

Ironically, India's first prime minister, Jawaharlal Nehru, had gone out of his way in the early 1950s to assist Maoist China, then a communist pariah to much of the world. Indeed, as late as 1954, Nehru had promoted the slogan "Hindi-Chini Bhai-Bhai," meaning that India and China are brothers, and in April of that same year, China and India had signed a mutual nonaggression pact.

Importantly, as part of that pact, Nehru had presented China with a frontier map that included Aksai Chin as part of India, and Chinese foreign minister Zhou Enlai had assured Nehru that China had no designs on this mountainous enclave or any other Indian territory. This assurance notwithstanding, China began to secretly build its strategic road across Aksai Chin as early as 1956.

In 1958, China would further escalate the budding crisis by marking Aksai Chin on official maps as Chinese territory. In this way, China sought to establish new facts on the ground and thereby legally bolster its sovereignty claim.

As we have documented earlier, this kind of "lawfare" and "mapfare" is now a common feature of China's *modus operandi* in claiming disputed territory—but it was quite new at the time. As to why India was originally willing to go to war over Aksai Chin in 1962, scholar Ashley Tellis of the Carnegie Endowment for International Peace describes the strategic problem posed by Aksai Chin's "western gateway" into India:

> While it is true that Chinese military forces coming out of Tibet can go peaceably into Xinjiang to the North, it is also true that they can divert towards the Southwest into India. So Aksai Chin is one key line

of advance that the Indians are very concerned about because it brings Chinese forces into the Indian state of Jammu and Kashmir and then, of course, southward into the mainland of India itself."[1]

Indeed, with New Delhi about as close to the Aksai Chin border as Washington, DC, is to Boston, China's rapid military buildup over the last several decades in both Tibet and Xinjiang has become a cause of great concern.

In evaluating the legitimacy of India's strategic concerns, it is important to note that historically, the high-altitude Himalayas formed a natural, almost impenetrable barrier between India and China. Today, however, China's military can now easily overcome this barrier through joint air and land operations.

China's growing threat to the Indian subcontinent comes not only from the stationing of as many as a half a million troops in Tibet and Xinjiang— their plains and plateaus now teem with Chinese army and air force personnel and bristle with advanced weaponry. This threat also emanates from a modern, military-grade road network in Tibet that features numerous axial roads, stretches for more than thirty-five thousand miles, and funnels right into Aksai Chin's land-invasion route.[2]

As a further strategic consideration weighing heavily on India, there is also China's growing ability to provide air support to any land-based assault emanating from Tibet and Xinjiang. As the tip of China's westernmost spear, Xinjiang houses the world's largest testing and training site for nuclear weapons and ballistic missiles, with the Malan facility alone occupying over one hundred thousand square miles.[3]

For its part, Tibet is home to five strategic airfields at Gar Gunsa, Gongar, Hoping, Linchi, and Pangta.[4] These bases house both large Chinese squadrons of fighter jets and bombers along with a growing arsenal of cruise and ballistic missiles. As Ashley Tellis grimly notes:

> The asymmetries between China and India with respect to ballistic missiles are stupendous: While China has a ballistic missile inventory that is measured in the hundreds of missiles, India's is measured in the dozens. And so if you look simply at an order of battle that compares Chinese missiles to Indian missiles, the Chinese have the advantage of both superior numbers and far more sophisticated missiles.[5]

What all this adds up to is a very credible threat to the Indian heartland, the strategic centerpiece of which is China's control of Aksai Chin.

★★★★★

As a second territorial dispute with quite similar strategic dimensions, there is also the Indian-held state of Arunachal Pradesh—what China calls "Southern Tibet." About the size of Austria, this "land of the dawn-lit mountains" and most northeastern part of India borders both Bhutan in the West and Myanmar in the east—as well as Tibet to the north, ergo China's appellation of "Southern Tibet."

In fact, more than fifty years after the end of the 1962 Sino-Indian War, Chinese troops continue to make periodic, and highly provocative, incursions into Arunachal Pradesh. From New Delhi's strategic perspective, if China were to successfully take this eastern gateway into India, it would offer a second line of military advance through the Brahmaputra Valley from China's heavily populated, and equally heavily militarized, Yunnan Province.[6]

Note, however, that it is not just matters of military strategy and national security that makes this particular dispute so contentious. In recent times, Arunachal Pradesh has been identified as containing what might be a treasure trove of oil now readily extractable with revolutionary new shale-oil "fracking" technologies.[7]

Ultimately—and this is a point lost on many analysts today—the real prize in any Chinese taking of Arunachal Pradesh may well turn out to be its water rights. To see why, we need to look more closely at the budding water wars between China and India.

Here, it must be said that for many people, it is difficult to imagine any two nations going to war over something as seemingly ubiquitous as water. Yet a careful review of history reveals simple H_2O to be a surprisingly diverse source of conflict.[8]

For example, Britain and France nearly came to blows in 1898 when a French expeditionary force sought control of the headwaters of the White Nile River upriver from Britain's colony of Egypt. Fast-forward to 1978 to Ethiopia's brash proposal to dam the Blue Nile River, and we may bear witness to this bellicose warning of then Egyptian president Anwar Sadat:

We depend upon the Nile 100% in our life, so if anyone, at any moment, thinks of depriving us of our life we shall never hesitate to go to war.[9]

Within the context of our own detective story, it should be further noted that water *diversion* projects are particularly "triggersome." For example, one of the subtexts behind Israel's 1967 Six Day War was a plot by Egypt, Jordan, and Syria to divert the Jordan River headwaters."[10]

As for any potential water war between China and India, it is not as implausible as it may seem. China and India account for almost 40 percent of the world's population but have access to only about 10 percent of global water supplies.

In addition, China's water scarcity is further compounded by a high degree of pollution—many of its lakes and rivers are dead zones and as much as 40 percent of the water in China's rivers is unfit for human consumption. For India, the situation is hardly any better. In a land heavily dependent on agriculture, it is projected by the World Bank to be "water stressed" as early as 2025 and "water scarce" by 2050.[11]

To these sobering facts, we must add this incendiary reality: China, through its forcible taking of Tibet, now has control over much of India's water supplies. In fact, the Tibetan Plateau is the "world's largest freshwater repository after the polar icecaps"[12] and a key watershed for fully ten of the largest rivers in Asia, including the Mekong running through Thailand, Laos, and Cambodia on its way to Vietnam and the Salween that winds its way through Burma.

As for how China's control of this Tibetan "water tower of the world" might actually trigger war, a rapidly growing Indian concern is Beijing's audacious proposal to divert as much as 60 percent of the waters of India's Brahmaputra River into China's increasingly parched Yellow River. To understand just how catastrophic such a diversion would be for India— and how the importance of Arunachal Pradesh as a war trigger jumps right back into the strategic picture—a little geography is in order.

At present, the waters of India's Brahmaputra River begin in the Kailas range of the Himalayas and head directly east for some 1,800 miles through Tibet before reaching the "Great Bend" just north of the border between Tibet and Arunachal Pradesh. At this point, in one of the most remarkable feats of nature, the river makes an abrupt U-turn and then winds its way through Arunachal Pradesh on its way first to become a main tributary of

India's sacred Ganges River and eventually to find the river's end in Bangladesh and the Bay of Bengal.

If China did indeed divert as much as two hundred *billion* cubic meters of this water annually to the Yellow River,[13] this obvious *casus belli* (cause of war) would be not just an environmental and economic disaster for India but also a cataclysmic event for India's downriver neighbor Bangladesh.

Of course, from this stark reality, we now see yet another reason— indeed, perhaps *the* most important reason—for China's increasing insistence that Arunachal Pradesh is Chinese, not Indian, territory. To wit: If China can impose its "Southern Tibet" claim on India either through coercion or force, India would have much less standing when it came to protesting the diversion of water from the Brahmaputra.

FROM THE TRIP WIRE OF PAKISTAN TO THE TRIGGER OF TIBET

Beyond these territorial and water disputes, there are also the perennial triggers, trip wires, and flash points associated with Pakistan and Tibet. On the Pakistan issue, India quite correctly blames China both for it substantial arms sales to Pakistan as well as for providing its archenemy with the expertise and technology to become a nuclear power. As Ashley Tellis frankly remarks:

> I think there is no Indian policy maker who has forgotten that the threats levied by Pakistan to India, particularly after the 1960s, have been conditioned substantially by Chinese assistance and Chinese support. And it's China's assistance both at the conventional [military] level and at the nuclear level to Pakistan that has been a source of great anxiety in India.[14]

As to why China is so cozy with Pakistan, it views the Islamic state both as a gateway to South Asia and as a buffer state against India itself. In fact, this is a strong and enduring relationship that dates back to the 1962 Sino-Indian War and the unraveling of strong relations between Nehru's India and Mao's China—hence China's need for a Pakistani buffer and hedge against India.

In addition, Pakistan has built a massive port at Gwadar that is likely to become an increasingly important port of call for China's growing navy. The "will there be war" problem here, of course, is that as China begins to project its naval power into the Indian Ocean and uses Pakistan as a basing area, the scope for a second Sino-Indian War will mount.

As for the perennial thorn of Tibet, when India's Nehru acquiesced to Mao's Tibetan conquest, he never imagined just how strategic Tibet would loom, both as a basing area for a possible Chinese ground and air assault on the Indian homeland as well as serving as a wellspring for India's water resources. For its part, China remains wary of alleged Indian support of Tibetan separatism, and Chinese leaders remain perennially incensed with India's harboring of what China regards as a "wolf in monk's clothing," Tibet's exiled Dalai Lama.[15]

The broader problem here is that as tensions continue to mount within Tibet over China's brutal hold on the indigenous population, China may begin to blame more and more of its troubles on alleged Indian interference and subversion.

As for whether India and China would actually ever really go to war over Tibet or water or anything else, some experts argue that this is impossible given that both states are very capable and well-equipped nuclear powers. However, Ashley Tellis believes that "all nuclear weapons do is ensure that China will not make the effort to engage in all-out conquest of India." In his view, "barring that extreme case, there is still a remarkable amount of space for a conventional conflict between the two countries."[16]

Chapter 27

AN IMPLODING CHINA WAGS THE DOG

Question: In the face of growing political dissent or social unrest, one country may decide to declare war on another country for which of the following reasons?

1. A war against an external foe may increase support for the ruling regime.
2. Wartime conditions may be used to justify the repression of political dissent.
3. A foreign war may distract the domestic populace from its original dissatisfaction with the ruling regime.
4. The new external threat may unify the country around the regime through a "rally round the flag" syndrome.
5. Any or all of the above.

In the classic film *Wag the Dog*, a US president finds himself embroiled in a sex scandal that threatens his reelection. To turn the situation around, the president's political consultant hires a Hollywood director to film a phony war for the media. The *faux* war does indeed rally the electorate around the seemingly courageous president.

Now ask yourself this question, dear detectives: Is the following event a case of life imitating "wag the dog" art?

To wit: In the midst of his own sex scandal—and curiously after viewing *Wag the Dog*—President Bill Clinton ordered no less than three military campaigns. These included missile strikes in Afghanistan and the Sudan barely three days after Clinton admitted having sex with a nubile aide, a bombing campaign of Iraq during a Congressional debate over his impeachment, and the strafing of Serbia just after Clinton dodged the

Senate impeachment bullet—Serb state television comically broadcast *Wag the Dog* in the midst of the bombing.[1]

While Hollywood hit a cynical nerve with *Wag the Dog*, the underlying logic of the film—that a regime's internal travails can trigger an external war—is actually formalized in an international-relations theory known as "diversionary foreign policy" or "diversionary war."[2] Scholars who have laid out this theory have identified "all of the above" as the correct answer to the question leading off this chapter.

Our next question, of course, is whether this diversionary war theory has any possible real-world application to Asia in general or China in particular. If so, one possible war trigger might be internal political dissent or social unrest that leads China's rulers down the wag-the-dog path. Let's look, then, at the diversionary war argument as it has been framed by at least some China watchers.

The argument's typical starting point is the observation that China is a country run by an unelected Chinese Communist Party with no real legitimacy to rule. In fact, this is a country of 1.4 billion people run by about 2,500 Communist Party members who basically elect themselves. Even more to the point, the Chinese Communist Party's grip on power comes far more from the world's largest army and internal police force than from any widespread popular support or unifying ideological theme.

On this latter point, prior to China's economic revolution in the 1970s, communism was the ideological glue that helped bind the populace together. However, since that economic revolution and the abandonment of communist and socialist principles, it is has become clearer and clearer with each passing day both within and outside of China that ideology has been replaced with a much simpler and often brutal brand of authoritarianism with distinctly Chinese characteristics.

It follows that, in the absence of any such ideological glue, one major concern of the diversionary-war theorists is that nationalism will replace ideology as a unifying force, and there is no better way to nurture and stoke the flames of nationalism than to create external enemies and villains in wag-the-dog style. Here, possible villains for the Chinese populace include an unrepentant and remilitarizing Imperial Japan; a philistine Philippines out to seize sacred and ancient islands in the South China Sea; a treacherous Vietnam stealing oil and natural gas from the territorial waters of the motherland; and of course, the damn Yankee imperialist out to contain, and perhaps even carve up, its "century of humiliation" Chinese victim—and so such wag-the-dog narratives in the government-controlled Chinese press may go.

That this is a potentially dangerous situation is compounded by the authoritarian nature of China itself. At least in the view of scholars such as Aaron Friedberg and Mark Stokes, the goal of the Chinese Communist Party is not the survival of China *per se* but rather more simply the preservation of Communist Party rule.[3] One clear implication of this assumption is that if their rule is threatened, Communist Party leaders will do whatever is necessary to erase the threat—no matter what the risks may be to the broader populace.

There is also another important difference between authoritarianism and democracy that further ups the wag-the-dog ante. In a democracy, the voters have a peaceful chance to "throw the rascals out." However, in an authoritarian regime, the rascals must police themselves, and this is often a recipe for corruption and plundering.

To be clear—and fair—China's leaders do have a strong incentive to ensure that the nation is safe and prosperous, if for no other reason than to help guarantee continued support from the populace. However, China's Communist Party members are also faced with a tremendous temptation to use the significant powers of their offices for self-enrichment. It is perhaps for this reason that even as China has enjoyed its unprecedented growth spurt, corruption, too, has flourished; today, China regularly ranks as one of the most corrupt large countries in the world.[4]

It is precisely China's hypercorruption that has become at least one major source of political discontent among a population that is increasingly exposed to dramatic and ever-rising levels of income inequality. Consider that the top 5 percent of households earn almost 25 percent of total household income while the bottom 5 percent account for just 0.1 percent.[5] Such a skewed income distribution is particularly remarkable in a country that at its communist birth less than seventy years ago at least putatively started with an equal distribution of income.

Today, however, in China, there are three basic economic strata. The first is the "super rich." They are China's version of the "one percent" in America, they number in the few thousands, and they are comprised of high-ranking Communist Party leaders and the corporate titans and top entrepreneurs that lubricate Party member bank accounts.

The second segment is an undeniably flourishing middle class that has been able to capture many of the trickle-down effects of China's economic miracle. While estimates vary widely, their numbers are anywhere from 100 to 250 million Chinese citizens, and they tend to be clustered along China's prosperous coast.

While the size of China's middle class seems at first glance very impressive, it is far less so when compared to China's total population of 1.4 billion. Indeed, despite the undeniable wealth that China's economic revolution has created, a full billion of China's citizens remain in poverty while more than half a billion of these quite literally dirt-poor souls live a Malthusian existence on subsistence farms.

It is not just extreme poverty, however, fanning the flames of rural discontent. It is also the rapacious practices of Chinese Communist Party officials who have turned brute-force landgrabs to fuel industrial development into a fine art. Here is how London's *Guardian* newspaper has described more than one million cases of illegal landgrabs as reported by the Chinese government itself:

> Sometimes it is little more than armed robbery as police and gangsters use force to drive people off their property. More often, it is fraud, when local officials—bribed by developers—cheat the farmers of fair compensation.[6]

While moving more and more of China's rural poor into its teeming cities may prevent a peasant revolt, such mass migration and a level of Chinese urbanization projected at fully 70 percent by 2035 may well create this entirely different, and highly ironic, conflict scenario: A classically pure Marxist "workers revolution" against the abominable sweatshop conditions of modern day China. On this possibility, there are already hundreds of millions of Chinese laborers who suffer from difficult and often horrific work conditions as they eke out a relatively meager existence—even as they watch with growing envy as their rulers and China's rising middle class flaunt their BMWs and Rolexes and newly acquired wealth.

It follows that doubling down on industrialization as a path to peace and prosperity may not be the smartest strategy for a Chinese Communist Party looking for stability and tranquility. Indeed, it is far too easy for Party leaders to imagine a scenario in which slowing growth in China, or even recession, creates a political clamor for regime change.

*****

Beyond the daunting economic demands of peasants and workers, the Chinese Communist Party must also grapple with a host of other problems fueling social unrest. Here, it is well worth noting that China has more than five hundred protests, riots, and mass demonstrations every single day.[7] Driving such unrest are problems that range from horrific air and water pollution and the aforementioned forced dislocation of peasants from their land, to poisoned food scandals and a ticking demographic time bomb.

For example, on the air-pollution front, China is home to sixteen of the twenty most polluted cities in the world. At the same time, China's rivers, lakes, streams, and oceans are inundated with all manner of toxins while "an estimated 980 million of China's 1.3 billion people drink water every day that is partly polluted."[8]

Regarding China as a ticking demographic time bomb, it has been said many times that China is a country that is growing older faster than it is getting rich. Consider that in 1980, the median age in China was a mere twenty-two—the classic definition of a young developing country. However, by 2050—thanks to China's much reviled and recently loosened "one-child policy"—the median age will be more than double that.[9]

As for the social turmoil this demographic time bomb is creating, there is a whole new generation of workers with their own aspirations that may not want (or be able) to shoulder the burden of financing the health care and pensions of large cadres of retirees. While Europe, Japan, and the United States face similar problems, China's is far more incendiary.

As a final source of internal turmoil, there are the growing numbers of dissidents themselves for which China's infamous lockups may eventually not be even big enough to hold. These dissidents include political groups pushing a prodemocracy agenda, religious groups hoping for more freedom to worship, pro-life forces vehemently hostile to China's one-child policy, and human-rights activists.

Add to these groups restive Tibetans and Uighurs subject to all manner of Chinese abuses and cultural genocide and China's Communist Party has a tiger of internal turmoil to ride—one that might eventually be addressed by an external wag-the-dog war against any one of a number of countries that China's government-controlled media has assiduously been building up as the "arch villain" out to once again humiliate China.

The escalatory problem with nationalistic fervor, however, is this: Once a population is whipped into a frenzy, compromise with any wag–the-dog enemy on thorny issues such as maritime rights or territorial boundaries becomes that much more difficult. This is because any such compromise exposes the government to charges of weakness rather than wisdom.

Thus, as a trigger or trip wire for war, "wag the dog" should never be underestimated. Given that other countries in the region, along with the United States, are all prone to their own internal problems, it may not even be China starting a wag-the-dog war.

Chapter 28

MADISON'S "MISCHIEF OF FACTIONS" WITH CHINESE CHARACTERISTICS

Question: Which of these statements best describes government decision-making in China?

1. The Chinese government is an authoritarian monolith tightly ruled by the Chinese Communist Party. Decisions are made from the top down and then loyally implemented by bureaucrats, military personnel, and commercial interests down the chain of command.

2. While not a democracy, the Chinese government and its Chinese Communist Party members are nonetheless subject to a wide range of special-interest pressures from bureaucratic, commercial, military, and provincial interests. This "mischief of factions" can lead to actions and decisions driven from the bottom up that can be highly escalatory.

W hile the popular conception of China is that of an authoritarian monolith a la answer no. 1 to our lead question,[1] long-time China Hands—like Stephanie Kleine-Ahlbrandt of the US Institute of Peace—who have had their "boots on the ground" throughout the country have raised the possibility that the Chinese government of today is more aptly described in answer no. 2. If this Madisonian reading of the decision-making tea leaves is more correct, this would be deeply disturbing news for the cause of peace. This is because a bottom-up Chinese government driven by an American-style "mischief of factions"[2] would likely be far more reckless and far less easy to negotiate, reason, and ultimately deal with than a top-down authoritarian monolith with a firm hand on the government wheel.

So what, then, do we know about the list of possible special interests that might have political sway over the rulers in Beijing or, more perniciously, even have the ability to operate beyond the sight and reach of these rulers? In truth, it appears to be a troublingly long list, and this Madisonian cast of actors may indeed go a long way toward explaining the uptick in Chinese aggressive behavior over the last decade. As Kleine-Ahlbrandt notes on this point:

> [O]ver the last five to eight years, there has been a proliferation of actors who are not direct foreign policy actors but who nevertheless have a large influence over how foreign policy is made. And that's in many different areas.[3]

Consider first China's much-condemned role in the development of North Korea as a nuclear-armed state. Rather than being the result of any grand Chinese strategy, as is the common view, this development may simply be the unwelcome fallout from the success of enterprising Chinese companies operating across porous borders to aggressively sell North Korea all of the gear and technology it needs to make what author Gordon G. Chang has derisively described as a "splendid nuclear weapon."[4]

In a similar "mischief of factions" vein, there is the gaggle of profit-maximizing provincial officials now helping to ratchet up tensions in areas like the South China Sea. As Kleine-Ahlbrandt tells it, in Chinese coastal provinces such as Guangxi, Guangdong, and Hainan, government officials out to boost tax revenues have pressured their fishermen to get bigger and bigger boats that can go farther and farther out into disputed areas. Such expansive activity jacks up fish yields and thereby increases growth and profits for the provinces—the bureaucratic goals. It also puts Chinese fishermen into increasing conflict with their counterparts from countries like the Philippines and Vietnam.[5]

And here may be the worst slice of Madisonian dissonance: Often times, provincial officials may take their provocative actions against the very wishes of Beijing. As Kleine-Ahlbrandt reports from the front lines:

The provincial officials that I've personally interviewed, both in Yunnan and other provinces, told me that their modus operandi is to act first, and if Beijing doesn't do anything, keep going. If Beijing does something, then slightly correct, but with the idea being to keep going anyway. And don't report up anything that's not necessary. Act first and take the initiative, and then issue corrective measures if necessary.[6]

In fact, there is a centuries-old tradition of ignoring the imperial dictates of Beijing dating back to the salad days of China's many dynasties. This tradition is embodied in the famous Chinese proverb that "heaven is high, and the emperor is far away." Metaphorically, this saying describes a dynastic world in which "far away" provincial actors act autonomously against the backdrop of a central government far removed from their daily lives.

✳✳✳✳✳

Beyond these problems of renegade Chinese entrepreneurs and provincial officials, there is also the dark phenomenon of a highly disconnected Chinese bureaucracy. A key issue here is that no single government agency holds complete dominion over Chinese foreign policy.

For example, the day-to-day management of North Korean issues is done through the US State Department and the Chinese Ministry of Foreign Affairs. However, according to Kleine-Ahlbrandt, China's Ministry of Foreign Affairs is not really a principal actor on North Korean issues at all. Instead, policy is made by the International Department of the Communist Party—with considerable input from the People's Liberation Army.

That this type of fragmentation is a recipe for conflict and miscalculation—and that negotiating with the wrong element of the Chinese bureaucracy can be maddeningly fruitless—is illustrated by China's taking of Scarborough Shoal from the Philippines in 2012. Recall from an earlier chapter that the United States came in as an "honest broker" during that confrontation and negotiated a truce that required both China and the Philippines to withdraw from the area and then attempt to settle their differences through peaceful negotiation. However, rather than withdraw as the Philippines dutifully did, China simply moved in and seized the shoal and holds it to this day.

As to how this poster child of bad-faith Chinese bargaining even happened, Kleine-Ahlbrandt explains that the truce agreement was negotiated between the US State Department and diplomats from the aforementioned Ministry of Foreign Affairs. However, this particular Chinese ministry is relatively weak within the Chinese system, and it was "easily over-ruled by other parts of the system."[7]

As a matter of fairness in relating this incident, Kleine-Ahlbrandt is quick to point out that the United States is equally prone to such bad-faith bargaining. She cites the repeated examples of American presidents making deals that the US Congress then refuses to fully ratify.

A case in point that still sticks in the Chinese craw is the 1979 Taiwan Relations Act. Congress took what President Jimmy Carter had negotiated with China and produced "a much expanded version of the act which nearly nullified normalization of ties with the People's Republic."[8] But that's the broader point, isn't it: While we in the West might expect a democracy like the United States to speak with different voices on issues, we likewise expect the monolith of China to speak with a single voice—but it very well may not.

Ultimately, to Kleine-Ahlbrandt, the key to successfully negotiating with China is to first understand where the centers of power are for any given issue. This is no small feat, however, as it requires an intimate knowledge of a bureaucracy that is anything but transparent.

Unfortunately, until this problem is solved, the world is likely to continue to see China break its agreements, not necessarily because of bad faith, but rather simply because of a broken bureaucracy. Regardless, the effect will be the same: China won't be trusted in the negotiation process; and if you can't talk through an issue, the likelihood that it will be settled by kinetic means obviously rises.

Chapter 29

THE EMERGING CHINA-RUSSIA THREAT VECTOR

Question: Which of these characterizations of Russian president
Vladimir Putin best captures the prevailing sentiment
today in China?

1. Vladimir Putin is an evil imperialist villain engaged in
   military adventurism in Eastern Europe who must be
   contained.
2. Vladimir Putin is a great national hero who is rightfully
   using Russia's military might to reclaim lost territory stolen
   from it by an imperialist and treacherous West.

Certainly, it is the "evil villain" of answer no. 1 that most accurately captures the prevailing view in much of the Western media as a United States–led coalition has struggled to contain Putin's expansionist and revisionist activities in Georgia and the Ukraine and other parts of Eastern Europe. However, within China, the "hero" characterization in answer no. 2 would likely win hands down as Russia's strongman is often referred to as "Putin the Great." Meanwhile, as the *Wall Street Journal* has noted, books about the former KGB chief have been known to "fly off the bookshelves" and frequently occupy China's bestseller lists.[1]

In fact, the hero worship of Vladimir Putin is fully consistent with a Chinese narrative in which the West, led by an imperialist United States, has systematically carved up the world at the expense of victim nations like Russia and China. In this narrative, Russia lost much of the territory that once comprised the Soviet Union only after Mikhail Gorbachev was "tricked" by Ronald Reagan. Now, it is only right and just that Putin the Great use Russia's growing military might to reclaim its lost territories.

Fig. 29.1. Is this the new axis of authoritarian evil? Here, China's president Xi Jinping and Russia's new "czar" Vladimir Putin strengthen ties. (Photograph by Kommersant Photo. Used with permission from Getty Images.)

Of course, the beauty of this Putin narrative is that it gives China permission to engage in precisely the same kind of coercive expansionism as Russia. The clear analogy: Because China was carved up during its own century of humiliation (including—and ironically—by Czarist Russia), it is also just that, as China grows its military might, it now exercise its historical right to recover the lands that were unfairly taken from it.

Within the context of our "will there be war" question, this is an obviously disturbing set of parallel narratives as they clearly sanction aggression in the name of justice. However, embedded in these narratives, is this even more disturbing possibility, namely: China and Russia might find common cause in their past history of victimhood and current status as the two most powerful authoritarian states in the world—and through such common cause, they may link together in a strategic military alliance arrayed against the United States and its democratic allies.

In thinking about the far-ranging implications of any such renewed Chinese-Russian military axis, it is well worth remembering this: While

Mother Russia has been stripped of former Socialist Republics in the Baltics, the Caucasus, Central Asia, and the Western Republics and no longer holds sway over client states like Czechoslovakia, East Germany, Hungary, and Poland, Russia nonetheless remains by far the largest country on the planet. In fact, the Russia landmass is almost double that of either China or the United States.

Within its ample borders, Russia is also blessed with the world's largest oil reserves, the second-largest coal reserves, 40 percent of the world's natural gas, one fifth of its timber, and an abundance of other minerals and metals such as aluminum, copper, lead, platinum, and tin.[2] On this basis alone, it would seem to make sense for the "energy superpower" Russia to throw its lot in with the world's undisputed factory floor of China. Such a convenient marriage of resources and manufacturing capacity is, however, hardly the only reason for a possible China-Russia alliance.

Fig. 29.2. Chinese and Russian warships on joint maneuvers in the East China Sea practicing antisubmarine warfare. (Photograph used with permission from Reuters.)

On the political front, Russia shares with China a common communist past as well as a current authoritarian form of government—Russia is a democracy in name only. On the military front, Russia is also China's leading supplier of highly advanced weapons systems; and any long-term marriage between Russian military technology and China's vast military forces offers the prospect of a pair of foes that, in an alliance, may have both "quantity" and "quality" on their side.

✱✱✱✱✱

While all these economic, political, and military ties would seem to make China and Russia natural allies, it must also be noted that there are equally compelling reasons why Russia over the longer term might instead choose to throw its lot in with the United States and its allies in a "balancing coalition" that would seek to contain China's rise. Perhaps the biggest reason for this possibility brings us back to one of the key motivators in Professor John Mearsheimer's theory of great-power politics, namely, *fear*.

Russia's fear of China begins with the fact that it shares the longest contiguous border of any in the world with a China that has a population almost ten times larger. Moreover, before the fall of the Soviet Union, China's Gross Domestic Product was only about one-third the size of Russia's. Today, however, China's heavily muscled economic engine is over four times larger.

Faced with these stark demographic and economic realities, many Russians now fear that Chinese immigration into Russia's Far East territories—both legal and illegal—will steadily erode Russia's hold on its own country.[3] A companion concern is that China's voracious appetite for Russian natural resources will eventually turn Russia into a Chinese "colony" in much the same way China has come to dominate most of Africa, parts of Latin America, and portions of Australia and Canada. Indeed, some in Russia even fear that an increasingly powerful China will eventually seek to take the riches of Siberia by coercion or force[4] under the flag of past Czarist territorial grabs from China—or even attempt to reclaim the port of Vladivostok under the banner of the unequal Treaty of Aigun that China was forced to sign in 1858 when it originally surrendered this key port.

From this perspective, the far better long-term strategy of Russia would be to join the United States balancing coalition. In fact, such an outcome would likely offer the world a far more stable and peaceful equilibrium than a Chinese-Russian axis that marries Russian technology and natural resources with the world's largest industrial base, military forces, and population.

The logic of such a US-led balancing coalition notwithstanding, a post-Crimea and adventurist Russia now appears to be moving in exactly the opposite direction—and right back into China's welcoming arms. This is certainly not a happy prospect for a world yearning for peace based on democracy and freedom, the rule of law, status-quo borders, and the non-violent resolution of any territorial or maritime disputes through the institutions and mechanisms of international law.

Part 4

SURVEYING THE BATTLEFIELD

Chapter 30

WHEN QUANTITY HAS A QUALITY OF ITS OWN

Question: Which statement most accurately reflects the military balance between China and the United States—and the likely outcome of any conventional war that might erupt?

1. America's technologically superior forces trump China's and the United States would be the clear winner today.
2. China is rapidly closing its technology gap with America so that over time, the likely winner will be more and more difficult to predict.
3. If China's economic growth continues to outpace America's, China will produce far greater numbers of weapons, and at some point, sheer quantity will likely trump any remaining American technological superiority.
4. In a regional conflict, China need not have a superior military force to win.
5. All of the above.

America's military position relative to that of China bears more than a passing resemblance to one of the most memorable quotes of the great baseball pitcher Satchel Page: "Don't look back, something might be gaining on you."[1]

Here, while it is certainly true today that the American military is the technologically superior fighting force, China is rapidly closing that gap. Moreover, China is closing that gap not through innovation in its own right but rather through a wide-ranging campaign of intellectual property theft—primarily, but not exclusively, from the US military itself.

As we documented in earlier chapters, this campaign includes a highly sophisticated combination of cyberespionage, traditional spycraft, and the reverse engineering of foreign arms purchases. The Pentagon's rapidly deteriorating relative advantage is being further accelerated by the ongoing offshoring of much of America's production to China and the collateral transfer of many "dual use" technologies to the Chinese military.

Consider that as a result of its cyberespionage, China can now field fifth-generation fighters comparable to that of the United States—with such fighters being the linchpin of air dominance in the skies of Asia. At the same time, China can now produce a dizzying array of "Designed in America" drones while China's cyberwarriors have also stolen what author Bill Gertz describes as the "the heart of the American navy"—the Aegis battlement-management system.[2]

As for China's old-fashioned, Russian-style cloak-and-dagger spy-craft, it has led to the acquisition of much of the technology that drives and guides those growing legions of ballistic and cruise missiles now aimed at American ships, forward bases, and cities. Perhaps the most unsettling fact here is that these missile arsenals with Chinese characteristics are far superior in numbers to those of the United States, if for no other reason than because of the restrictions faced by America in its disarmament trea-ties with Russia.

And speaking of Russia, as we have also previously discussed, China now ably defends its air spaces with Russian systems that are the best in the world. Through the acquisition of yet more "dual use" technologies from "friends" of America like Australia, France, and Germany, China can also now deploy virtually undetectable conventional diesel-electric sub-marines and advanced helicopters along with a growing fleet of extremely deadly cruise-missile-equipped catamaran boats.

Here, former Pentagon analyst Michael Pillsbury philosophically reflects on America's waning qualitative edge:

> The old way of thinking used to be: "American technology is by far the world's best. Our ships, our fighter aircraft, our missiles have circuit and communications capabilities that no one can touch for twenty years." That was all true. It wasn't a mistake to think that way. The problem is that as the controls on our technology have loosened, the basis of our military superiority has been slowly transferred, sometimes by espionage

and illegal means, but often just by direct sales. At the same time, we've also cut our own defense research and development budget so that we've eaten our seeds, as some military officers like to say. What this means is that the very discoveries that made us have the best satellites, the best radio communications, the best encryption, and the best fighter planes are now gone.[3]

To this grim assessment, Brookings Institution scholar Michael O'Hanlon adds:

The nature of the technologies we are buying and building today make it easier for the Chinese at any plausible level of military spending to threaten our assets in the Western Pacific. And we can try to build missile defenses and we can spend ten times as much on missile defense as they spend on offensive weapons; but the offense still has a bit of an advantage in this kind of competition. So even if we keep our defense budget bigger than theirs, the shifts in technology are going to make it hard for us to operate in the western Pacific with impunity the way we've become accustomed to.[4]

On top of all this—and providing perhaps the biggest question mark at the end any hubris-laden American claim of perpetual military superiority—there is the potentially decisive role that China's rapid economic growth may eventually play in any future combat scenario. Indeed, if China's growth simply continues to outpace that of the United States at current rates, at some point its sheer military mass should be able to simply overwhelm the technologically superior forces of the United States—recall yet again Josef Stalin's astute observation that "quantity has a quality of its own."[5]

To understand the problem that Chinese mass poses for US naval force projection in Asia, let's return to the Aegis battle-management system. This system is built around a high-powered radar system that can track incoming threats from hundreds, if not thousands, of miles away. Aegis, as its Greek name signals, is quite literally the digital shield for America's aircraft-carrier strike groups in the Asia-Pacific.

According to US Naval War College professor Toshi Yoshihara, China's clear strategy to defeat Aegis—and thereby gain control of key battle zones like the Taiwan Strait—is to simultaneously swarm supersaturation salvos of antiship ballistic missiles, sea-skimming cruise missiles, and high-altitude hypersonic missiles, with each coming at Aegis-equipped ships from different directions and different vectors. Under such an onslaught, even the vaunted Aegis shield is likely to shatter.[6]

In reflecting upon the ultimate military balance in Asia, it must finally be noted that America's biggest foe may not be China *per se* but rather simply the "tyranny of geography." To put it most starkly, Asia is seven thousand miles away, and no combination of forward basing, aircraft-carrier strike groups, and long-range bombers is likely to offset the intrinsic ability of a successfully modernized and well-equipped Chinese military to fight on its home turf with nearby supply and logistics lines—even if that military remains the technologically inferior force.

Unfortunately, these are all truths that, like the name of the villain in the Harry Potter series, few in Washington policy circles dare speak. In fact, there are very good political reasons for this "see no Chinese evil" perspective.

For starters, neither the White House nor Congress wants to publicly acknowledge that a rising China is steadily closing the military gap. Such an acknowledgement would require action at a time when the American public is war weary and the budget situation is already dire. Indeed, to acknowledge the rising China threat would be to force uncomfortable "guns versus butter" budget choices in a political system already sharply polarized.

At the same time, it is far more popular for both US politicians and our military leaders to beat their chests and extol the superiority of the American military than to acknowledge a possible relative decline. To do otherwise would serve little purpose other than to further embolden China's salami-slicing tactics in the East and South China Seas—and perhaps on the Indian subcontinent.

Finally, the myth of a perpetual American military superiority also fits in well with the narrative favored by commercial interests in the United States that rake in large profits from the China trade. In this narrative, which is particularly popular in America's financial press and amongst the cable-news narrative grinders, China is a "friend" that only seeks to peacefully trade with the United States.

Never mind that many of these same commercial interests—Boeing, Caterpillar, GE, General Motors, and so on—are willingly transferring "dual use" technologies to China in exchange for the right to operate on Chinese soil. Of course, the "dual" in the "dual use" description means that these American technologies inevitably find their way into weapons pointed at US soldiers, sailors, and pilots.

At the end of the day, if the correct answer to our lead question of this chapter regarding the rapidly shifting military balance between the United States and China is indeed "all of the above" as the facts we have discussed would seem to suggest, this sobering reality brings us right back to a Mearsheimer future in which the more China sees itself gaining on the US military, the more likely it is to press its hegemonic agenda in Asia. Of course, part and parcel of this agenda will be a collateral attempt by China to push the reigning US hegemon out of Asia.

It follows from these sobering observations that our next two questions necessarily must be: (1) How really vulnerable are America forces in Asia to China's asymmetric weapons and growing military might, and (2) against the backdrop of any such vulnerability, what might be the best strategy to deal with a Chinese attack on American ships, planes, and forward bases in Asia? It is to these questions we now turn to in the next several chapters.

Chapter 31

THE FORWARD BASE AS A SOFT, FIXED TARGET

Question: How vulnerable are America's forward bases and aircraft-carrier strike groups to Chinese attack?

1. Not vulnerable at all
2. Somewhat vulnerable
3. Extremely vulnerable

At least within Pentagon circles, there is this rapidly growing realization: China's massive military buildup—particularly in its ballistic- and cruise-missile arsenals—is rapidly turning America's forward-base fortresses and vaunted aircraft-carrier strike groups into, if not sitting ducks, then at least extremely vulnerable targets. Such vulnerability begins with the fact that the Pentagon has essentially bet the strategic farm in Asia on a relatively small handful of large forward bases arrayed along the First and Second Island Chains of defense.

Take Guam, for example. As we have already documented, this American territory anchoring the Second Island Chain fairly bristles with the best weapons America has in its arsenal. However, as Princeton professor Aaron Friedberg has warned:

> Although at the moment Guam is outside the range of Chinese conventional precision strike systems, China is in the process of developing and deploying new weapons that will soon bring Guam well within range.[1]

As for other key American forward bases now anchoring the First Island Chain, they are already firmly in the crosshairs of China's Second Artillery Corps. Key facilities include the Sasebo and Yokosuka Naval Bases and Yokota Air Force Base on the home islands of Japan, the Kadena

Air Force Base and Torii Station Army Base on Okinawa, and the Osan Air Force Base and Daegu Army Base in South Korea. Again, Professor Friedberg minces no words about the vulnerability of these bases:

> They're fixed. They're not going anywhere; and they can conceivably be struck repeatedly by Chinese conventional weapons. So our posture in that part of the world is somewhat precarious; and the strategic policy question is how to make it less so.[2]

At particular missile risk are not just the planes that will be destroyed on the runways but also critical elements of the military supply chain. As US Naval War College professor Toshi Yoshihara clinically puts it:

> Many of these facilities can be seen right on Google Earth. They are very visible from the air; and they are soft, fixed targets. So the Chinese can just punch in the coordinates, salvo the missiles, and thereby make sure that our ammunition depots and our oil supplies and other elements of logistical support are simply destroyed. Of course, that would greatly complicate America's ability to sustain its operations along the First Island Chain.[3]

It is also well worth noting here that America's penchant for leaving its military assets out in the naked open is in sharp contrast to China. Since the days of Chairman Mao and the numerous Cold War–era threats from both the Soviet Union and the United States to "nuke" China, the People's Liberation Army has had an absolute obsession with hard shielding as many of its military capabilities as possible—just recall our chapter on China's Underground Great Wall replete with missiles or our discussion of China's cavernous submarine base on Hainan Island, and you get the clear strategic picture across the length and breadth of the Chinese mainland.

As to what the US solution is to its growing vulnerability, there appears to be as much of a consensus about what must be done as there is a lack of political will to actually do it. Beyond the obvious goal of enhanced missile defense systems, this consensus focuses on a three-pronged strategy that includes: (1) the "hardening" of existing bases and targets, (2) a "disperse and diversify" strategy involving the dispersion of bases within existing host countries in tandem with the opening of additional facilities in other Asian countries, and (3) a "force restructuring" strategy that deemphasizes the large-surface capital ships of aircraft-carrier strike groups in favor of an undersea attack submarine and sea mine approach designed to turn the asymmetric warfare tables back on China.

The goal of such a three-pronged strategy is to make American assets in Asia far more resilient. As Professor Yoshihara explains, the idea of resilience is to "make sure that the United States can, in fact, absorb the first blow from a Chinese missile attack—especially against the basing infrastructure across the First Island Chain."[4]

As to the actual specifics of a "hardening" strategy, this means moving fuel supplies and weapons caches deep underground, siloing aircraft, and pouring literally tons of concrete on literally tons more of steel rebar to fortify runways and buildings and barracks and piers. It also means having specialized equipment on hand that can quickly repair runways and clear the inevitable rubble that will come from swarms of missile salvos. As Professor Friedberg notes on the value of such mundane endeavors:

> Things like equipment that can patch craters in runways can be extremely important. They're not high up on the list of priorities. They're not the fancy new systems that military services generally want to buy, but they could be essential in preserving our capacity to use bases and facilities in the context of a conflict.[5]

As for a "disperse and diversify" strategy, this can be pursued in two ways. The first is to further disperse the bases within those countries already hosting a substantial American presence. Here, Professor Yoshihara explains how such dispersal and implicit diversification of risk might work in Japan—the country most likely to be receptive to the idea because of the intense coercive pressures that China has been applying. Says Yoshihara:

> Redeploying high-value assets like bases and ships across the entire Japanese Archipelago would make targeting a much more complicated issue for the Chinese. For example, the Ryukyu island chain—the string of islands that constitutes the Japanese territories—stretches for about a thousand kilometers; and it has, in fact, a whole host of port facilities as well as airfields that can be used by the air and naval forces of the United States and its allies. Being able to disperse those forces, say, even across the southwestern islands of the Ryukyu Island chain would enormously complicate Chinese targeting.[6]

As a second form of dispersal and diversification—and the one likely to encounter the most Chinese resistance—there is also the option of expanding American bases and facilities into countries not currently hosting a large American presence. As American Enterprise Institute scholar Dan Blumenthal notes: "If Chinese decision makers all of a sudden have to think about hitting many targets in many countries, that is a far bigger deterrent rather than just having to hit a few bases in Japan or a US aircraft carrier."[7]

While Vietnam is likely to be most open to such an embrace of the American defense umbrella given its rapidly escalating resource and territorial disputes with China, this type of expansionist diversification does indeed run the risk of crossing one of China's "red lines." As Brookings scholar Michael O'Hanlon has warned about the need to tread ever so lightly:

> The number of new bases America might build is a delicate matter, but especially in new countries. So, for example, if we were to put five airfields into Vietnam in order to disperse US forces throughout the region, that's more than a simple dispersal strategy. That's developing a new ally right on China's border. It's going to feed into Chinese fears of containment; and I would only do that under very extreme circumstances.[8]

As for the imperative to engage in "force restructuring," consider the extreme vulnerability of the crown jewels of the US-naval-fleet deployment—the vaunted aircraft carrier and its "picket ships." Indeed, in this new era of Chinese antiship ballistic and hypersonic missiles, rocket mines, cruise-missile-equipped catamarans, and ultraquiet diesel-electric submarines, America's crown jewels have now also become China's biggest and juiciest targets. Nor does the People's Liberation Army make any bones about the fact that its entire asymmetric weapons strategy is calibrated on vanquishing—or at least neutralizing—American aircraft-carrier strike groups, particularly in the Taiwan Strait.

Given this increasing vulnerability of America's crown-jewel capital ships, the obvious battlefield conclusion to draw is that while the United States has built a very fine force to fight the last war, China has been extremely busy preparing for the next war. Of course, one obvious solution to this problem is indeed a force restructuring that deemphasizes America's reliance on "sitting duck" aircraft carriers.

As to just what such an effective force restructuring might look like,

Professor Yoshihara reiterates that it must be based on turning the asymmetric warfare tables right back on the Chinese. The goal must be to strike at the very heart of China's weakness in the Asian theater—the extreme vulnerability of China's merchant and military fleets to interdiction at the many choke points along the ally-controlled First Island Chain.

To Yoshihara, this means a renewed emphasis on submarines, particularly attack submarines, even as the carrier fleet is downsized. The rationale for taking America's force projection in Asia undersea is underscored by this simple asymmetric math offered by Yoshihara:

> Part of the beauty of China's anti-access/area denial strategy is that it relies on really very striking cost asymmetries. For example, an aircraft carrier costs billions of dollars while a salvo of Chinese missiles is priced in the millions; and it may take only one Chinese missile getting through to score a mission kill. So if you think of the cost asymmetry there, it's not a competition that the United States can win. The Chinese can build many more missiles than the Americans can build capital ships.[9]

To Professor Yoshihara, the submarine is particularly key in any force restructuring because it is a deadly "double-edged sword" that strikes right at the heart of China's biggest vulnerability. As Yoshihara puts it:

> We are the best submarine force in the world; and the Chinese have historically demonstrated a weakness in anti-submarine warfare. So at the same time that America is taking advantage of its inherent strengths, it is also exploiting one of China's inherent structural weaknesses.[10]

Echoing this theme, Cambridge professor and former White House advisor Stefan Halper insists that:

> We have to take China's commitment to its area denial strategy very seriously; and taking it seriously means being aware of the limitations of using large naval platforms like aircraft carriers within range of their missiles and other ordinance that can take them down. It also means that we have to emphasize our submarine force because we need to be able to reinforce our friends and our allies, without putting these major assets in play.[11]

On the wisdom of a force restructuring scenario favoring more submarines, Halper adds: "the political effect" of losing an aircraft carrier to a Chinese attack "would limit our options going forward and compel us to a very forceful attack on Chinese mainland facilities. So having an aircraft carrier struck or a major capital vessel struck and sunk would be an option-limiting event that could be very dangerous in terms of escalation."[12]

As for how a beefed up submarine presence in Asia might strategically turn the asymmetric warfare tables on China, in Yoshihara's vision, one of the key roles that attack submarines could play would be to serve as gate-keepers around the choke points along the First Island Chain so that any Chinese merchant or military ship attempting to go through a choke point could be sunk. In this way, the United States would be able to exert exactly the same kind of coercive pressure on China that China is now trying to exert on the US surface fleet with its "carrier killing" arsenal.

Of course, the major downside of any such a shift to an undersea strategy is that America would lose the important symbolic value that aircraft-carrier strike groups provide in advertising American force projection. Yoshihara, himself, is the first to acknowledge this downside. As he explains:

> While American submarines are great anti-access weapons, they cannot fundamentally demonstrate American resolve through a show of force. Only aircraft carriers can do that job by showing up off the coast of a country or in the vicinity of a contested island to say "America means business." In fact, there is a huge demand signal from American allies for precisely this particular aircraft carrier role. So America has to very carefully weigh the tradeoffs because the things carriers can do, submarines can't, and vice versa. And so this is not going to be an easy force restructuring decision because our allies are going to be looking at aircraft carriers as the primary sign of America's security commitment to them.[13]

As for the feasibility of implementing any three-pronged strategy of hardening, dispersing, and restructuring, it is well worth noting that any base-dispersal strategy is likely to be met by grassroots political opposition in the host countries. Here, tensions over existing American bases are already quite high in Japan and South Korea while such grassroots opposition was at the core of the American military's eviction from the Philippines in 1992.

As a further political complication, one must also consider the upheaval any restructuring would foment within the US military. This is a fighting force notorious not just for its interservice rivalries but also for its intraservice battles between, for example, in the navy, the "carrier guys" and the "sub guys." Frequently lost in these rivalries is the goal itself—to win, and to preferably do so without fighting. On this sore political point Professor Friedberg notes:

> The military challenge that China poses to the United States requires the development of some military systems capabilities that have not, historically, been those the US military services prefer. The Navy likes aircraft carriers—yet carriers look increasing vulnerable and we probably need more submarines. The Air Force likes relatively short-range fighters really not designed for the kind of theater that we have in Asia where the ranges are extraordinarily long and the access to bases is limited; but we probably need more unmanned aerial vehicles and a new stealthy bomber to replace the B-2. [However,] these have not been the systems that the Air Force has typically wanted to invest in.[14]

✵✵✵✵✵

If winning without fighting is indeed the goal of an American military presence in Asia, it would seem prudent to pursue the three-pronged "harden, disperse, and restructure" strategy that has been outlined. However, over time, such a strategy might well wind up in the "woulda, coulda, shoulda" bin for the aforementioned reasons.

In the meantime, America's forward bases and aircraft-carrier strike groups remain extremely vulnerable to a well-coordinated missile attack from the Chinese mainland. In the next two chapters, we will explore the two major schools of strategic thought as to how America should respond to any such attack given the precarious chessboard its forces are moving on. As we shall see, dear detectives, this "Air-Sea Battle" versus "Offshore Control" debate constitutes one of the deepest levels of our mystery.

Chapter 32

THE ONGOING BATTLE OVER AIR-SEA BATTLE

Question: If the People's Liberation Army fires missiles from the Chinese mainland targeted at American ships at sea or at American forward bases in places such as Guam or Japan, what should be the American response?

1. Launch counterstrikes on the Chinese mainland aimed at blinding battle networks, disabling long-range strike systems, and destroying intelligence, surveillance, and reconnaissance capabilities
2. Impose a blockade on China's military and merchant fleets and thereby strangle China's economy by cutting off its energy imports and trading exports
3. Both 1 and 2

Let us first stipulate that the very premise of this question—that China would ever attack American naval vessels or forward military bases— is deeply unsettling. However, if you have read all of the previous chapters in this detective story, you may have reasonably concluded that the probability of such an event is considerably higher than the high level of economic interdependence between China and the US would suggest.

Because this scenario is possible—if not, as some would argue, probable—the US Pentagon has necessarily had to confront our lead question in this chapter. In the process, Pentagon strategists have proposed two radically different strategies to the threat China's growing military arsenal poses to America's forward posture in Asia.

The first strategy, embodied in answer no. 1 above, has been dubbed "Air-Sea Battle." Emanating from the Pentagon's Office of Net Assessment, it does indeed involve counterstrikes on the Chinese mainland in response to a conventional attack on US naval vessels and forward bases—a response that opponents of Air-Sea Battle like Professor Amitai Etzioni of George Washington University have immediately branded as an escalatory invitation to nuclear war between China and the United States.[1]

The second strategy, embodied in answer no. 2, goes by various names that include the bland "Offshore Control" and the far more evocative "War-at-Sea." As proposed by American advocates such as Colonel T. X. Hammes of National Defense University and Captains Jeffrey Kline and Wayne Hughes of the Naval Postgraduate School, this approach would simultaneously turn the waters within the First Island Chain into a "no-go zone" for Chinese merchant and military ships—America's own version of area denial—while choking off China's global trade routes through a more distant blockade.

The central premises of this strategy—for simplicity, we will herein-after call it Offshore Control—are that the *threat* of economic strangulation may be sufficient to deter Chinese aggression while *actual* economic strangulation in the event of Chinese aggression should be sufficient to force China to surrender any territorial gains it might initially achieve.

Of course, just as with Air-Sea Battle, Offshore Control has its own host of critics. Claiming "blockades never work" and warning of Chinese *faits accomplis*, they have decried it as a weak and ineffective strategy that will turn China into a sanctuary from which it can pummel American military assets with missile salvo after missile salvo without fear of direct reprisal.[2]

Still a third "hybrid" strategy, embodied in answer no. 3, involves some combination of Air-Sea Battle and Offshore Control, raising the question as to whether this approach combines the best—or perhaps worst—of the Air-Sea Battle and Offshore Control worlds.

Because this debate is so central to our "will there be war" question, it is important that we systematically work our way through the pros and cons of each of the strategic responses. In the remainder of this chapter, we will therefore focus on the rationale for, mechanics of, and potential problems with Air-Sea Battle. In the next chapter, we will give Offshore Control a similar treatment and then try to come to some conclusion as to which, if either, might be the best approach and whether a hybrid strategy com-bining features of both may ultimately be the more feasible or desirable.

WHY AIR-SEA BATTLE?

The rationale for Air-Sea Battle flows from three fundamental premises. The first is captured in these words by one of the lead architects of Air-Sea Battle, former Pentagon analyst Andrew Krepinevich. In the Pentagon report that started the whole debate, he and several coauthors write:

> For well over half a century, the United States has been a global power with global interests. These interests include . . . extending and defending democratic rule, maintaining access to key trading partners and resources, and reassuring those allies and partners who cooperate with the United States in defending common interests. The United States' ability to project and sustain military power on a large scale has been, and remains, essential to this endeavor.[3]

One can, of course, argue with the need for the United States to continue its role as a global superpower "cop" defending everything from democracy and free trade to its many regional alliances. In fact, we will explore the neoisolationist counterarguments later when we discuss possible pathways to peace.

For now, however, let's assume Krepinevich is right about the need for the United States to play this global policeman's role. What, then, is the second premise of his argument? Again, in the words of him and his coauthors, we have:

> [T]he US military's ability to operate in an area of vital interest, the Western Pacific, is being increasingly challenged. . . . Currently there is little indication that China intends to alter its efforts to create "no-go zones" out to the Second Island Chain, which extends as far as Guam and New Guinea. Unless Beijing diverts from its current course of action . . . the cost incurred by the US military to operate in the Western Pacific will likely rise sharply, perhaps to prohibitive levels, and much sooner than many expect.[4]

In this scenario, Krepinevich assumes the Chinese are preparing to chase the US military out of the Western Pacific. In fact, there should be little debate about this premise. As we saw when we inventoried China's growing military capabilities in previous chapters, the People's Liberation

Army is clearly building an impressive asymmetric arsenal of anti-access, area-denial weapons that range from missiles, subs, and mines to cyber- and space-based capabilities. Moreover, Chinese leaders themselves dating back to the days of Admiral Liu Huaqing openly acknowledge that China is building up its military explicitly to deny the US access to the Western Pacific—or at least dramatically increase the costs and risks of the United States to operate freely in the region.

Of course, Krepinevich's third premise immediately follows from the first two. Specifically, Krepinevich et al. claim that America's strategic choice is:

> [Either] to risk a loss of military access to areas vital to its security and those of key allies and partners to whom it is committed by treaty or law OR to explore options that can preserve the stable military balance that has seen the region enjoy a period of unparalleled peace and prosperity.[5]

At least to Krepinevich, Air-Sea Battle provides the best option available to the Pentagon. Conceptually, it consists of two distinct parts— one eminently sensible, the other as controversial as it is logical.

The sensible aspect of Air-Sea Battle simply involves much greater coordination and integration between the US Navy and Air Force in theater. If you are tempted to say "oh duh" at this point, feel free, but please know that traditional interservice rivalries amongst the four major branches of the US military have been endemic since at least World War II and there- fore have always made such integration difficult.

As for just what kinds of coordination and integration Krepinevich has in mind, here's a typical Krepinevich *quid pro quo*:

> The Air Force conducts counter-space operations to blind China's space- based ocean surveillance systems and thereby prevents China from tar- geting high-value Navy ships like aircraft carriers. In return, the US Navy uses its Aegis radar ships to help defend Air Force forward bases in Japan against Chinese missile attacks.[6]

As for the second component of Air-Sea Battle—the one that is both logical *and* controversial—this involves direct nonnuclear strikes on the Chinese mainland in response to any nonnuclear attack from that mainland on American ships or bases in the region. Specifically, Air-Sea Battle calls for a sequence of counterstrikes that commence as soon as China launches any first strike.

Here's how a leading critic of Air-Sea Battle, Professor Amitai Etzioni has described what he sees as the fatal and cataclysmic logic of the process:

> In the opening "blinding campaign," the United States attacks China's reconnaissance and command-and-control networks to degrade the PLA's ability to target US and allied forces. Next, the military takes the fight to the Chinese mainland, striking long-range anti-ship missile launchers. Given that this is where the anti-ship missiles are located, it is only logical that the United States would target land-based platforms. And to go after them, one of course needs to take out China's air defense systems, command and control centers, and other anti-access weapons. In short, AirSea Battle requires a total war with China.[7]

Lest anyone be confused about whether Air-Sea Battle actually incorporates American precision strikes on the Chinese mainland, Krepinevich includes in his Pentagon report a very handy map of many of the targets envisioned. These targets, which span the full length and breadth of China, include the Beijing Aerospace Command and Control Center, the large phased-array radar and antisatellite weapons facilities in Xinjiang Province, additional antisatellite weapons facilities in Hefei and Mianyang, and all five of China's major satellite launch and monitoring facilities in Hainan, Jiuquan, Taiyuan, Xian, and Xichang.

This is "Old Testament" strategy at its purest—an eye for an eye and a counterstrike for any strike; and at least from a purely military perspective, such counterstrikes on the mainland are eminently sensible. Indeed, absent such counterstrikes, China would be shooting at US ships and bases like fish in the proverbial barrel and doing so from a heavily armed sanctuary. At least to Air-Sea Battle proponents, the existence of such a sanctuary would make it virtually impossible for the United States to defend its interests in the region. Notes Princeton professor Aaron Friedberg on this vexing problem:

> We are not going to initiate a war by attacking China. If China initiates a conflict by attacking our forces and bases or our allies who we are sworn to defend, I don't think we can afford to allow them a sanctuary or to let them believe that they would have a sanctuary in which they could continue to carry out those kinds of attacks.[8]

Indeed, to Friedberg, such a sanctuary would also likely increase the probability of a Chinese attack given that the United States is providing China with a "free pass" to do so.

Of course, the problem with Air-Sea Battle is that what looks sensible, simple, and logical on battle maps becomes much more complex upon a second and deeper glance. The overarching problem—and the biggest hurdle any American president would ever have to leap over in ordering implementation of an Air-Sea Battle plan in the event of war—is the possibility (critics say the high probability) of a nuclear response by the Chinese. Of course, once China drops nukes on US soil—or sends a tactical nuke at an American forward base or aircraft carrier—the United States would likely have to respond with nukes of its own.

This textbook case in escalation is even further complicated by the close integration on the Chinese mainland between China's conventional- and nuclear-missile arsenals. The abiding fact here is that both programs are run by China's vaunted Second Artillery Corps, and there appears to be little evidence that the Second Artillery Corps segregates China's missiles by location according to conventional versus nuclear warhead types.

Why is this observation relevant to our detective story? Simply because a conventional attack by US forces on the Chinese mainland which has the *limited* goal of destroying China's ability to launch conventional warheads at American ships and forward bases may wind up also, and quite accidentally, taking out some or all of China's nuclear capabilities. Thus, when faced with the prospect of Air-Sea Battle, the Chinese may rightly fear the loss of their own second-strike nuclear deterrent.

And here's the escalatory rub: The entire rationale for the doctrine of "mutually assured destruction," which is supposed to guarantee the nuclear peace, rests on the ability of each country with nuclear weapons to respond with a second strike if another country hits it with a first strike. Thus, if a country like China were to lose its second-strike capability—or even fear that it might because of an attack by an America planning an Air-Sea Battle campaign—the temptation might be to launch a preemptive first strike.

It follows—at least to critics– that even planning for Air-Sea Battle is highly escalatory, while actually launching an Air-Sea Battle campaign itself would be an open invitation to a fearful China to respond with nuclear weapons.

As a final critique of Air-Sea Battle, there is also the hardly inconsequential matter of whether it would even be effective. According to Professor T. X. Hammes of National Defense University—a leading proponent of the competing Offshore Control strategy—Air-Sea Battle fails the effectiveness test in at least two dimensions.

First, the probability that America can blind China's battle networks—the most essential part of the plan—is extremely low. The problem here is that even if the United States were able to knock out China's conventional satellites and command and control centers—a very tall order in a country as large as China—new technologies such as drones produced in massive numbers, high-altitude aerostat balloons, and cheap, microsized satellites known as "CubeSats" make it extremely difficult to achieve the necessary level of blinding.[9]

Second, Hammes believes the probability that the United States can hit China's mobile missile systems is even lower than that for blinding China's battle networks. He bases this assessment partly on the sobering fact that during the 1991 Gulf War, the United States was unable to hit a single Iraqi Scud missile on the ground before launch despite repeated attempts.[10]

Here, it must be noted that this Scud failure occurred long ago and targeting technologies have improved dramatically. Nonetheless, if China's Underground Great Wall can truly move missiles around with the speed and agility that we discussed in an earlier chapter, Hammes is likely to be right on this point—calling into question the viability of the entire strategy.

Given all of these various possible drawbacks with Air-Sea Battle, our next question necessarily must be whether Offshore Control fares any better as a battle plan when it comes to responding to the rise of China's anti-access, area-denial threat to America's presence in the Asia-Pacific. It is to this task we now turn to in our next chapter.

Chapter 33

A NET ASSESSMENT OF OFFSHORE CONTROL

Question: Which of these elements make China highly vulnerable to a blockade strategy?

1. Economics
2. Geography
3. Both 1 and 2

W e have discussed China's "tyranny of geography" at length before. However, it is well worth a reprise in any net assessment of an Offshore Control strategy.

Geographically, China is a continental power almost perfectly contained or encircled by a First Island Chain of American allies and democracies that Beijing's authoritarian rulers must stare forebodingly out at every day from mainland shores. In effect, this "Great Wall in Reverse" runs from Japan's home islands and through Japan's Okinawan territories out to the midpoint of Taiwan; it then continues to the Philippines and through to the Indonesia Archipelago where it culminates in the globe's ultimate naval-blockade choke point, the narrow and perilous Malacca Strait.

The Malacca Strait is, however, hardly the only choke point Chinese merchant and military vessels must worry about in the event of a blockade. For example, at the eastern end of the First Island Chain, there is the Soya Strait between the northern tip of Japan's home islands and the southern tip of the Kuril Islands. It is one of just two passageways from the Sea of Japan to the Pacific Ocean.

In addition, the entire run of islands along the "Ryukyu Island arc" that constitutes Japan's Okinawan territories represents one of China's most difficult hurdles to reaching the Western Pacific. Yet another key choke point along this arc is the Miyako Strait located about 190 miles from Okinawa.

At present, the Miyako Strait is a preferred route for China's navy, and particularly its submarines, from the East China Sea into the Western Pacific.[1] However, on the west side of this strait, over the strong protests of China, Japan has added an arsenal of Type 88 surface-to-ship missiles to its already elaborate radar installation. These missiles can easily range any Chinese surface ships passing through the Miyako Strait.

Moving further west, there is also the 160-mile-wide Luzon Strait between Taiwan and the Philippines. It played a key role first as an invasion route in Japan's conquest of the Philippines in 1941 and then as a critical choke point for America's naval and air blockade of Japan toward the culmination of World War II.

Of course, once China's merchant or military ships transit into the South China Sea and begin to seek an exit into the Indian Ocean, numerous other choke points abound. These include the two major alternative routes to the Malacca Strait as a gateway to the Indian Ocean—the equally perilous Sunda and Lombok Straits in Indonesian waters.[2]

Taken as a whole, these numerous choke points would make it very difficult for both Chinese merchant and military vessels to access the deeper waters of either the Pacific or Indian Oceans in the event of a naval blockade by the United States and its First Island Chain allies. Moreover, this difficulty stems not just from the threat of submarines and over-the-horizon aircraft-carrier strike groups but also from the ability of China's enemies to lace those choke points with mines—a "turnabout is fair play" gambit if there ever were one given China's major emphasis on mine warfare.

As for China's "tyranny of its economy," this stems from its exceedingly heavy reliance on both imported oil for its energy and selling exports to the world for its economic prosperity. As part of this tyranny, China's "factory floor to the world" also needs vast amounts of everything from copper and iron ore to nickel, tin, and lumber. Most broadly, China's heavily export-dependent economy depends on global trade for more than half of its entire Gross Domestic Product growth—while its citizenry is increasingly dependent on the importation of food and agricultural products such as corn and soybeans.

Given these economic and geographic tyrannies, it would appear China is indeed highly vulnerable to a blockade, and it is upon this strong

premise that experts like Colonel T. X. Hammes of America's National
Defense University and Captains Wayne Hughes and Jeffrey Kline of
the US Naval Postgraduate School have built their strategy of Offshore
Control.[3] Here's how Captains Kline and Hughes describe its "ends, ways,
and means":

> The war-at-sea *strategy* is to deter Chinese land or maritime aggression
> and, failing that, deny China the use of the sea inside the "first island
> chain" . . . during hostilities. The *ways* are distant interception of Chinese
> shipping, widespread submarine attacks and mining inside the first island
> chain, offensive attacks by a flotilla composed of small missile-carrying
> combatants to fight in the China seas and patrol vessels for maritime
> interdiction at straits and choke points, and Marine expeditionary forces
> positioned to hold the South China Sea islands at risk, with no intention
> of putting ground forces on China's mainland. The *means* are a force
> structure with a better combination of conventional air forces, battle-
> group ships, and submarines, and a forward-deployed flotilla of U.S. and
> allied small combatants.[4] (emphasis added)

This is indeed nothing short of, in Colonel Hammes's ice-cold
phrasing, "a war of economic strangulation." To Hammes, the strategy's
elegance lies in seeking "to force China to fight in ways that maximize US
strengths while minimizing China's strengths"[5]—a theme echoed by Kline
and Hughes who describe the strategy as "plying long-standing American
maritime strengths against China's dependence on the seas."[6]

✶✶✶✶✶

At this point, it may be useful to ask: Just what is the strategic goal of Offshore Control beyond economic strangulation? That is, what is the "theory
of victory?"

To Hammes, the goal is not to vanquish China. In fact, he believes
the complete defeat of a thermonuclear power in today's times is not just
impossible, but that it will be a "pyrrhic event" in which both sides take
each other down in a final paroxysm of nuclear exchanges.[7]

To avoid this cataclysm, Hammes argues that "victory" should lie
simply in first stopping, and then rolling back, whatever China's territorial

grab may have been to start the war in the first place—a Taiwan conquest; a Senkaku Islands invasion; the taking of oil and natural gas or fishing rights from the Philippines or Vietnam, a blitzkrieg seizure from India of Arunachal Pradesh, the denial of freedom of navigation or overflight to the United States, and so, we have learned, our possible triggers, trip wires, and flash points for war may go.

As a second aspect of Hammes theory of victory, he also presumes that the global economy is going to need China's 1.4 billion consumers and massive production capacity if the world is to continue to grow and prosper. That Offshore Control does no damage to China's infrastructure precisely because it refrains from any Air-Sea Battle–type strikes on the mainland thus is the superior approach on this ground. As Hammes points out: "By not destroying Chinese infrastructure, this facilitates restoration of global trade after the conflict."[8]

Still a third part of Hammes's argument rests on the famous Clausewitzian trinity of "passion, chance, and reason" as causes for war. From this Clausewitzian perspective, Air-Sea Battle makes the fatal mistake of inflaming the passions of the Chinese people with direct strikes on their homeland—and thereby ensures a long war with little prospect of settlement.

As Hammes frames the problem against the nationalistic backdrop of China's century of humiliation:

> When you bomb China, it becomes a passion over reason issue, making it harder to get China to negotiate a peaceful settlement. Bombing makes it so much harder to return to the status quo before the conflict.[9]

Echoing this sentiment, Captain Mark Morris of America's National War College notes in his favorable assessment of Offshore Control:

> Direct attacks on the homeland change the legitimacy equation of the Chinese Communist Party to that of the defender of the Middle Kingdom against the foreigners.[10]

As a final pillar of Offshore Control, there is this virtue: The strategy's various pressures can be applied slowly and in stages—more akin to a python rather than the quick strikes on the mainland of an Air-Sea Battle rattlesnake. As Captains Kline and Hughes note:

The capacity for sea denial within the First Island Chain and executing a distant blockade would provide American leadership graduated options before undertaking the potentially escalatory step of strikes on mainland China.[11]

To both Hammes and the duo of Kline and Hughes, this python approach allows enough time and space for critical negotiations to begin between the two warring parties before the missiles start to fly; and in this way, Offshore Control is likely to be far less escalatory than the much faster moving trajectory of an Air-Sea Battle engagement.

✵✵✵✵✵

While Hammes makes a persuasive case, there is, as with Air-Sea Battle, no shortage of potential problems with Offshore Control. For starters, while China may be highly vulnerable to a naval-blockade strategy at this particular point in time, its leaders clearly understand this vulnerability. In response, they are rapidly developing land-route alternatives to moving both energy and tradable goods from and to world markets.

For example, as an end run around its "Malacca Dilemma," China has built both oil and natural-gas pipelines linking Burma's deepwater port of Kyaukphyu in the Bay of Bengal with Kunming in China's Yunnan Province. In a similar risk-hedging vein, China is also well into the process of constructing an elaborate Trans-Eurasian air, road, rail, and pipeline network in the hopes of fashioning a new "Silk Road Economic Belt" that bypasses any blockaded seas entirely.

This new Silk Road already links China via its Xinjiang Province to Central Asian states like Turkmenistan and Uzbekistan. At the same time, China has already inaugurated a direct rail line that passes through Moscow on its way to Hamburg, Germany—thereby cutting the transit time for Chinese exports from fully five weeks at sea to a mere twenty-one days.[12]

As a second significant issue with Offshore Control, there is also this sobering reality: While it is all well and good for American naval vessels to pull back to deeper waters well outside the range of China's anti-access, area-denial capabilities, that still leaves America's forward bases in Japan, South Korea, and Guam as sitting ducks for intense missile salvos. In the face of such punishing salvos, it would be hard for US politicians and military commanders to resist Air-Sea Battle–like counterstrikes on the mainland. Indeed, absent such counterstrikes, China may be able to inflict enough damage to allied air and naval power and their logistical support that it would make it impossible for the United States to enforce the "no-go zone" within the First Island Chain—at which point Offshore Control may fall apart.

Fig. 33.1. American B-52s on the runways of Guam—"sitting ducks" for a Chinese missile attack. (Photograph from the Andersen Air Force Base website.)

Third, as Hammes readily acknowledges, any blockade would take considerable time to have the desired effect on the Chinese economy and political landscape. In this waiting game, the economies of the United States and its key blockade allies of Australia, Japan, and South Korea would suffer crushing blows. While Hammes argues that over time, global trade would recover as other nations around the world found alternatives to the China trade, it is difficult to imagine that a nuclear-tipped China would tolerate being left out in the global-market cold for any extended period.

Perhaps more to the point, this observation raises the even more fundamental question as to whether America and its allies would even stay the course as a cohesive Offshore Control unit. Would, for example, South Korea and Australia be willing to sacrifice their economies for the preservation of Taiwan's independence? Similarly, would Japan stand by America if it came to the aid of its treaty ally, the Philippines? As Professor James Holmes of the US Naval War College has framed the problem:

> Prolonged economic warfare cuts both ways. It exhausts not just the enemy but friendly powers, not to mention one's own constituents who depend on foreign commerce for their livelihoods. Keeping the populace and the allies on the same sheet of music while their economic self-interests suffer poses a challenge, to say the least.[13]

As a final problem[14] with Offshore Control—and perhaps its true Achilles' heel—there is also the uncomfortable truth that a "waiting game" blockade strategy blows the door wide open to Chinese *faits accomplis*.

Indeed, it is far too easy to imagine that after significant lives and treasure have been lost and the global economy has been pushed to the brink of collapse, America and its fractured alliance will simply throw in the towel and allow China to keep whatever prize it took that started the war to begin with—Taiwan, Japan's Senkaku Islands, the Philippine's Second Thomas Shoal, India's Arunachal Pradesh, Vietnam's oil and gas rights, and so on. Of course, with Taiwan in particular, it would be hard to imagine China ever surrendering its so-called renegade province once it successfully occupied it.

✖✖✖✖✖

From our review of Air-Sea Battle versus Offshore Control in these last two chapters, it would seem then that as choices go, this is one that lies between the proverbial rock and a very hard place—or for those with a literary bent seeking an appropriately maritime setting, a choice that seeks to sail between Scylla and Charybdis.

While it is easy to get lost in the complexity of this difficult choice, the following may well be the most salient point for our detective story: While Air-Sea Battle may well offer the fastest escalatory route to nuclear war— that's one of the big imponderables—it does have the virtue of denying China any mainland sanctuary from which to launch missile salvos with impunity at the ships and military bases of America and its allies. Accordingly, it may be unwise to take retaliatory strikes on the Chinese mainland completely off the table *before* any possible conflict starts. Uncertainty in the Chinese mind may well be a friend of American deterrence here. As Professor Toshi Yoshihara of the US Naval War College notes on this point:

> What kind of signal would we be sending to the Chinese if we simply said: "Yes, you can attack our forward military bases on allied soil; and your targets on the mainland are, essentially, off-limits." That doesn't mean deep strikes against the mainland will be automatic, but we need to at least preserve the option to maintain that level of strategic ambiguity so that there is at least some doubt in the minds of the Chinese. Here, the more ambiguity and the more caution that we can impose on the Chinese, the more sturdy deterrence will be.[15]

This observation leads us to our last question on this critical strategic issue: Should Air-Sea Battle and Offshore Control perhaps be used in tandem as an American response to an attack by Chinese forces? That's a question perhaps best left on the table to ponder until we arrive at that part of our inquiry focusing on possible pathways to peace.

Suffice it to say for now that while both strategies may have their virtues, the best way to avoid the pitfalls of each is to prevent any conflict to begin with. While that is a very tall order, we must do our very best in this inquiry to at least give peace a chance.

That said, before we move to our final "pathways to peace" section of our inquiry, we must close this part of our detective story with an analysis of just what "victory" might look like if war does indeed break out. In fact, this candid assessment should serve as the ultimate motivation for finding ways to avoid any military conflict with a rapidly rising China.

Chapter 34

WHAT MIGHT "VICTORY" LOOK LIKE?

Question: What is the most likely outcome if a conventional war breaks out between China and the United States?

1. A conventional war will not escalate into nuclear war; it will be a very *short* war with a decisive victor, and there will be relatively little damage to the broader global economy.
2. A conventional war will not escalate into nuclear war, but it will be a very *long* war, likely with no clear winner. There will be significant damage to the Chinese and US economies as well as to the broader global economy.
3. Any such conventional war will rapidly escalate into a nuclear war with catastrophic consequences.

As we end part 4 of our detective story, it may be useful to once again stop and briefly assess where we are in our investigation before attempting to answer our lead question above—yes, we all hope against hope that answer no. 1 is the correct one.

On the intentions question, we have determined that China is seeking to expand its territory and maritime rights in the East and South China Seas based on a series of historical claims that date back at least to its century of humiliation. It is equally clear that these revanchist activities are bringing China into increasing conflict with neighbors like Japan, the Philippines, and Vietnam, and, to a lesser extent, Brunei, Indonesia and Malaysia.

We have also seen that China is pushing hard against the envelope of both freedom of navigation and freedom of overflight. This push (and occasional shove) is similarly bringing China into increasing conflict with American military forces in Asia.

Finally, against the volatile backdrop of rising Indian nationalism, there is mounting evidence that China has territorial designs on Indian's state of Arunachal Pradesh—what China claims as "Southern Tibet." Nor has an increasingly angry India ever relinquished its own claim to the now Chinese-held Aksai Chin.

The reality of these myriad disputes is not in question—the evidence does not lie. There is, however, a very deep perceptual divide over whether China's expansionism constitutes the offensive behavior of an aspiring regional hegemon or simply the legitimate defensive actions of a country seeking to defend its trade routes and guard its homeland.

From China's perspective, its actions are fully consistent with its doctrine of "active defense." Through this prism, China sees control of the East and South China Seas (as well as perhaps Arunachal Pradesh) as a means to both help solve its natural resource needs and resolve its "Malacca Dilemma." Chinese control of the East and South China Seas—and by implication, the driving out of the American military from the region—would also greatly enhance China's ability to defend its coastline and homeland.

From the perspective of those state actors now at the tip of China's coercive spear, however, China's behavior doesn't look like "defense" at all—"active" or otherwise. Rather, China's multivectored advance looks (and feels) like offensive behavior in every sense of the word. Senior Advisor Bonnie Glaser of the Center for Strategic and International Studies has almost perfectly captured this deep perceptual disconnect with this frank psychological profile:

> China does not put itself in the shoes of other countries and understand how other nations view China and its actions; and this is the problem that I think China has. That's why I often call China the autistic power. It just does not seem capable of understanding how its behavior really scares the rest of the region.[1]

The broader point to be gleaned from this reprise of our facts and clues and conclusions is simply that conflict is becoming increasingly possible. As for what we have learned from our brief survey of the potential battlefield in this part of our story, we have determined at least two salient facts.

First, American forward bases and naval forces are highly vulnerable to a Chinese attack, and they will continue to be so until the United States implements an appropriate "hardening, dispersing, and restructuring" strategy. America's vulnerability, in turn, makes the probability of a Chinese attack higher because the prospect of victory is commensurately higher as well.

Second, neither Air-Sea Battle nor Offshore Control as possible American responses to a Chinese attack provide the United States and its allies with any magic bullet to deter China. Both strategies involve nasty complications, and neither provides any true guarantee of success.

Given this battlefield and chessboard, it behooves us now to come back to the lead question of this chapter and seek to determine what "victory" might look like in the event that a conventional war breaks out in Asia.

Of the three likely options—short war, long war, or nuclear holocaust—clearly the first option is the most preferable (although it raises the question of what the world would look like if China won). The problem, of course, is that a short war with a clear victor that does little damage to the global economy is the least probable of our three options. Just why might this be so?

The basic reality here is that we have two very large continental powers with vast resources to wage war. If a war were to remain below the nuclear threshold—a big if—both sides could pummel the other with conventional weapons for a very, very long time, likely without either achieving a definitive victory.

It follows from this observation that no one should get sucked into dreaming, as President George W. Bush once did, of unfurling a banner that can legitimately claim "mission accomplished" shortly after the bullets begin to fly. Indeed, if a large nation like the United States can get bogged down in much smaller wars in countries like Afghanistan, Iraq, and Vietnam for a decade or more, it is unlikely the United States would be able to quickly subdue a country as powerful as China—nor would China likely quickly vanquish the United States.

This fantasy of a short war notwithstanding, it must nonetheless be said that it is a very dangerous dream for either side to entertain. This is because if either side believes a short, winnable war is possible, the probability of that side starting a war rises dramatically.

Unfortunately, this short-war fantasy is exactly the kind of dream underpinning the doctrine of Air-Sea Battle. In this fantasy, China attacks the United States first. Then, through the miracle of technology, the United

States uses its arsenal of weapons to simultaneously knock out China's command and control systems, destroy its missile launch sites, shoot down any incoming missiles, and thereby very quickly bring China and its Communist Party leaders to their knees.

It is equally unfortunate that certain segments within the Chinese power structure may have this same short-war fantasy. Indeed, there are increasing signs in everything from China's strategic military literature to government press releases of the belief that China's growing military juggernaut may soon be able to knock out rivals like Japan or the United States quickly and decisively.

Here, Professor T. X. Hammes of America's National Defense University uses an important chapter in history to reflect on the possible dangers of such hubris, particularly within the ranks of a Chinese military that now has a lot of shiny new weapons at its disposal but has not fought a major war in more than three decades and may have forgotten what one's own spilled blood tastes like. Says Hammes:

> I think it is very important that military officers are honest and say these are going to be long wars. There is no such thing as a short war. If you look at World War I, the Germans faced a strategic problem they thought was getting worse; and the military said: "Yes, we can clean this up. Give us a couple of months; and we'll get that. Bam!" If they had just come in and said: "Yeah, four years, a million dead, shatter your economy, we'll be there, probably the [German] leadership would have said "No thanks!" That's the danger with the Chinese leadership: They may be convinced that they can get a quick win.[2]

On this point, US Naval War College professor Toshi Yoshihara wishes to underscore how important it is for the United States to strongly signal to the Chinese that "they will not be able to get away with a quick decisive victory."[3] To Yoshihara, convincing the Chinese of the bleak and uncertain prospects of a long war would go a very long way to bolstering deterrence and thereby avoiding war to begin with.

✶✶✶✶✶

Given that a short war is likely not in the cards, the second-best option should war break out may simply be a long and economically crippling conflict with no clear victor—or perhaps an inconclusive Korean War *redux* followed by a new Cold War age.[4] However, such a depressingly grim option is "best" only because option 3, a rapid escalation of a conventional war into a nuclear holocaust, is clearly unthinkable.

As to why this "unthinkable" option could become reality, one major problem is the obvious schism between the people of China and their own authoritarian government. It has been said many times by many different China experts and already revealed in this investigation that the goal of the Chinese government first and foremost is not to advance the welfare of the Chinese people but rather to maintain the tight grip of the Chinese Communist Party on power.[5]

It follows that if, during a conventional war, China begins to find itself on the losing end and Communist Party leaders believe their regime may soon be on death's ground, it is no short leap for these leaders to opt for nuclear war—and hope, then, to ride things out in China's many bomb shelters that crisscross the country.

For this reason—and because a short war is improbable and a long and highly damaging conventional war is similarly unthinkable—we must, dear detectives, in the final two parts of our story, methodically work our way through the various possible pathways to peace.

Part 5

PATHWAYS TO PEACE THAT (PROBABLY) WON'T WORK

Chapter 35

SHOULD AMERICA BEAT A NEOISOLATIONIST RETREAT?

Question: Which of these justifications for an American military
presence in Asia do you agree with?

1. America's ships, troops, and forward military bases are
   necessary to protect the sea lines of communication in the
   fastest growing region of the world and thereby facilitate
   the trade that creates new American jobs.
2. America's forward bases and its defense alliances with
   key nations like Australia, Japan, and South Korea
   provide the United States with a critical first line of
   defense against an attack of the American homeland.
3. If America withdrew its troops and ships from Asia, the
   probability of war between bitter historical rivals like
   China and Japan or North and South Korea would rise
   dramatically.
4. The United States has a strong moral obligation to defend
   flourishing democracies like Japan, the Philippines, South
   Korea, and Taiwan that it has entered into long-term
   defense treaties with.
5. All of the above.
6. None of the above.

I f you are a neoisolationist—or perhaps simply a war-weary American
taxpayer—few if any of the above arguments are likely to deeply reso-
nant. Instead, from the neoisolationist perspective, the most direct pathway
to peace—at least peace between China and the United States—is for
America to bring its ships and troops home and thereby eliminate the

growing friction between the two superpowers. On this point, American Enterprise Institute scholar Michael Auslin observes that:

> Recent polls have shown clear majorities of Americans who want a reduced American presence around the world; and that's due not just to financial and fiscal fatigue but also to the results of a decade of a war on terror that seems to be somewhat inconclusive—and quite honestly, a period of forty years of quote unquote fighting the Cold War. You know, this country has been upholding the international order uninterruptedly since 1945; and we may be at a tipping point where the American people say "enough is enough. There are a lot of other rich countries out there that should be doing more to protect themselves and be doing more to confront the bullies in their own backyard. Why do we have to do it?" And it's particularly difficult when you're talking about the Asia-Pacific. It's far away, and the majority of Americans don't have an ancestral or a cultural connection to it. It is also the one area that has a true potential great power rival which we don't want to mess with.[1]

In truth, it is in many ways far easier to make the neoisolationist case than it is to persuasively argue for maintaining a strong American military presence in Asia. As Professor John Mearsheimer notes on the historical implications of this point:

> The case for isolationism is not to be underestimated. It's why the interventionists in our policy establishment go to such great lengths to discredit it, because the logic is so powerful. [President Franklin] Roosevelt had a devil of a time defeating isolationism, and it wasn't until Pearl Harbor that it was defeated. And the reason is: It's just such an attractive ideology.[2]

Consider for example, the "sea lines of communication" argument. The easy isolationist rejoinder here is that China depends on trade even more than America—so why would it disrupt those sea lines and peaceful commerce?

Similarly, the argument that America's forward bases help protect the American homeland appears to ring hollow as soon as one points out that Asia is half a world and seven thousand miles away from an American homeland perennially protected by huge oceans on both its east and west coasts.

As for the argument that a bunch of Asian countries might fight each other, well, isn't that their business? And let's not try to scare anyone with the specter of nuclear bombs dropping all over Asia—no country would ever be insane enough to do that. Right?

Finally, in the moral dimension, many American citizens and taxpayers are just plain tired of the United States trying to play superpower "cop" and Crusader Rabbit to the world. Nor does the obvious hypocrisy of American foreign policy help much here. To wit: If the United States is so "moral" and "exceptional," why does it prop up repressive regimes in countries like Bahrain and Saudi Arabia? Oh, that's right, we need their oil or to locate our military bases there.

Yes, it is relatively easy after more than a decade of failed wars in the Middle East and a domestic landscape featuring high unemployment, rising budget deficits, and political gridlock to make the neoisolationist case. The real underlying question, of course, is whether withdrawing American troops from Asia would really be in the broad interests of peace and the narrower economic and national-security interests of the United States?

To answer this question, let's take a deeper look at each of the various rationales for a continued, and perhaps even beefed up, military presence in Asia, starting with the jobs and trade issue.

Here, it is indeed true that in this new century, Asia will likely be the fastest growing region of the world. Home to 60 percent of the globe's population, it is a region teeming with commerce and trade. It is equally true that in order for the United States to prosper, it must find at least some of its growth in the trading arena, and Asia, far and away, provides the best opportunities when matched up against the stagnation of Europe and the relative poverty of Latin America.

Ultimately, however, the economic case for an American military presence in Asia rests on something that cannot be known with any certainty. That is: How would China behave in the absence of that presence? Would it continue to allow American merchant ships unimpeded access to Asian markets? Would it abide by the rules of free trade or simply expand the mercantilist and protectionist practices it already engages in to further skew trade in its favor? Would it allow the export of key raw materials out of the region? Might it even seek to establish a regional "condominium" with other countries in Asia that conduct trade on its terms to the competitive disadvantage and detriment of the United States?

These are all questions that really can't be answered unless America pulls its troops out of Asia; and the clear risk is that China might not provide the answers that Americans like. Here, Princeton's Aaron Friedberg sounds a distinctly cautionary note:

China may want to set up a regional system in which the United States is on the sidelines; and that would be harmful to our economic interests— aside from our other concerns strategically.[3]

So, at least in the economic dimension, this is an argument around which much uncertainty revolves. All one can say with certainty is that China has historically exhibited strong mercantilist tendencies, and, in the absence of a firm American presence in Asia, Chinese mercantilism might even more fully bloom. The question here, then: Is that a risk Americans want to take?

As for the argument that America's forward bases and its alliance partners play a critical role at the front lines of America's national defense, this may be far more clear cut—the "half a world away" neoisolationist argument notwithstanding. The abiding fact here is that we are in an age of supersonic ballistic missiles, and it is now abundantly clear that nuclear warheads shot either from the silos of China's Underground Great Wall or from the hills of North Korea can now reach Portland, Minneapolis, or Baltimore in a matter of minutes. As Michael Green of the Center for Strategic and International Studies reminds us:

The Pacific Ocean is not a barrier to threats against us. North Korea is developing nuclear weapons, and they're developing ballistic missiles. Over the next decade, they want to put those nuclear weapons on ballistic missiles; and it's not to hit Europe. It's to hit the West Coast of the United States.[4]

The equally abiding fact here, as author Gordon G. Chang has phrased it, is that "America's first line of defense is not Alaska and California but rather South Korea and Japan."[5] The salient point is that America's forward bases first in South Korea and Japan and then in Australia and Guam play important roles in an early-warning matrix that helps the US missile-defense system detect incoming threats.

Equally important is America's ability to promptly retaliate against any first strike from bases within Asia. Simply because of this deterrent, there is far less likelihood that any Chinese or North Korean missiles will be launched to begin with—and one need look no farther than the attack on Pearl Harbor for a reason to be forward-leaning in Asia.

As for the important role an American military presence has played in keeping the peace in Asia for more than seventy years, Dr. Patrick Cronin of the Center for a New American Security has framed the argument in this way:

> When you think about the consequences of the United States pulling back, you have to then appreciate the sweep of history. The United States has been the dominant power in the Asia-Pacific since the end of World War II. It has ensured that deep historical grievances between countries have not come to the surface. If we pull our troops back, we are guaranteed that some of these historical animosities, some of the distrust, some of the racism, some of the bad blood that has been spilled between these countries and peoples, will definitely come out. That's why we see tensions right now between Japan and China. That's why we see tensions between Vietnam and China. Those tensions are there, but they are suppressed. So we deter open conflict from breaking out with our presence.[6]

Echoing this theme, Gordon G. Chang flags this important indivisibility between America's economic security and its national defense:

> You can only have prosperity during times of prolonged peace; and the reason why East Asia has had both peace and prosperity is because of the presence of the United States. Without America there, this never would have happened; and that's why countries in the region want us to be there. That's why they're demanding us to be there. So we Americans can't say: "Oh, we'll just trade with Asia" without also having the military and security relationships that we have. These are indivisible. One follows the other. You cannot divide peace from prosperity.[7]

Now, what can be said about the neoisolationist argument that if Asian nations want to go to war, then that's their business—and it won't affect our business? Here, it really doesn't take much deep reflection to see how dangerous this argument may be.

The most obvious problem is that Americans live in a globalized economy where any disruption in the world's supply chain caused by war in Asia would quickly redound to American shores. To understand this economic sensitivity, just consider what happened after a massive flood hit Thailand and shortly thereafter Japan was rocked by an earthquake and tsunami. The result was an only slightly less massive shock to the global supply chain that led to acute shortages in both the electronic and automotive industries, sent thousands of manufacturers around the world scrambling for replacement items, and created significant unemployment in the two countries at the epicenters of the shocks.[8] Imagine, then, what a *conventional* war in Asia would do to the ability to conduct commerce.

As for any *nuclear* war between Asian combatants, there are these simple matters of geography and meteorology to consider: The fallout from any such conflagration would travel along the jet stream and reach American shores in a mere seven short days. Moreover, if enough weapons were detonated, a nuclear winter might engulf the whole world. Is that a risk anyone wants to take by removing America's protective nuclear umbrella from Asian allies—an umbrella that has kept the peace for more than seventy years?

Now what about the companion isolationist argument that no country in Asia would actually use nuclear weapons because of their devastating consequences? In truth, this is simply naïve.

For example, if South Korea were abandoned by American troops and the US nuclear umbrella, two things are certain: First, South Korea would quickly use its highly sophisticated technological base to develop its own nukes; here it is well worth noting that South Korea agreed to abandon its nuclear weapons program in 1975 only *after* the United States promised it protection.[9] Second, South Korea would surely not hesitate to use its nukes on North Korea if a million North Korean soldiers began to stream over the demilitarized zone or the supreme leader in Pyongyang ordered a nuclear weapon dropped on Seoul—and as we have demonstrated, literally anything is possible when it comes to the "wild card" and "wild child" of North Korea.

Of course, there is a similar escalatory dynamic working with Japan. As previously noted, Japan's decades-long experience in the nuclear-power industry has given it both the expertise and fissionable material to quickly build a large arsenal of highly sophisticated nuclear weapons should

America abandon it. Faced with humiliation or subjugation by China, this land of the kamikaze, the samurai, and true Yamato spirit may then well choose nuclear war as the nobler alternative, perhaps even gambling that if it could knock out the Communist Party leadership in Beijing, the rest of China might come to its senses.

Finally, on the moral question, this is indeed a toss-up—particularly in light of the aforementioned American hypocrisy in supporting some authoritarian regimes even as it seeks regime change in others. This is a toss-up until one acknowledges that what a Realpolitik America does under the twin banners of morality and democracy is often nothing more than actions taken to promote America's self-interest.

So let's be candid here: While America's presence in Asia may allow democracies like Singapore, South Korea, and Taiwan to flourish and may help small, weak nations like the Philippines avoid subjugation, it is also true that such alliances are the backbone of the American presence in Asia; and it is this presence that may well be necessary to facilitate future economic prosperity and ensure homeland security.

Ultimately, to former Yale professor and current American Enterprise Institute scholar Michael Auslin, this question of an American presence in Asia all comes to the question of what is America's "red line"? To explain the red-line concept—and the dangers of complacency and neoisolationism—Auslin draws these historical parallels to the march of a rising China today:

> We saw signs all through the 1930s, we let a ton of territory go, and we ignored it. We ignored Hitler, we ignored Mussolini, and we ignored the Japanese. And then suddenly Pearl Harbor came, and we hit our red line. We hit our red line again on 9/11. We had a decade-plus of warnings that something like this was coming. We had the USS *Cole*. We had the African Embassy bombings. We had bombings around the world, and we didn't take them seriously.
>
> What's going to change our world next? We don't know; but what we don't want to do is think seriously and hard about it. We're tired. We want to focus on what feels good; and we don't want to commit to keeping our forces around the world that have kept stability; but we've been disproven every time that we've taken that position.[10]

Chapter 36

WILL ECONOMIC ENGAGEMENT KEEP THE PEACE?

Question: Which statement about the role of economic
engagement in promoting peace in Asia do you agree
more with?

1. Economic engagement is turning China from an
   authoritarian regime into a liberal democracy less prone
   to violence and aggression, and therefore such economic
   engagement is a force for peace.
2. Economic engagement has only served to strengthen
   the Chinese Communist Party's authoritarian grip on its
   citizenry even as it has helped finance China's military
   rise.

A merica and its Asian allies have certainly made a big bet on the
power of economic engagement to transform China from a bellig-
erent, authoritarian regime into a peace-loving liberal democracy. In fact,
as big bets go, it certainly seems to have had a reasonable chance of paying
off—at least when this bet was first made back in the 1970s.

Consider that since that time, other Asian nations like Singapore,
South Korea, and Taiwan have all come over to the liberal-democracy side
from the dark passenger of authoritarianism—largely on the wings of free
trade and the economic engagement such trade inevitably brings. In other
parts of the world, economic engagement has likewise seemingly worked
its magic, with formerly authoritarian countries like Argentina, Chile, and
Ecuador in Latin America and Hungary, Poland, and the Czech Republic
in Europe now full, if not always flourishing, democracies. Surely, then,
China must eventually follow suit—or so the perennial hope has been.

Not only does the authoritarian grip of the Chinese Communist Party seem to be tightening, but economic engagement is providing China with a supercharged economic engine to drive its military buildup. As we have documented, with this new strength, China is exhibiting increasingly aggressive behavior. This is not how the economic-engagement story was supposed to unfold after President Richard Nixon and Secretary of State Henry Kissinger ushered in an era of "Ping-Pong diplomacy" in 1972.

At that seemingly propitious time, neither Nixon nor Kissinger had any grand plan to use economic engagement to specifically pacify and liberalize China. Instead, the deal between Chairman Mao Zedong and President Nixon was far more pragmatic—and both sides got exactly what they bargained for.

On the principle of "the enemy of my enemy is my friend," Nixon and Kissinger wanted to align with China to help offset the growing power of the Soviet Union—which China had little qualms about doing given Mao's growing rift with Soviet Premier Nikita Khrushchev. Kissinger, in particular, also wanted China's help in bringing North Vietnam to the Paris bargaining table so he could engineer an exit strategy from the Vietnam War, if not with honor at least with expediency.

As for China, with Mao's power fading, more pragmatic leaders like Premier Zhou Enlai were waking up to the need for international trade after the twin disasters of the Great Leap Forward and Cultural Revolution. Thus, as its *quid pro quo*, China sought an end to America's economic embargo and access to the global economy.

In contrast to this Nixonian pragmatism stands Bill Clinton's grand and idealistic vision of the taming power of engagement. At the tail end of his presidency in 2000, it would be Clinton, with the strong support of America's corporate community, who would champion economic engagement as a tool to transform China into a peaceful, Western-style democracy.

In perhaps one of his most famous campaign slogans on behalf of promoting such economic engagement through China's entry into the World Trade Organization, Clinton would piously intone: "I don't believe that we will have more influence on China by giving them the back of our hand." To this hope, Clinton would add this homily:

> Economically, this [World Trade Organization] agreement is the equivalent of a one-way street. It requires China to open its markets with a fifth

of the world's population, potentially the biggest markets in the world. For the first time, China will agree to play by the same open trading rules we do. Never happened before. For the first time our companies will be able to sell and distribute products in China made by workers here in America.[1]

Perhaps no American president has been more wrong about so much with such devastating economic consequences. In the wake of China's joining the World Trade Organization, Clinton's corporate backers would begin a massive offshoring exodus to China that would help lead to the closing of over seventy thousand American factories; the number of unemployed and underemployed workers would eventually swell to over twenty-five million; and America's massive trade deficit would swell to over $300 billion annually, leaving America in debt to China to the tune of trillions of dollars.

Of course, engagement with China may have been worth all of the economic hardship it has imposed on the American people (and much of the rest of the world) if it had achieved its goal of turning China from an aggressive, authoritarian regime into a peaceful liberal democracy. However, as economist Ian Fletcher has noted: "Economic growth in China has not led to its becoming more democratic. It has simply led to a more sophisticated, better-financed form of authoritarianism."[2]

Here, US-China Commission[3] member Dan Slane adds this revealing requiem:

> When the United States allowed China to enter the World Trade Organization in 2001 and opened up its markets without any corresponding opening up of the Chinese markets, we knew we would take a huge economic hit. However, many of our leaders thought that hit would be worth it because increased trade would take China and turn it into a democracy. As it turned out, that never happened. Instead, China has taken advantage of every opportunity to game the free trade system, maximize their own trade to build up their economy, and, in the process, they've done severe damage to our own economy.[4]

As to why economic engagement with China has thus far not borne its much hoped for and highly anticipated liberal democracy fruit, it certainly can't be blamed on the Chinese character or culture. If nothing else, the successes of both the Singapore and Taiwan democracies have proven that.

So just what *has* gone wrong here—and perhaps might it eventually go right? The answers may be found in the three main pillars of the economic-engagement argument—and the intriguing possibility that the rhetoric of economic engagement may simply be a ruse for corporate interests to expand globally at the expense of domestic workers.

As to where these three pillars of the economic engagement argument may be found, one can perhaps do no better than visiting the website of USA*Engage.[5] This is a self-described broad-based coalition of agricultural and manufacturing interests whose members include a veritable "who's who" of multinational Americana—from Apple, Boeing, Caterpillar, and ConAgra to Union Carbide, Westinghouse, and Xerox.[6] To these multinationals, an authoritarian China represents not just a huge market but also the world's premier offshoring destination with a seemingly endless supply of cheap labor, a dramatically reduced tax burden, and the virtual absence of any meaningful environmental or health-and-safety regulations.

Of course, in the political arena, corporate lobbyists are never going to make the argument for economic engagement on the basis of higher profits, more pollution, and worker abuses. Instead, that argument is going to rest on the promise of a more peaceful and prosperous world. Enter stage right the three logical pillars of engagement.

First, there is the power of the "rising middle class" to effect change. Here, USA*Engage expansively asserts that:

> [M]arket-oriented economic development causes social changes that impede authoritarian rule. These include widespread education, the opening of society to the outside world, and the development of an independent middle class.[7]

According to USA*Engage, it follows that "a government faced with this change must seek the support of the middle class and must respond to middle class demands for greater political freedom, the rule of law, and the elimination of corruption."[8]

This is indeed a persuasive argument. However, in China, the prosperity that has flowed from economic engagement has tended to act much more like a *pacifier* of the middle class than as a promoter of free speech. The tacit deal in China between the Chinese Communist Party and China's rising middle class seems to be this: In exchange for the government helping to make you rich, you keep your mouth shut. That's perhaps why, on the whole, China's middle class is one of the least, not most, vocal in the political arena.

As for the second "independent organization" pillar of the engagement argument, USA*Engage invokes the wisdom of Stanford scholar Seymour Martin Lipset. Opines Lipset:

> Economic development also tends to alter the relationship between state and society, to increase the number and variety of independent organizations that check the state and broaden political participation, and to reduce corruption, nepotism, and state control over jobs and opportunities to accumulate wealth.

Of course, the problem here is that the Chinese government devotes considerable resources to an Orwellian security apparatus that keeps exceedingly close tabs on any "independent organizations" that might spring up to challenge government authority. Make such a challenge too strongly as an environmental, human-rights, free-speech, or Tibetan-issues advocate, and you are likely to simply disappear into the "Laogai"— China's intricate network of forced-labor camps explicitly modeled after the Russian "Gulags" built by Stalin.[9]

Turning to the final "information is power" pillar of economic engagement, this assertion from yet another Stanford scholar Henry Rowen captures the essence of the argument:

> [O]pening an economy to the outside world vastly expands the flow of information. The internet, television, books, newspapers, copying machines, foreign magazines, all the various forms of popular entertainment and intellectual thought begin to flow, spreading ideas like democracy, human rights, and the rule of law.

Here again, however, standing in the way of democratic change is China's massive security apparatus—particularly its "Great Firewall." With an army of over fifty thousand "cybercops" and using surveillance technologies provided by foreign corporations like America's Cisco Systems,[10] China is able not just to restrict the flow of information, particularly from the Internet, but also shapes that information flow in a way consistent with its authoritarian messaging.

It follows from these observations that, at least in the case of China, the world would do well not to pin too much hope on economic engagement as a force for peace in Asia. To the contrary, economic engagement seems to be the primary well from which China's new found military might seems to have sprung—and in direct contradiction to the "engagers for peace," one possible option to curtail China's military rise may well be to *reduce* the level of economic engagement with China.

Before considering such a Draconian step, however, we must next evaluate an argument that is often made synergistically with economic engagement, namely, that the high level of *economic interdependence* between China and the rest of the world makes war highly unlikely. It is to this task in the next chapter we now turn.

Chapter 37

WILL ECONOMIC INTERDEPENDENCE PREVENT WAR?

Question: Is a country heavily dependent on global trade more
or less likely to go to war with its trading partners?

1. Less likely
2. More likely
3. The correct answer may depend on the goods being traded

At least when it comes to China, the conventional wisdom today seems to clearly favor answer no. 1—a *pax mercatoria* or peace that comes from trade. Indeed, from Wall Street and Main Street to the "liberal school"[1] of international relations, a loud chorus continues to assert that war is far less likely with China because the costs in lost trade to everyone would be far higher than any benefits that might be gained from war. As the French political philosopher Montesquieu put it long ago:

> Peace is the natural effect of trade. Two nations who differ with each other become reciprocally dependent; for if one has an interest in buying, the other has an interest in selling; and thus, their union is founded on their mutual necessities.[2]

Of course, those in the competing "realist school" quickly reject the notion that "trade will always trump invade."[3] To support their view, they just as quickly jump to history's most glaring *pax mercatoria* failure— World War I—along with one of history's worst prognostications. Consider that just months before the start of the "Great War," Stanford University president David Starr Jordan, in all his liberal glory, piously made this prediction:

> What shall we say of the Great War of Europe, ever threatening, ever impending, and which never comes? We shall say that it will never come. Humanly speaking, it is impossible.

Of course, within months, the "impossible" morphed into an all-too-real conflict that would all but destroy the global economy while killing millions of soldiers and millions more civilians. In explaining why a *pax mercatoria* failed in this particular case, the realist school offers a far more nuanced view of the power—or lack thereof—of economic interdependence to keep the peace.

In this more nuanced view, if a country is heavily dependent on global trade for goods vital to national security such as food, energy, or other natural resources for manufacturing, that country may actually be *more* likely to go to war. In fact, it is precisely this more pernicious variation of economic interdependence that leads us right back to World War I—and a very interesting set of parallels that may be drawn between pre–World War I Kaiser Germany and the China of today.

As a first parallel, consider Kaiser Germany and its own variation on China's modern "Malacca Dilemma." In the decades leading up to the Great War, a rapidly rising Germany was becoming increasingly dependent on oil imports to fuel its growing manufacturing capabilities. So it was that Kaiser Wilhelm and his advisors watched with mounting alarm—and considerable anger—as the British Empire conspired with *both* Imperial Russia and a quasi-imperialist United States to effectively lock Germany out of the Middle East and its vast oil reserves.

As to whether China believes there is a similar conspiracy against it today, there is this troubling fact: When Chinese president Hu Jintao originally coined the term "Malacca Dilemma" in a 2003 speech, he did indeed warn that "certain major powers" might seek to control oil flow through the Malacca Strait.[4]

As a second parallel between Kaiser Germany and today's China, there is also their shared status as rapidly rising powers heavily dependent on the importation of other natural resources to feed their growing industrial bases. As realist-school professor Dale Copeland tells the German story, when a protectionist French government stepped in to limit ore exports to Germany, it wasn't long before German industrialists began to speak openly "of the need to lay their hands on the iron ore basin of French Lorraine; [and] war seemed to them a matter for industry."[5]

As to whether China's numerous state-owned enterprises of today might similarly seek to "lay their lands" on foreign resources through war, that is at least one reasonable interpretation of Chinese expansionism—recall our discussion of the Madisonian "mischief of factions" that may be helping to propel Beijing's revanchist agenda. Indeed, in both the East and South China Seas, China's usurpation of natural resource rights is a common theme and thread in the emerging conflicts, and it is not uncommon to see the massive oil rigs of Chinese corporations like the China National Offshore Oil Corporation ringed by Chinese warships leading the revanchist charge.[6]

Such spectacles notwithstanding, it is the third parallel between Kaiser Wilhelm's pre–World War I Germany and today's China that is perhaps the most interesting. This parallel is their shared fear of a naval blockade.

In Germany's case, in the twenty years leading up to World War I, its food imports began to grow even faster than its rapidly growing population. The grim result was an arms race between Germany and Great Britain that, according to Professor Copeland "reflected fears on each side that the other might blockade imports to starve the adversary into submission."[7]

Nor was this any paranoia on Kaiser Germany's part. As Copeland notes: "British plans for such a blockade were well-advanced in the last decade before [World War I]," and "the shared fear [within Germany] was that German industry, increasingly dependent on outsiders for vital goods, would be strangled by the growing economic restrictions imposed by adversaries."[8]

Of course, it is an open question as to whether China's business and government will eventually succumb to the same kind of "shared fear" that brought the world to its knees at the turn of the last century—that was then, this is now. But when one compares the "economic strangulation" rhetoric of modern blockade supporters to the German experience, any such shared fear in China would be quite legitimate, indeed quite prudent.[9]

The broader point of these historical parallels is to simply underscore the realist conclusion that countries like pre–World War I Germany or today's China that are heavily dependent on trade for goods vital to national security may indeed lash out. That said, there is a much more modern history that provides additional support for the idea that economic interdependence is no absolute guarantee of peace.

✱✱✱✱✱

This thoroughly modern history involves Russia's expansionist activities in Crimea and the Ukraine and, more broadly, across Eastern Europe. Here, we have an authoritarian Russian nation that is heavily dependent on trade with Europe and on the financial system of the West, particularly the United States. Yet this interdependence has done little to stop a revanchist Russia from its repeated attempts to regain territory lost with the dissolution of the old Union of Soviet Socialist Republics.

Of course, the obvious parallel to draw here is that, like Russia, a revanchist China might also use its military might to right what it perceives to be historical wrongs. What is perhaps most interesting, however, has been the Western response—watched very closely by China—to Russian aggression.

In particular, rather than send in arms and troops to support the Ukraine or try to push Russia out of the Crimea, the United States and a coalition of European nations simply chose to fight this undeclared war solely with economic sanctions. Here, however, is the rub:

To the extent that sanctions may have had some mild deterrent effect on Russian aggression—that is certainly open to debate—they have only worked because America and its allies are far less dependent on trade with Russia than Russia is on America and its allies. If, however, China has its own "Crimea moment" and for whatever reason, it decides to take disputed territory such as the Senkaku Islands or Taiwan or Second Thomas Shoal or Arunachal Pradesh by force, economic sanctions by the United States and its Asian allies are likely to fail miserably.

Just why is this so? Because, unlike in the Russian case, any such sanctions regime would do as much or more damage to the economies of the American alliance as they would do to China. Moreover, because this is so, it is unlikely economic sanctions against China would even be attempted.

What all this means within the context of our "will there be war" question is this: At least with China, the nonkinetic tools of economic and financial sanctions are largely taken off the table. This is because China has as much power to harm the economies of the American alliance as the alliance does of harming China's economy. Of course, once *nonkinetic* economic sanctions are taken off the peacekeeping table, the probability of kinetic warfare in the face of a Chinese Crimea moment must *rise*.

✱✱✱✱✱

In light of this both old and new history, perhaps the best we can say about economic interdependence is that it is a double-edged sword. Under some circumstances such as symmetrical trade of goods not vital to national security, economic interdependence may well help keep the peace—the fruits of trade will indeed trump the costs of invade. However, under other circumstances such as an overreliance on tradable goods vital to national security by a fearful combatant, economic interdependence might actually help *escalate* conflict.

This suggests that counting on economic interdependence to keep the peace in Asia is a strategy that may be based more on hope than upon any sober analysis of either past history or present circumstances. As Princeton's Aaron Friedberg notes: "Look at the relations between China and Japan right now. These are two countries that have extremely important trade and investment relations, but that hasn't prevented the Chinese from taking steps to raise the risk of conflict with Japan."[10]

Because this is so, and because there are also other less rational elements that can lead to war, it may be appropriate to give Professor Toshi Yoshihara of the US Naval War College and Princeton's Friedberg the last words in this chapter. Says Yoshihara:

> I'd like to think that economic interdependence would create this rational cost-and-benefit analysis that would tend to have a self-deterring effect on both sides since a war would obviously destroy that interdependence and lead to enormous economic costs on both sides; but we've seen in history that there are other factors that lead countries to go to war—things like fear and honor. These are two major drivers in terms of how states determine whether they need to use force to defend what they consider to be their vital national interests. And so I think if you include these more intangible elements of why states go to war, it would be prudent for us not to rule out the possibility of a crisis and maybe even conflict between China and the United States.[11]

To this Friedberg adds:

People have believed for a long time that trade is a source of stability and peace and, I think, in a large sense, that's true and on average, historically, that's been true. Unfortunately, it's not a guarantee. Countries that have intense trading relationships do not necessarily have good strategic or political relationships; and, historically, countries with intense trading relationships have sometimes gone to war with one another.[12]

Chapter 38

WILL NUCLEAR WEAPONS DETER CONVENTIONAL WAR?

Question: Nuclear weapons in the hands of both America and
China significantly decreases the probability that
China may initiate a conventional war in Asia.

1. True
2. False

This is indeed a vexing question, dear detectives. For just as the conventional wisdom has been that both economic engagement and economic interdependence act as forces for peace, so, too, is it with nuclear weapons. However, as with engagement and interdependence, there are strong counterarguments that suggest China's growing nuclear capabilities may actually provide it with an effective shield behind which it can actually engage in more aggressive behavior, including conventional war.

Let's work our way, then, through both sides of the argument and see where we stand at the other side of that enquiry. To begin, let's look at the premier example of "nukes prevent conventional war"—the four-decade-long rivalry between the Soviet Union and the United States during the Cold War.

Here, it may be said quite accurately that although proxy wars abounded, these two superpowers never directly engaged each other in either conventional *or* nuclear war; the reason most often given for this icy peace was the existence of massive "mutually assured destruction" nuclear arsenals on both sides.

In a related vein, there is also the 1962 Cuban Missile Crisis. Aside from the CIA–backed and grossly undermanned Bay of Pigs invasion by Cuban exiles in 1961, the United States never attempted to militarily invade Cuba and violently overthrow the Fidel Castro regime. However, if there ever were a time to do so, it would have been during the Cuban Missile Crisis.

In the months leading up to that crisis, the Soviets had planted on Cuban soil strategic nuclear weapons capable of quickly striking any city in America—an obvious *casus belli*. That the United States never launched a conventional-war invasion of Cuba either during or after that crisis is likely due to the extended nuclear-defense umbrella the Soviets offered Castro.

As still a third telling example bolstering the "nukes for peace" argument, there is India versus Pakistan. These two bitter rivals went head to head in conventional wars in 1947, 1965, and 1971, and the conflicts in both 1965 and 1971 in particular involved fierce fighting and heavy causalities. However, since both India and Pakistan became nuclear powers, they have fought only one conventional war—one far more limited in scope and quickly resolved diplomatically.

It follows from these various examples that a strong historical case exists for the proposition that "nukes prevent conventional war." So why, then, should we be worried that China would ever launch a conventional war in Asia given the current nuclear balance between China and America? The answer lies in making a deeper and more textured assessment of the nuclear-deterrence chessboard—and digesting a few more slices of history.

Consider, for example, an incident we discussed in an earlier chapter: China's attack on the Soviet Union in 1969. At the time, China was not yet a capable nuclear power while the Soviet Union had enough missiles to destroy every major city on the Chinese mainland—yet China had absolutely no qualms about launching a conventional attack on Soviet forces. Instead, in the midst of that conflict, Chinese leaders openly talked about how they would not submit to "nuclear blackmail"[1] in seeking to right a historical wrong perpetrated by Imperial Russia during China's century of humiliation.

In a related territorial dispute equally tinged with nationalism and the redress of a historical wrong, there is the war between a nuclear-armed Great Britain and a nonnuclear Argentina over the Falkland Islands in 1982. In the midst of growing civil unrest, Argentina's "wag the dog" military junta ordered the invasion of what Argentines call the "Malvinas Islands"—and Great Britain's nuclear capabilities appeared to have played absolutely no role in the Argentinian decision to launch its conventional strikes.

As yet a third and quite-rich slice of relevant history, there is also the Taiwan Strait Crisis "trilogy." In both the first crisis of 1954–1955 and the second crisis of 1958, China obviously showed no hesitation in engaging in conventional war despite the fact it was as yet without nuclear weapons and faced a daunting nuclear power in the United States.

Here, while repeated American threats to "nuke China" did cause China to back down in the first crisis, the existence of America's nuclear threat did not prevent China from jumpstarting the second crisis in 1958. However, what is perhaps most interesting about this second crisis is that it only ended because Taiwan's military gained the upper hand on the *conventional-war* battlefield—it was America's provision of the magic bullet of Sidewinder air-to-air missiles that allowed the victorious Nationalists to strike the decisive blow over the skies of the Taiwan Strait.

Perhaps needless to say, a "Taiwan defeats China" scenario is unlikely to be repeated today. This is not just because of China's massive military modernization but also because of the ongoing reluctance of the United States to provide Taiwan with the latest weapons technology to strike another "decisive blow."

As for the Third Taiwan Strait Crisis, this one may offer the most insight of all. Once again, the threat of being "nuked" by America did not prevent a now nuclear-armed China from attempting to hijack Taiwan's electoral process in 1995 and 1996 through a campaign of intimidation. Moreover, China only retreated after American aircraft-carrier strike groups arrived on scene. This likewise is a result not likely to be repeated given China's military buildup and the increasing effectiveness of its asymmetric warfighting capabilities.

These observations logically lead to a discussion of perhaps the most important ingredient of an effective deterrent capability—the *credibility* of that deterrent. In fact, for American deterrence against Chinese aggression in Asia to be effective, it must be credible in at least two dimensions.

First, China must be convinced that America and its allies have the military capabilities to defeat China—or at least fight China to a draw. Otherwise, China has little reason to fear that its rivals will be able to inflict the kind of "severe punishment" that, according to Professor Kenneth Waltz, is the hallmark of effective deterrence.[2] Of course, this form of credibility is increasingly in doubt as China arms itself with both traditional and asymmetric weapons.

Second, in order to be deterred from conventional war, China must also believe that its opponents have the will and resolve to both fight a conventional war if they need to and use nuclear weapons if they must. It is in this dimension that another key concept in deterrence theory takes center stage—the perceived "rationality" of the potential combatants.

The importance of rationality can be highlighted using one of the most important tools of deterrence analytics, namely, game theory. Consider, then, this typical deterrence game offered up by Nobel Laureate Thomas Schelling as it might be framed in a China-US context.

If China does not act according to America's conventional assumptions, America will consider China's behavior "irrational," and China's perceived irrationality might result in it winning the competition. However, if China is not really irrational—or mad—but is using its unconventional behavior as part of a conscious bargaining or competitive strategy, then this so-called irrationality is effectively rational in relation to the game's "payoffs."[3]

In other words, the feigning of "madness" can be "wickedly rational," as one expert has framed what has come to be known as the "madman theory."[4] Lest any of you think this may be a fanciful idea, please know this:

The most famous practitioner and disciple of the "madman theory" was not China's Chairman Mao Zedong but rather the American president Richard Nixon. He purposively feigned angry and erratic behavior as a strategy to convince the North Vietnamese to agree to American terms during the Paris peace negotiations. In describing his "madman theory" in private to an aide, Nixon said:

> I want the North Vietnamese to believe I've reached the point where I might do anything to stop the war. We'll just slip the word to them that, "for God's sake, you know Nixon is obsessed about communism. We can't restrain him when he's angry—and he has his hand on the nuclear button" and Ho Chi Minh himself will be in Paris in two days begging for peace.[5]

As applied to our present case, if American leaders truly believe China is crazy enough to push the nuclear button, America may be more hesitant to respond to a conventional war initiated by China for fear of nuclear escalation, and this will be particularly true because such a conventional war is unlikely to directly threaten American soil. In this way, China's perceived irrationality and the condition of uncertain retaliation[6] it entails may not only make conventional war in Asia possible, but it may make such a war even more probable as China believes it will get a free nuclear pass so long as it avoids directly attacking American soil. As scholar Ashley Tellis of the Carnegie Endowment for Peace has warned:

> There is a clear risk that despite the presence of secure second strike capabilities on both sides, China and the United States could well find themselves in a serous military conflict in the years to come; and the risk of such conflict arises because China has now steadily acquired the capabilities to prevent the United States from coming to the assistance of its friends in Asia if Chinese political objectives demand such a campaign.[7]

Here, Professor Toshi Yoshihara of the US Naval War College drills down into this vexing problem:

> If there is mutually-assured denial at the strategic nuclear level between China and the United States and if the Chinese can, essentially, superimpose their anti-access strategy along the near seas against US naval forces, that might essentially create strategic space for China to conduct conventional offensive military operations within the Asian maritime theater. This is what theorists have called the "stability-instability paradox." In other words, while having an assured nuclear retaliatory capability on both sides may create strategic stability at the highest nuclear level, this then opens up space for either proxy wars or lower-level conventional wars under the umbrella of mutually assured deterrence. And so, having nuclear weapons does not necessarily ensure that there will be no war. It simply opens up different avenues for different kinds of wars.[8]

Now here's the worst part of this deadly game: If China misreads the American side and underestimates the will of its leaders and thereby pushes too hard on the conventional war button, it may wind up inviting the very nuclear response it believed was not possible.

From this discussion, you can see why China will always prefer a "rational dove" like Barack Obama as an American president rather than a perhaps "irrational hawk" like Ronald Reagan or George W. Bush. At least to the Chinese, the "doves" lack the requisite will and resolve even as the "hawks" are more likely to fit the madman ruse—if it really is a ruse. But you see what I mean here about uncertainty—can anybody really be sure about China's rationality and intentions, particularly given its history of Maoist excesses and exorcisms?

✴✴✴✴✴

As for other reasons why a nuclear-deterrent capability might not restrain China from launching a conventional war, there are two others well worth noting to end this chapter. Of no small matter, first is the chilling question of who *really* is in charge of the People's Liberation Army. There is considerable debate on this subject and no real consensus.[9] Nevertheless, the nightmare scenario here is that some rogue military faction may trigger a conventional war that quite literally mushrooms into nuclear war.

In addition, there is this equally chilling game-theoretic possibility: Chinese leaders may indeed be perfectly rational and simply approach the decision to wage conventional war in pure Clausewitzian "war by algebra" terms. In such a calculus, a rational China may one day conclude that its military buildup has reached that defining moment where it can inflict sufficient costs on the American side to force its retreat from Asia. If, however, an equally rational American side believes any such retreat might entail unacceptably high economic, moral, and national-security costs, then it is "game on" in the worst possible kind of miscalculating World War III way.

At the end of the day, all we can say, then, is this: There appears to be no certainty that the now roughly offsetting nuclear capabilities of China and the United States will in any way deter conventional war in Asia. Both the historical record as well as the insights from deterrence theory are simply too mixed to offer us a clear picture or any guarantee of a lasting peace.

Chapter 39

CAN WE NEGOTIATE
OUR WAY OUT OF THE
THUCYDIDES TRAP?

Question: Which of these statements most accurately
characterizes China's perspective on transparency,
negotiations, and the rule of law?

1. China likes to build direct communication links to minimize
   tensions and avoid miscalculations.
2. China favors transparency when it comes to revealing its
   military capabilities.
3. China prefers to operate in a multilateral, rather than
   bilateral, negotiating framework and does not seek to
   gain leverage over smaller nations.
4. China plays strictly within the rules of international
   organizations such as the United Nations and World
   Trade Organization.
5. China has a strong track record in abiding by the
   agreements that it negotiates.
6. None of the above.

One of the big reasons nuclear bombs never fell during the Cold
War is that the United States and Soviet Union were willing to talk
with one another. At the highest level, the American president and Soviet
premier shared a hotline. At the front lines and on the open seas, naval
commanders would regularly engage in bridge–to–bridge communications.

In addition, the Americans and Soviets had a tacit agreement not
to disrupt each other's satellite networks so as to preserve each other's
second-strike capabilities and therefore the nuclear deterrence that comes

from "mutually assured destruction." Toward the end of the Cold War, the two sides even engaged in treaty negotiations that led to a truly astonishing transparency with regards to their nuclear arsenals—and ultimately to a revolutionary breakthrough in nuclear disarmament. Of equal importance, when the two sides entered into agreements, they generally kept them, thus making future agreements possible.

Unfortunately, none of these "circuit breakers" exists today in any meaningful way between China and the United States, and that "none of the above" is likely the correct answer to our lead question hardly bodes well for the use of negotiations as a pathway to peace. It is therefore important that we probe more deeply into this area to see if there is any way to cut through this particular Gordian knot.

To begin, it is important to understand that China's perspective on the communications and negotiations process represents not just a clash of cultures but also a quite-different strategic calculus. To see this, consider the contrasting perspectives of China and the United States on the role of transparency in deterrence within the context of what might aptly be described as a global game of poker.

At one end of the strategic gaming table is the superpower of America. As former US Assistant Secretary of Defense Kurt Campbell has described it:

> The United States is all about showing what we've got. Look how powerful we are. You don't want to screw with us.[1]

From the American view, such transparency is not based on egotism or bravado. Rather, it is a rational strategy based on the presumption that if it lays all of its military cards on the table and shows it is holding four aces, everyone else will fold. In this way, a completely transparent US military force will keep the peace—or so much of the thinking at the Pentagon and White House typically goes.

At the other end of this high-stakes global poker table, however, there is a rising China pursuing an exact opposite strategy of *nontransparency*. As Campbell notes:

> China seeks deterrence often through uncertainty leaving potential adversaries with questions as to just how capable they are.[2]

Of course, from the perspective of China—the historical "folder" over issues like Taiwan in America's great power game—this is an equally rational strategy. Indeed, when China refuses to disclose how many nuclear warheads it may have beneath its Underground Great Wall *or* what weapons it might be launching into space *or* whether its antiship ballistic missiles can really hit an American aircraft carrier at sea, it raises uncertainty in the minds of its rivals. Such uncertainty, in turn, is apt to create doubts and hesitation in times of conflict. In this completely nontransparent world, America in particular thus must ultimately worry that a Chinese "straight flush" of asymmetric weapons might actually trump America's four aces— so an opaque China would be a fool to ever show its hand.

Here's how Professor David Lampton of Johns Hopkins University has aptly summed up the situation—which looks more like a stalemate and a stare down than a viable pathway to peace:

> So we have us believing clarity leads to deterrence, and China thinking that obscurity and non-transparency will.[3]

Of course, China's posture toward nontransparency might change as its military might grows and it reaches a point where it believes that it has equaled or surpassed the United States. Past that threshold, it may well want to "strut its stuff" for the same reason the United States does now— to overtly intimidate would-be rivals. However, there is no guarantee of any such future transparency. For now, we are stuck in a polarized world in which a transparent America faces an opaque China without any real prospects of negotiating meaningful treaties in such important areas as arms control and the nonweaponization of space.

✷✷✷✷✷

There is also a similar clash of cultures and strategies when it comes to direct communications between China and the United States on more rubber-meets-the-military-road matters. Particularly troublesome here is the lack of adequate bridge-to-bridge communications when Chinese and US military ships cross each other's bows in the East and South China Seas—as they are increasingly wont to do.

From the American point of view, such forms of communication are critical to prevent any miscalculations that might trigger a war. China, however, has a very different strategic perspective. As Kurt Campbell has described it:

> It is American forces that are deployed very close to the Chinese homeland; and they don't want those American forces to have a degree of confidence that in a crisis, there are communication procedures worked out in advance and the Americans will have a "get out of jail free card."[4]

As both Campbell and Institute of Peace expert Stephanie Kleine-Ahlbrandt have explained it, to China, such communications are simply "seatbelts for the speeders."[5]

From this perspective, Chinese military commanders believe it is far better for their American counterparts to worry about what a Chinese response might be as this will breed more caution. If the price of that lack of direct communication is a possible *mis*calculation and things escalate, then so be it. As Campbell notes, however, the problem with China's refusal for more communication channels is that "things can get out of hand" and "lead to really unprecedented challenges."[6]

As for the negotiating process itself, one major problem in the area of resolving the myriad of territorial disputes it has in the East and South China Seas is China's predilection for bilateral, rather than multilateral negotiations and a concomitant aversion to using international bodies for any type of binding arbitration. There certainly is no mystery as to why China prefers such an approach; it will obviously have far more leverage going head-to-head with smaller countries like the Philippines and Vietnam than allowing these countries to band together in an effort to seek common ground.

A case in point is offered by the perennial "code of conduct" dance between China and the ten nations that have banded together in the Association of Southeast Asian Nations. These ten ASEAN members include Brunei, Cambodia, Indonesia, Laos, Malaysia, Myanmar, the Philippines, Singapore, Thailand, and Vietnam. Over a decade ago, China and ASEAN signed a declaration designed to be the first step in adopting a rules-based code of conduct for relations between all of the nations in Southeast Asia.

According to Asia experts like Bonnie Glaser of the Center for Strategic and International Studies, if such a code of conduct were actually adopted and adhered to by China and ASEAN, it would virtually eliminate military friction over territorial disputes in the South China Sea. This is because the cornerstone of any such code would be a proviso that no country would unilaterally attempt to change the status quo by force or coercion, and that any disputes over land features or maritime issues would be arbitrated in international courts.[7]

In these ways, a code of conduct would prevent the kinds of takings that China has already engineered in both the Paracel and Spratly Islands as well as at Scarborough Shoal. More broadly, such a code of conduct would ensure that all disputes be resolved through peaceful means.

The problem here, however, is that since signing the original declaration of intent, China has done nothing but drag its heels on getting to a final deal. One likely explanation for this delay tactic is that China believes it is only a matter of time before its growing military capabilities will allow it to dictate terms to its lesser rivals. Accordingly, there is no real reason to actually sign a binding treaty—and every reason to drag the process out until such time as it reaches critical military mass in the region. At such a point, all other nations in the region—as well as perhaps the United States—will be forced to negotiate on China's terms.

In fact, China's gaming of the ASEAN negotiating framework is symptomatic of a broader pattern of abuse of key international institutions in the global order that are committed by charter to the rule of law and the cause of peace. For example, as a permanent member of the United Nations Security Council, China has the power to veto any UN resolution. Unfortunately, over the last several decades, China has earned a very well-deserved "rug merchant" reputation for using that veto simply as a bargaining chip to acquire a wide range of natural resources in war-torn or troubled areas of the world. Here, perhaps the most glaring example is that of China's efforts to block UN sanctions against the Sudan for its Darfur genocide in exchange for Sudanese oil rights.[8]

As a final, and perhaps fatal, impediment to using the negotiation process as a pathway to peace, there is this vexing issue: China is prone to breaking agreements outright that it has entered into.

The poster child of this problem is the previously discussed US–brokered pact in 2012 between China and the Philippines. Recall that both parties agreed to withdraw from Scarborough Shoal and negotiate a solution. However, after the Philippines honored its commitment, China simply moved in and consolidated its hold on the shoal. It is a fair question as to how anyone would ever trust China to keep its word after this kind of charade.

The bottom line? It is unlikely that China, at least in the near future, will play either the "transparency game" or "negotiations game" fairly—if at all. Because this may be true, we are likely going to have to seek other pathways to peace.

This is not to say that the rest of the world should not continue to reach out to China. As Professor David Lampton has opined:

> I think we need to avoid a polarized discussion—that you either can talk to the Chinese or you can't. I would say you can but it's difficult . . . therefore we've got to persist.[9]

To American Enterprise Institute scholar Michael Auslin, however, any such persistence must be matched with a much needed, and long overdue, dose of realism. As Auslin reflects:

> In the west, we have this idea of how international relations are supposed to work. First of all, everyone respects everyone else's sovereignty, we all deal with each other as equals, and the best way to resolve all these problems and deepen understanding is with dialogue. So we get into a dialogue dependency trap, and I think that's where we are with China. The goal is simply to talk. It's not to solve the problems. It's not really to articulate our own interests or, I would argue quite honestly, understand theirs. [Instead], it is "We just have to talk. What's the next meeting? What are we going to do the next time?" And that's why I think it's a little bit of a Potemkin village. We're very happy to look at the facade of all of these talks; and then we say "look how pretty these houses are. They've got wonderful shutters and doors." [But] you walk through them, and it's a howling desert beyond.[10]

Chapter 40

IS A "GRAND BARGAIN" WITH CHINA FEASIBLE?

Question: Would you support the following "grand bargain" for the cause of peace? The United States withdraws its defense of Taiwan. In exchange, China gives up all its other territorial claims in the East and South China Seas and also recognizes the right of the American military to maintain a presence in Asia.

1. Yes
2. No

One of the most seductive ideas in diplomacy is the notion of a "grand bargain." That is, an agreement that ends all disagreements among adversaries who often have sharply different ideologies and agendas and just as often hold deeply entrenched positions.

Over the course of history, grand-bargain phraseology has been used to describe everything from the successful Peace of Westphalia in 1648 to the failed Treaty of Versailles in 1919 that set the stage for World War II. The term "grand bargain" has even been used to characterize the implicit deal China made with its people—prosperity in exchange for silence—after the 1989 Tiananmen Square massacre crushed China's prodemocracy movement.

In truth, the idea of a grand bargain is so seductive precisely because it offers the promise of a silver bullet and a severed Gordian knot all rolled up into one big happy ending. The question before us now, dear detectives, is whether such a grand bargain might once and for all settle the increasingly sharp differences between China and the United States—and thereby serve as an ultimate, one-stop-shop pathway to peace.

As to what such a grand bargain might look like, George Washington University professor Charles Glaser has put perhaps the most concrete—and controversial—proposal on the table.[1] Because this proposal, summarized in the lead question to this chapter, offers a very specific pathway to what may well be a permanent peace—and because a deeper analysis of the proposal's pros and cons will further illuminate the complex nature of tensions in Asia—it is well worth our strong consideration.

Professor Glaser's "Grand China Bargain" begins with the realist-school assumption that countries like the United States pursue "grand strategies" to advance their national interests. In Glaser's view, America's grand strategy may be characterized by the pursuit of a hierarchy of at least three major goals.

At the very top of this hierarchy is national security. This is, of course, the most important pursuit not just of the United States but of any nation.

Next, and only slightly less important, is that of economic prosperity. To Glaser, these two goals—national security and economic prosperity—are, and very well should be, the major driving forces of US foreign policy today.

As a third, but significantly lower-ranked, pillar of US foreign policy, Glaser also sees the pursuit of a set of ideals associated with the ideology of "American exceptionalism." These goals are defined by the belief that the world will be a better, safer, more prosperous, and more just place if it is organized according to democratic principles in the political arena, free trade and free markets in the economic arena, and free expression and free will at the individual level. Implicit in these ideals is the collateral belief that America has a strong moral obligation to protect weaker nations from tyranny and to help individuals during global humanitarian crises.

It should be immediately clear that Glaser's realist assumptions immediately open the door to a coldly pragmatic America willing to sacrifice its ideology and moral obligations on the altar of achieving its economic and national security goals. In Glaser's world, while we have "an interest in supporting democracies and promoting them, it's not our highest interest." This means that in some cases "on net, we will be better [off] breaking our commitment."[2]

As to where Taiwan and its thriving democracy come into this strategic calculus, Glaser starkly portrays the dispute over the island as the single most important irritant in the US-China relationship. In his words:

It is not only the possibility that down the road we will actually protect Taiwan in a military confrontation. The commitment itself strains the relationship because the Chinese see us as meddling in their affairs. That's not our view, but it is their honest view. So it strains the relationship and it strains the relationship even more when we sell arms to Taiwan.[3]

Now here is Glaser's ultimately key grand-bargain assumption: Because Taiwan is of such paramount importance to China—a "core interest" in China's diplomatic parlance—it should be willing to deal on the issue. Glaser further assumes that the territorial disputes China has with other countries like Japan in the East China Sea and the Philippines and Vietnam in the South China Sea do *not* rise to the level of a core interest that China is willing to go to war for.

Based on these assumptions, it follows that China should also be willing to effectively renounce all its other claims in the East and South China Seas in exchange for the ultimate prize of Taiwan. In addition, China should be willing to recognize a permanent American presence in the region, if for no other reason than the American navy has played a stabilizing role and thereby facilitated economic trade and growth. As for the United States, in Glaser's realist world, it should be equally willing to sacrifice Taiwan on the altar of a lasting peace.

In evaluating the prospects of any such grand bargain ever being struck, Glaser readily admits that it would require big, and likely quite painful, political sacrifices on the parts of both Chinese and US leaders. In China's case, its leaders would have to convince its citizens—including a rabid community of nationalists that the Chinese government has already whipped into a frenzy—that such a deal would not constitute any surrender on China's part or, worse, yet another "humiliation" at the hands of foreigners.

As for the United States, the American president and US Congress would have to renounce what has been often portrayed as a "moral" commitment to Taiwan. By abandoning Taiwan, the United States would also have to confront the likely severe damage any such cold and calculating grand bargain would do to America's other defense-treaty alliances, not just in Asia but also in Europe.

In the end, however, Glaser view is that:

If we get a Grand Bargain, I think that it would be an unhappy one but a very good deal.[4]

The two big questions, of course, surrounding any such "very good deal" are: (1) whether the deal would actually work in practice to keep the peace; and (2) would China and the United States ever really sell their respective nationalist and moral souls to the Grand Bargain devil and sign on the dotted line of any such treaty?

To answer these questions, let's look at what some of our other experts specifically have had to say on the matter—starting with one of the most preeminent Taiwan scholars in the world, Richard Bush of the Brookings Institution. In Bush's decidedly unminced words:

My initial impulse when I hear a suggestion like a Grand Bargain is to pull my hair out because it's just not going to work. First of all, the Taiwan people have a say in the outcome that's being proposed. Second, China has its own reasons why it is pushing out into the East and South China Seas. It wants to have greater strategic depth as a way of building its national defense and to propose a Grand Bargain would be to ask China to act in ways that are contrary to its own conception of its own interests.[5]

Raising the issue of bad faith, Bush further notes:

The Chinese are very good at taking a deal and interpreting it in ways that suit them and in ways that are contrary to what we think the deal means; and so deals like this just end up in more disagreement and argument."[6]

This problem of bad faith is further compounded by the fact that, as Bush tells it, "the United States and China right now" simply "don't trust each other," and "China has serious doubts about our intentions."[7] So even if Washington proposed a grand bargain, to Bush:

Beijing would probably see this as a trick that somehow is designed to fool them, and simply for that reason, they would not be interested.[8]

As for any moral obligation of America to defend Taiwan and its flourishing democracy, former US Assistant Secretary of State Kurt Campbell expresses his own form of outrage:

I do not believe it is in the US strategic interest to even contemplate nineteenth century-like deals like: "We'll give you Taiwan in exchange for some other regional set of circumstances." I mean, who does that?[9]

There is also the very real issue of how America's allies would view any such American abandonment of Taiwan. On this point, Heritage Foundation scholar Dean Cheng is unequivocal:

The idea that the United States would walk away from a commitment that it has maintained for some 40 years is absolutely the sort of thing that would make America's allies, not just in Asia, but around the world, deeply question our willingness to be there. This is the sort of thing that would affect not just America's position in Asia, but America's position in Europe.[10]

Brookings Institution scholar Michael O'Hanlon drills down even deeper into this theme of destabilized American alliances:

Yes, we do have a commitment to Taiwan largely on moral grounds which gets you in an uncomfortable place: Are you really prepared to risk American lives for a moral commitment in this kind of situation? But even if you were prepared to abandon Taiwan, what's the rest of the world and the rest of America's Asian allies going to do? What are they going to deduce? And how many of them are going to build nuclear weapons along the way? And Taiwan itself is going to be tempted to start building a nuclear weapon which China has already said in advance would be a cause for war. So, by trying to avoid danger, you actually increase the danger.[11]

Here, Professor John Mearsheimer is equally clear in explaining how both rising Chinese nationalism and what Beijing may now view as its inevitable march toward supremacy would likewise cut against the grain of any grand bargain. Asserts Mearsheimer:

The Chinese are simply not going to be willing to make the concessions that are necessary to placate the United States and its allies. They are not going to be willing to give up on the Senkaku/Diaoyu Islands. They are not going to be willing to make concessions on the South China Sea.

There are two reasons for this. One is just good old-fashioned nationalism; the Chinese believe that this territory belongs to them, and they're not interested in compromising. But furthermore, the Chinese believe that time is on their side, and they will eventually become so powerful that they can dictate the terms of any settlement.[12]

Perhaps the most philosophical critique is offered up by long-time Pentagon advisor Michael Pillsbury. He describes the idea of having a grand bargain with China to be "a very American approach":

To put it in a common phrase, let's make a deal. Why can't we make a deal? And this approach has been tried with many difficult problems in the past, where unfortunately the outcome has been war. . . . And some of the assessments of the origins of World War I and World War II are very similar to that. There were good willed people, who proposed: "Can't we work together?" And this was misunderstood by the other side in a way that had tragic consequences.[13]

In light of these expert critiques, it is unlikely that Professor Glaser's grand bargain would ever gain traction in the real world of Asian diplomacy, making it the proverbial "nonstarter." Nonetheless, Glaser's proposal does serve a very important purpose in this inquiry. This is because it more brightly illuminates the very clear strategic and ideological differences that exist between China on the one hand and America and its Asian allies on the other hand.

Through such brighter illumination, Glaser's grand bargain reinforces perhaps the most important insight that has emerged thus far in our enquiry. To wit: The rising tensions in the "cauldron" of Asia are not primarily the result of any cultural misunderstandings, any misreading of China's intentions, or any strategic miscalculations on the part of the various would-be combatants. Rather, these tensions are the result of very real and stark differences between China and much of the rest of Asia regarding China's increasingly strident territorial claims and its apparent quest for hegemony in the region. As Georgetown University professor Oriana Mastro has put it in seeking her own version of a pathway to peace:

The sooner that we are honest about the fact that it's not that we [China and America] misunderstand each other's positions but that maybe we just don't like them, I think the sooner we can move past some of these tensions and actually move to some of the areas of cooperation.[14]

The question before us therefore remains: What are the appropriate policy responses to China that will help us best "move past some of these tensions" and ensure the peace? Unfortunately, from our "pathways to peace" chapters thus far, we have only been able to rule out a number of otherwise promising options.

In particular, we have learned that economic engagement, economic interdependence, and nuclear weapons are unlikely either alone or together to keep the peace. We have also determined that a neoisolationist US–military withdrawal may well lead to more, rather than less, conflict and instability while fruitful negotiations with an opaque and truculent China are likely to be very, very difficult.

It follows from these sobering conclusions that if a grand bargain is also infeasible—indeed, perhaps well-nigh impossible—the only option seemingly to consider is that of "peace through strength." It is to this pathway—and the many dangers it may bring as well—that we turn to in the next and final part of our detective story.

Part 6

PATHWAYS TO PEACE THROUGH STRENGTH

Chapter 41

THE LOGIC AND ARCHITECTURE OF PEACE THROUGH STRENGTH

Question: Which of these statements do you agree with?

1. Weakness invites aggression.
2. Strength deters aggression.
3. Any American attempt to enforce a peace in Asia purely through *military* strength will likely result in an escalatory arms race and an increased chance of war.
4. All of the above.

To begin, let us strongly affirm the obvious proposition that weakness does indeed invite aggression. Whether in modern, medieval, or primitive civilizations, the strong have always preyed on the weak; the lions have never lain down with the lambs; and weakness will never deter aggression by a much stronger adversary intent on expanding its territory. Here, and centuries long ago, Thucydides had it exactly right when, in his reflections on the Peloponnesian War, he opined that the question of what is "right" is only a question that can be settled between "equals" while "the strong do what they want and the weak suffer what they must."[1]

The fact that weakness invites aggression does, not, however prove the opposite, that strength will always deter aggression. That is a far too simplistic formulation, which is why we must also entertain a third possible answer to our lead question, namely, that attempts to achieve a peace purely through *military* strength may sometimes have the perversely unintended consequence of increasing the probability of war.

In fact, we have already seen ample evidence in support of this seeming paradox during our analysis of the "security dilemma." Recall that when one nation's attempt to bolster its defense is mistaken for an aggressive attempt to build offensive capabilities by another nation, the unwelcome "security dilemma" result is an escalatory arms race that rapidly increases the probability of war—even as such a race often impoverishes the countries and their taxpayers that have to pay for it.

How, then, do we square the circle drawn in our lead question and thereby find a true pathway to peace based on strength? The answer lies first in developing a far more textured understanding of why any nation's real strength far transcends mere military might.

In fact, the Chinese themselves have a name for such real strength. They call it "comprehensive national power."

The critical insight behind comprehensive national power—*zonghe guoli* in the Chinese language—is that the real strength of any nation is rooted not just in its "hard power" military and nuclear-weapons capabilities. Rather, true national strength is just as critically dependent on a wide range of "soft power" metrics that take into account everything from the strength of a nation's economy, the skill of its labor force, and the stability of its political system, to the depth and breadth of its natural resource base, the quality of its educational system, the state of scientific discovery and corresponding rate of innovation and technological change, and even the nature and strength of the nation's diplomatic and political alliances. As Chinese Vice Premier Deng Xiaoping aptly put it long ago: "In measuring a country's national power, one must look at it comprehensively and from all sides."[2]

What is perhaps most remarkable about China's incredibly precise calculations of comprehensive national power to Pentagon analyst Michael Pillsbury is that military capabilities are rated at only about 10 percent of *overall* power.[3] As Pillsbury notes:

> The Chinese focus on Comprehensive National Power is really quite different from the way the Pentagon thinks about who might win in a conflict from the very beginning. This is true in terms of both what you are going to measure and what kind of metrics you are going to use.[4]

Pillsbury's clear implication is that the Pentagon in microcosm, and the American policy establishment writ large, are simply not thinking globally enough about how to build and maintain an effective defensive shield against a country like China—while the United States plays military-capabilities checkers, the Chinese play comprehensive-national-power chess.

In fact, China's concept of comprehensive national power is deeply rooted in our now oft-repeated Sun Tzu maxim that "to subdue the enemy without fighting is the acme of skill."[5]

Here, Wu Chunqiu, a noted strategist at the People's Liberation Army's Academy of Military Science, provides the critical intellectual link between Sun Tzu's ancient dynastic Middle Kingdom and the expansionist quest that a rapidly militarizing China is on today. To Wu:

> Victory without war does not mean that there is no war at all. The wars one must fight are political wars, economic wars, science and technology wars, diplomatic wars, etc. To sum up in a word, it is a war of comprehensive national power. Although military power is an important factor, in peacetime it usually acts as a backup force and plays the role of invisible might.[6]

In fully embracing the importance of comprehensive national power in helping to ultimately keep the peace, Professor David Lampton of Johns Hopkins University has argued that when America is healthy along the key parameters of comprehensive national power—economics, education, technology, human resources, research and development, and so on—the Chinese will respect the United States. However, if America is declining in in these areas, "the Chinese are going to be more difficult to deal with."[7]

Former NATO Supreme Commander and General Wesley Clark offers his own version of this assessment when he writes in the *New York Times*:

> If we are to retain our global leadership, and be a constructive, counter-vailing force as China rises, America needs a long-term strategic vision of our own: a strong, growing economy built on a foundation of energy independence; a vibrant, effective democracy; assertive, patient diplomacy backed by supportive allies; and a military capable of standing toe-to-toe with China in a crisis.[8]

As for Professor Lampton, he goes on to advise that America "may be at a point in its history where it relatively has to pay more attention to its domestic circumstance."[9] To Lampton: "By creating the long-term basis for renewed American power, America will therefore be more effective" at deterring an aggressive and expansionist China.

In fact, the pivotal role of comprehensive national power in the "peace through strength" equation can only be truly understood by cultivating a much deeper understanding of how each of the various hard- and soft-power metrics of comprehensive national power fit together *synergistically* to create the type of overwhelming force that may be used against overt aggression by countries like China (or North Korea or Russia or Iran) and for a lasting deterrence.

Consider, then, the synergies required to build up a nation's military capabilities. Such synergies begin with the need for a strong economy both to manufacture the actual weapons as well as to generate the tax revenues necessary to finance such military expenditures. However, for a nation to have a strong economy, it necessarily must have a highly skilled work force and also enjoy the ongoing fruits of innovation and technological change.

Of course, to produce a high-quality labor force, one needs a strong education system. At the same time, rapid innovation and technological change can only take place in the presence of an education system geared toward science, math, and engineering; a financial system capable of delivering the capital investment to drive research and development; and a tax system that rewards entrepreneurship and innovation.

Nor will any *domestic* economy be able to prosper in today's global financial system without free and ready access to *foreign* markets. Of course, such access not only requires strong alliances among trading partners; it also demands freedom of navigation along the trading routes of the world—which brings the synergistic process right back to the need for a strong military to keep the seas (and skies) open for trade.

This is not the whole synergy story, however. As the national foundation for any such synergies, there must also be a well-functioning political system. This system must provide not just social stability; it must also produce the kind of wise public choices that will lead to the provision of the infrastructure and "public goods" a nation needs to support its private sector growth—modern roads, bridges, air-traffic control, mass transit, water and sewer works, and so forth.

✱✱✱✱✱

In thinking about how all of these various hard- and soft-power elements synergistically mesh and how they ultimately all contribute to comprehensive national power, it nonetheless remains important to always remember this: While a nation's military strength may be only one element of national power, it will always be *the* most important element when the wolf—or dragon—is at the door.

To frame this truth in the language of mathematics, while all the other elements of comprehensive national power are *necessary* conditions for the achievement of true national strength, it is ultimately military strength that is the *sufficient* condition. In its simplest Clausewitzian terms, a poorly armed nation with a strong economy, a fine education system, a stable political order, a wealth of natural resources, and a superb labor force will nonetheless still be totally defenseless against, and therefore easy prey for, any well-armed adversary with malicious intentions.

In fact, this is a brute force lesson the Romans first taught the Greeks several hundred years before the birth of Christ, and the Barbarians then returned the favor to the Romans several centuries later. It is also a lesson that a succession of Chinese dynasties quite painfully learned trying to fight off Mongol hordes from the steppes of Central Asia.[10]

It follows from all of these observations that the ultimate answer to our "will there be war" question may ultimately only be found by clearly identifying the various steps that America and its allies in Asia must take to build a peace through strength coalition based on the strong deterrent of comprehensive national power. It is to this exploration that we must now turn in the final chapters of our detective story—with these observations from Dan Blumenthal of the American Enterprise Institute and Patrick Cronin of the Center for a New American Security helping to guide the way. Says Blumenthal:

> I believe that the United States has gotten into wars when other countries have questioned our resolve and will; and I think that this case can be made across many US wars. So I believe the best way to avoid war is to have a very strong military, a very strong set of alliances, and have the potential adversary convinced that the United States has enough stake in whatever the two countries are having a dispute about that the United States would actually use force as a last resort.[11]

Adds Cronin:

The perception in the region is the United States simply does not have the capacity to enforce the rules. And that's the world we're living in right now. It is a world where it's not clear who enforces the rules. And when nobody knows who makes the rules, guess what happens: people make up the rules.[12]

Chapter 42

ON THE PRIMACY
OF PEACE THROUGH
ECONOMIC STRENGTH

Question: Which of these statements do you believe to be true?

1. China relies on a diverse set of unfair trade practices such as currency manipulation, illegal export subsidies, intellectual property theft, and protection of its own markets to strengthen its manufacturing base and drive its export-driven growth.
2. China's economic growth and strong manufacturing base have provided it with a wealth of resources to build up and modernize its military forces.
3. China has used its superior economic strength to coerce Asian neighbors such as Japan, the Philippines, Taiwan, and Vietnam on issues ranging from trade to territorial disputes.
4. Since China joined the World Trade Organization in 2001 and gained unfettered access to American markets, the United States has lost over seventy thousand manufacturing facilities and seen its economic growth rate cut by more than half.
5. Slow economic growth and a weakening of its manufacturing base is making it increasingly difficult for the United States to maintain a military force large and modern enough to ensure its national security and fulfill its treaty obligations, particularly in Asia.
6. All of the above.

I f all the above statements are indeed true—and a strong factual case has already been made in this inquiry for each—then reducing the dependence of America and its allies on "Made in China" products would seem to be an obvious policy step to improve both US national security as well as the prospects for peace in Asia. After all, such a step to "rebalance" the China trade relationship would slow China's economy and thereby its rapid military buildup. Such trade rebalancing would also provide America and its allies with both the strong growth and manufacturing base these countries need to build their own comprehensive national power. On this point, University of Chicago professor John Mearsheimer notes:

> What really makes China so scary today is the fact that it has so many people, and it's also becoming an incredibly wealthy country so that our great fear is that China will turn into a giant Hong Kong. And if China has a per capita GNP that's anywhere near Hong Kong's GNP, it will be one formidable military power. So a much more attractive strategy would be to do whatever we can to slow down China's economic growth— because if it doesn't grow economically, it can't turn that wealth into military might and become a potential hegemon in Asia.[1]

What seems like an easy and obvious step to take in the interests of fostering peace through economic strength may, however, be far harder to do because of a variety of economic, political, and ideological obstacles.

Economically, if America were to reduce its Chinese import dependence through, say, the imposition of countervailing tariffs to offset China's unfair trade practices, there would surely be an uptick in the inflation rate. This would necessarily occur as American consumers replaced cheaper "Made in China" goods with more expensive products made in America or imported from other countries.

Beyond this inflationary effect, there is also this difficult political matter in equity: Reducing the flow of cheap, illegally subsidized "Made in China" products into American markets would hit the poorest segments of American society disproportionately hard—a prospect that at least the American Left would likely heavily criticize.

As for the role of ideology in dampening any "Not Made in China" movement, many Americans with an abiding faith in the benefits of free trade—particularly on the American Right—remain reluctant to support any policies that might be viewed as "protectionist." However, in defense of a policy of "defensive tariffs" to fight Chinese mercantilism, US-China Commission member and Republican Dan Slane has opined:

> We have a weak economy because we have allowed ourselves to get into a trade deficit with China . . . and until we can get control of our trade deficit and start producing our own products, we're going to have enormous economic problems in this country.[2]

Whether these economic, political, and ideological obstacles might ultimately be overcome in a concerted policy effort to rebalance the China trade is an open question. However, what should be clear and unequivocal is this cold Clausewitzian "war by algebra" epiphany: Whenever we buy products made in China—and by "we" I mean citizens not just in America but also in other countries now grappling with a rising China like India, Japan, the Philippines, Singapore, South Korea, and Taiwan—we as consumers are helping to finance a Chinese military buildup that may well mean to do us and our countries harm.

If we as individuals cannot collectively translate that "war by algebra" epiphany into concrete steps both at the ballot box and at the cash register to reduce our economic dependence on an authoritarian and increasingly militaristic China, then we will have only ourselves to blame when the bullets and missiles begin to fly—or when China simply takes what it wants because it can.

On this critical point, former US-China Commission member Pat Mulloy explains why an American reliance merely on a *military* pivot to Asia may be a huge misstep:

> Now the president says we have to pivot toward Asia. Why? Because we have a rising China. Well, why is China rising so rapidly? It's because we're running massive imbalances of trade and rapidly transferring our investment and technology. So as their capabilities are strengthening, ours are weakening. So then we say okay, let's [militarily] pivot to Asia to reassure our allies because of this rising China. Well, wouldn't it make more sense to simply rebalance our trading relationship with China and not continue to have American consumers feed China's rise? That would be the truly smart way to pivot toward Asia.[3]

As to how America may actually execute that kind of more nuanced and economically oriented pivot, Mulloy's colleague on the US-China Commission Michael Wessel makes this argument on behalf of establishing a "China Policy Czar" within the upper echelons of the American government:

> First of all, we have to get serious. There is really no one in charge in the US government looking at US-China relations. To date, everything has been viewed simply as an opportunity to sell to a billion consumers under the assumption that China has similar interests to us in terms of being a good stakeholder in the world economy. However, I think we've seen over the last 10 or 20 years that China has very different interests and wants to promote those interests to the exclusion of others. That's their right, but the question is whether we are going to challenge that. So first of all, we need to put somebody in charge who looks at both the economic and national security implications of the US-China relationship and recognizes that they are inextricably intertwined. For example, if you allow China to manipulate its currency, they're going to build up budget reserves and then they can use that money to go out and buy whatever weapon systems they need to defeat us. And we've seen that year after year after year.[4]

✱✱✱✱✱

While rebalancing the trade relationship with China is certainly one of the most direct routes to both strengthening the economies of the United States and its allies in Asia while simultaneously weakening the ability of China to finance its war machine, such a trade rebalancing is certainly not the only "peace through economic strength" strategy America might pursue.

A second policy lever to pull—one, however, that is as politically contentious as that of trade rebalancing—is that of tax reform. Such reform is particularly critical for the United States, which presently has the highest corporate tax rate in the world. The practical effect of this high corporate tax rate is to literally push American manufacturers and American jobs offshore. There is a very simple reason for this: Any company that takes its factories and jobs off American shores gets an immediate tax cut through the ability to evade the higher American corporate tax.

Still a third possible policy initiative would be to dramatically increase the protection of the kinds of military and private-sector intellectual property now being plundered with regularity by China—up to, and including, a "zero tolerance" policy on the theft of both economic and military secrets by China.

Of course, one of the most direct routes to retaining American intellectual property would be for the US government to crack down on China's illegal policy of forcing American companies operating in China to turn over their technology. This forced technology transfer is a crystal-clear violation of the World Trade Organization rules, but even the biggest of the American corporations that have been victims of such technology blackmail have been reluctant to protest for fear of being excluded from the Chinese market. However, as Commissioner Slane notes on this key contributor to comprehensive national power:

> You cannot have a superior military force without superior technology. So when you have [American] companies like Boeing and General Electric transferring technology to the Chinese, you put yourself at an enormous disadvantage because what makes us such a powerful global power is our technology and our innovation and our weapon systems that are far superior to any other country in the world.[5]

Finally, there is the prickly matter of rebuilding—or more likely restructuring—an education system that, at least in America, is currently in disarray all the way from K through 12 to the student-debt-ridden halls of higher education. Clearly, for any nation to succeed it must train its children well for the jobs of the future—without burdening them with a crushing debt, and while education reform is clearly well beyond the scope of this detective story, this is a status quo likewise in urgent need of urgent care.

✷✷✷✷✷

In thinking most broadly about all of these possible pathways to economic strength—and therefore enhanced comprehensive national power and improved deterrence—the common thread that runs through them all is the need for political consensus on any requisite changes. This is a topic we will return to in our final chapter. In the meantime, let's move now to the military side of the "peace through strength" equation—but not before allowing former US Assistant Secretary of Defense Kurt Campbell and Dean Cheng of the Heritage Foundation to have this chapter's eerily similar last words. Says Campbell:

> People often ask me what's the most important thing that the United States can do to sustain its leadership on the global stage; and people think sometimes that [thing] is about how to do this sort of military move or how to engage in this region. I will tell you the most important thing is to get our own domestic house in order.[6]

Echoes Dean Cheng:

> Well, the first and foremost thing we need to be doing is getting our own economic house in order. All else follows from that. If we do not get our own economic house in order, if we don't reduce our debt, we will not have the ability to match China. And more than anything else, this is within our power. This is something that the American people and the American government can do, and Beijing can do nothing about it.[7]

Chapter 43

TOWARD A NEW STRATEGY FOR PEACE THROUGH MILITARY STRENGTH

Question: At present, which country has the superior military strategy in Asia?

1. China
2. The United States

True peace through military strength in Asia can only come about if the United States and its allies are able to demonstrate a collective level of capabilities that, on the one hand, are not directly threatening to China, yet on the other hand are unassailable by any imaginable display of Chinese force. That delicate balance must be the gold standard of any quest for peace through military strength—for it is only under those circumstances that Chinese expansionism can be deterred without any actual resort to violence on either side.

As for finding and maintaining any such balance, this is problematic on at least two grounds. First, and most obviously, even as China's military capabilities are rapidly increasing, the capabilities of America and its allies are in relative decline. Second, and more subtly, the American alliance appears as yet to have no clear response to what is emerging as a likely superior Chinese military strategy.

To be crystal clear here, China's strategy is not really a strategy at all. Rather, it is a *counter*strategy aimed at operationalizing yet another famous Sun Tzu maxim: "What is of supreme importance in war is to attack the enemy's strategy."[1]

It is precisely China's counterstrategy—or counterintervention strategy in the Chinese parlance—that is now taking dead aim at the three main strategic pillars of American military dominance in Asia. These pillars include: (1) overwhelming force projected by US aircraft-carrier strike groups to achieve air and sea dominance, (2) a small number of large American forward bases along the First and Second Island Chains that serve as both launchpads for attack and as nodes for logistical support, and (3) a space-based system that provides battlefield awareness to American forces through cutting edge "C4ISR," that is, command, control, communications, computers, intelligence, surveillance, and reconnaissance.

China's plan to destroy these three American strategic pillars, in turn, rests on three strategic pillars of China's own: (1) a proliferation of relatively inexpensive asymmetric weapons capable of destroying or neutralizing America's very expensive aircraft-carrier strike groups along with its fixed "soft target" forward bases; (2) China's mass production of its own aircraft-carrier strike groups aimed at meeting American military mass with superior Chinese mass over the longer run; and (3) space dominance to eliminate America's C4ISR advantage as achieved both through the destruction of America's satellite system and the construction of China's own competing satellite network.

At present, China is methodically executing its counterstrategy with great precision while the United States and its allies have been very slow to respond to the rapidly changing battlefield. If events continue to move in this same direction, China's superior strategy is likely to tip the military balance in Asia within several decades—and perhaps far sooner. This is, of course, a very dangerous trend because if China gains the upper hand in Asia—or even prematurely believes at some point that it *has* gained the upper hand—this will constitute an open invitation to further aggression in the region. The question, of course, is: What should the Pentagon do about a chess game that looks like it is moving inexorably to checkmate if America keeps making the same old predictable moves?

To answer that critical question—and thereby find a true pathway to peace through military strength—we must now, dear detectives, systematically work our way through each of the emerging vulnerabilities in the American strategy now being targeted by China. As we do this, we will necessarily have to reprise many of the points that have been made in earlier chapters. However, the whole point of making those points earlier was to get to this point in our investigation where we can hopefully figure a peaceful way out of our "will there be war" box.

✵✵✵✵✵

Let's begin, then, with perhaps the easiest and relatively cheapest of the vulnerabilities to address—that of the soft, fixed sitting-duck targets that America now calls its forward bases. As we have previously discussed, any solution here first and foremost requires "hardening" these bases. As has been noted, this can done through techniques such as moving fuel supplies and weapons caches deep underground; siloing aircraft; and fortifying runways, buildings, barracks, and piers with tons upon tons of concrete and steel.

At the same time, solving America's sitting-duck, fixed-base problem will also require dispersing some of the heaviest concentrations of US military might now on bases such as Guam and Okinawa's Kadena to much smaller and far more numerous locations throughout Asia. The goal here of what is effectively a hedging and diversification strategy is to vastly complicate China's task of targeting American bases.

As for the increasing exposure of America's space-based assets to China's broad range of antisatellite weapons, America's "eyes and ears in space" must likewise be "hardened" against attack in the same spirit as America's forward bases. Likewise in the spirit of forward-base diversification, the United States should also greatly proliferate—and shrink the size of—its available space-communications nodes. This kind of space-asset diversification can be done relatively easily and cheaply through a variety of new technologies such as miniaturized satellites known as "CubeSats", high-altitude "aerostat" balloons, and the increasingly ubiquitous drones.

Ultimately, however, the best way to protect and preserve the American military's ability to communicate in a conflict may be to build redundant systems not dependent on space at all. As a practical matter, this means having the capability to go "old school" using well-established technologies like surface-search radar and high-frequency radio should a conflict erupt.

As a final comment on the space-based-asset front—and this is as regrettable as it is unavoidable from an arms-race perspective—the United States will almost certainly have to further develop its own antisatellite capabilities aimed at knocking out China's competing satellite networks. The interesting strategic point here is that as much as the US military is dependent on space for its communications, the Chinese over time may become even more so.

In fact, China's increasing vulnerability in this area may be traced to the very centralized nature of its own command and control systems. Such centralization is a by-product of China's own authoritarian leadership and a collateral great fear of letting Chinese military commanders have anywhere near the same degree of decentralized autonomy that American military officers currently and routinely have on the high seas and in the skies. What such micromanagement from Beijing means as a practical matter is that if the United States can find and destroy the main nodes of space communications, it may be able to more quickly compromise or paralyze Chinese command centers in the event of a conflict.

✶✶✶✶✶

While America's forward-base and space-based vulnerabilities appear to be both manageable and relatively inexpensive to solve, the same cannot be said of the rapidly increasing exposure of America's aircraft-carrier strike groups to Chinese attack. This vulnerability obviously stems from the growing Chinese mass of both asymmetric- and traditional-weapons capabilities as well as more subtly from the rapidly improving technological quality of the overall Chinese arsenal.

To reprise, on the quality of weapons front, China's ability to hit a moving aircraft carrier with an antiship ballistic missile launched from a thousand miles away is an obvious game changer. So, too, in its own Mach 10 way, is a new hypersonic Chinese glide vehicle quite capable of literally blowing American ships out of the water with tremendous force.

As for America's "quantity having a quality of its own" problem that we have already put several exclamation points to, it is well worth repeating that China's factory floor is already producing its latest asymmetric weapons in record numbers. With such growing mass, China may eventually be able to use a combination of salvoing and swarming missile tactics to overwhelm American defense systems—remember, it only takes one warhead out of a thousand launched to achieve a mission kill.

It is also well worth repeating here that it is not just asymmetric weapons that China is churning out. Its "factory floor to the world" is also prodigiously producing large quantities of all of the aircraft and ships necessary for China to field its own fleets of aircraft-carrier strike groups with global reach.

Equally alarming, having stolen the technology, China can now also produce its own fifth-generation fighters in far greater numbers than America's budget-deficit-plagued F-35 and F-22. In particularly lamenting the decision of the US Congress to halt F-22 production, American Enterprise Institute scholar Michael Auslin has issued this "quantity has its own quality" warning:

> The F-22 flies high, it flies very fast, and it has a low radar cross-section so it's hard to pick up. But one day, their air defenses will get better. They'll have radar that looks higher, that can track faster objects, and is more sensitive; and, on that day, they may not be able to see the F-22 right away, but they'll see it sooner than they can see it today. That affects everything, which is one reason you still need numbers. If you only have two of these great planes, no one is particularly scared of you. If you can darken the skies of an adversary, like we did in World War II with an armada in the air, that's credible. Unfortunately, that's not what we're doing; and it's not what we're going to do.[2]

Of course, the prospect of dogfights in the sky between China and a potentially overwhelmed American force calls into further question the ability of the United States to maintain air dominance over the skies of the Pacific. Recall here the admonition of Dean Cheng of the Heritage Foundation that: "You may not win with air superiority, but you will certainly lose without it."[3]

✱✱✱✱✱

Given this grim battlefield assessment, we must return to the question of: What should America do to address its growing vulnerability? To experts like Toshi Yoshihara of the US Naval War College, the answer lies in turning the asymmetric warfare and area denial tables right back on China—thereby attacking China's own strategy just as Sun Tzu advises.[4]

First and foremost, such a "turnabout is fair play" strategy will require a US force restructuring that begins with using attack submarines as the basic building blocks of an impregnable undersea "Great Wall in Reverse."

The idea here, as Yoshihara describes it, is to array such attack submarines along the major choke points of the First and Second Island Chains and thereby better control the access of both Chinese military and merchant ships to the Pacific in time of crisis.[5]

To Yoshihara, this "submarine as the tip of the spear" strategy should provide a powerful deterrent to Chinese aggression because China will know that any such aggression can only end with as much or more damage to its own economy and military forces. As US Naval War College professor James Holmes has noted on the wisdom of such a move:

> Submarine warfare is a key area of advantage for the United States, and it has been for many years. It's where we excelled during the Cold War, and it's where we still excel today. The Chinese, for whatever reason, have not to date put a lot of effort into anti-submarine warfare, and so therefore I think this is an advantage that will prove durable for the United States for quite some time to come.[6]

Note, however, that the submarine alone must not carry the entire weight of America's undersea "Great Wall in Reverse." Instead, both the United States and its allies must also develop more extended asymmetric mine-warfare capabilities.

Armed with such capabilities, the American alliance may then "tit for tat" just as easily mine the waters leading into the harbors of Shanghai or Dalian or Fujian should China threaten the use of mines to isolate Taiwan or the Senkaku Islands or any number of maritime features in the South China Sea.

As these mine and submarine capabilities are deployed, the US alliance must also significantly up its game in the areas of antisubmarine warfare, which it has historically been good at, and antimine warfare, which it now by and large ignores. Here again, the overall result should be improved deterrence and maintenance of the status quo—the American version of "winning without fighting."

✭✭✭✭✭

Beyond these various measures to reduce America's strategic vulnerabilities in Asia, there are several additional steps that must be taken along this pathway to peace through military strength. First, it is absolutely critical that the United States get its moribund space program back off the ground. Absent such action, America will cede the strategic high ground to China simply by default; and once that high ground is lost, it is unlikely it will ever be regained.

Second, it is equally critical that America produce in substantially larger numbers both the F-35 fifth-generation fighter and the new Long-Range Strike Bomber now under development by the Air Force. Both of these programs will be very expensive—yet both are critical to the peace-through-strength and improved-deterrence calculus in their own unique ways.

Regarding the F-35, its technological prowess is essential to maintaining air dominance in the Pacific theater, and these relatively short-ranged fighter jets need to be deployed and dispersed tactically throughout the region. Here, numbers do indeed count, particularly given the aforementioned ability of China to swarm its own versions of fifth-generation fighters.

As for the Long-Range Strike Bomber, advocates like the American Enterprise Institute's Michael Auslin argue that it must be built to cope with the increasingly difficult challenges posed by the kind of modern integrated and automated air-defense systems now being deployed by potential adversaries such as China, Russia, and Iran. This bomber not only constitutes an important insurance policy in the Asian theater against the possibility that China might neutralize or destroy America's aircraft-carrier strike groups and forward bases in time of war; it also offers a far safer alternative to relying on unmanned intercontinental ballistic missiles. As Auslin explains:

> Right now, America's only choice is to send in bombers that can't survive in Chinese airspace. So what do we do? Start launching missiles off submarines or from silos in the Midwest? Well, the Chinese aren't going to wait to see what's on the ends of those missiles. They're going to launch their own. So as crazy as it sounds, as retrograde Cold War era as it sounds, a bomber like the Long-Range Strike Bomber that can penetrate deep into Chinese airspace or Russian airspace is actually a very stabilizing element. You can send them up in the air; you can recall them. They're very visible. In contrast, once you launch a missile, that's it. You're done.[7]

Most broadly, Dr. Patrick Cronin of the Center for a New American Security argues that:

We need a balanced force for the 21st century between sea power and air power and fairly traditionally assets in large enough numbers. So I need my carriers. I need my aircraft. But I also need submarines. I need stealth. I need to be able to patrol the sea lines. At the same time, I need to keep investing in cyber and space technologies, and unmanned aerial vehicles, and long range unmanned systems because those technologies could be game changers as they say. So we need a balance of innovative technology and pretty traditional technology.[8]

In thinking about the considerable expense of all these weapons systems, it may be useful to remember this pearl of deterrence wisdom from Auslin: "The reason we build these weapons is not to use them."[9]

As Auslin notes on this point:

It's amazing to think that our youngest B-52 bomber is fifty years old and that we've had close to three generations of pilots flying the same planes—grandfathers, fathers and sons. They are wonderful airplanes, but they can't survive today against today's automated modern missile defense systems. Plus, we only have twenty B-2 Stealth Bombers remaining in service, and they're actually getting old now as well. So we need a new bomber, and we need the F-35 in far greater numbers to be able to clear the ground and the skies if need be, and we need to do this as much for military reasons as for political reasons; and it'll actually bring more stability to Asia, not less.[10]

Finally, beyond all these concrete steps, there is an important policy principle that Georgetown professor Phillip Karber believes is essential to building a deterrent capability based on strength. To Karber:

What we need is a policy, vis-à-vis China and I think with other countries, frankly, of reciprocal response. You go into arms control and you reduce your forces, then we reduce our forces. You start doing provocative things like adding more and more missiles and threatening our bases and our allies, we will respond. And we need to get that principle out. Up until now we've basically given the Chinese a free ride.[11]

Chapter 44

PIVOT SOFTLY AND CARRY A FIRM ALLIANCE STICK

Question: Which of these statements do you agree with?

1. America needs its alliance partners in Asia to defend its own economic and national-security interests.
2. America's alliance partners in Asia need the United States security umbrella to defend against Chinese expansionism.
3. A breakdown of the American alliance in Asia would lead to more instability in the region.
4. All of the above.

These are the best of times for American efforts to build its alliances in Asia. They are the worst of times as well.

These are the best of times because China's expansionist activities, particularly since 2008, have rudely awakened China's Asian neighbors to the need to build a strong balancing coalition against a rising China. Since this awakening, existing American allies like Japan and the Philippines have been seeking stronger ties with the United States. Other nations ranging from India and Indonesia to Malaysia, Singapore, and Vietnam have likewise sought to align (or realign) themselves more closely with the American security umbrella.

Such favorable political developments for US diplomacy notwithstanding, these may well also be the worst of times for building an effective alliance. The core problem here is one of false promises, neglected relationships, limited engagement, and often intemperate or empty rhetoric. It is a problem that may be laid squarely at the doorsteps of a US Congress, Pentagon, and White House that have all been mightily distracted by events elsewhere on the globe.

The poster child for these worst of times has been America's so-called "pivot" to Asia. In 2011, in belatedly recognizing the economic and national security importance of the region, President Barack Obama, at the urging of then Secretary of State Hillary Clinton, announced with great fanfare that the United States would make the Asia-Pacific the primary focus of national-security policy.[1] As part of this pivot, the Pentagon announced it would increase the percentage of its total naval fleet dedicated to the Pacific to some 60 percent.[2]

Such announcements have, however, turned out to be false promises and empty rhetoric because the United States has failed in spectacular fashion to "walk the pivot talk." The problem may be traced to some simple pivot math.

This math starts with the observation that the US naval fleet has been steadily shrinking from its high of more than five hundred ships during the Reagan years of the 1980s down to the less than three hundred today. Moreover, because of continued and massive defense-budget cuts, the fleet now seems destined to fall into the two-hundred-ship range.[3]

What this steadily shrinking fleet means to experts like Professor Toshi Yoshihara of the US Naval War College is this: By the year 2020, the United States will have the "same amount of combat power" as when the pivot began in 2011. This is because while the *relative* distribution of ships may indeed shift to the Pacific, the *absolute* numbers are declining. In math terms, 60 percent of a smaller fleet will lead the US pivot exactly back to the grossly inadequate place in Asia where it started.[4]

As to how such a smaller fleet may radically affect the American risk calculus in Asia—with disastrous results—Yoshihara provides this perspective:

> The basic argument for dramatically shrinking the US fleet is that our weapon systems are far more capable than systems even 10 or 15 years ago and so our increased quality will make up for any decline in quantity. However, I go back to the dictum that quantity has a quality all its own; and a sunk ship is indeed a sunk ship. So if we have fewer assets that we will be able to use in theater, we will be less and less willing to risk a smaller fleet that, per unit, is more valuable to us. And what that means is we're going to play right into China's strategic calculus which is to raise our perceptions of our cost and risks in intervening in issues that China

cares more about. This makes it even more likely that we might hem and haw and decide not to act at all over some contingency involving China including, say, a war over Taiwan.[5]

To this sobering conclusion, Yoshihara's coauthor and colleague at the Naval War College, James Holmes, has added this further pivot twist: Many of the ships that the Pentagon will be counting in the pivot-to-Asia column in the future will be small shore-hugging ships that are not "high end combat assets."[6] To Holmes:

> As diplomatic signals go and as deterrent signals go, this makes the pivot a pretty bush-league thing.[7]

What we appear to have here, then, is the exact opposite of one of the most famous phrases ever uttered by an American president: "Walk softly and carry a big stick." Indeed, instead of following Teddy Roosevelt's deterrence dictum, the United States is pivoting loudly—and merely angering Beijing—while waving the smallest of pivot sticks.

Here, Senior Fellow Seth Cropsey of the Hudson Institute drills down further on this little-stick problem when he observes that:

> The United States has already cut its defense budget by half a trillion dollars and is aiming for another half a trillion.[8]

To Cropsey:

> That does not send a signal to those in Asia who look to us for security and friendship and support. That doesn't send a signal to them that we're serious.[9]

And at least in Cropsey's worldview:

> Weakness is always an invitation to aggression.[10]

As for the broader problem that falling defense expenditures create for the ultimate goal of deterrence, Heritage Foundation Research Fellow Dean Cheng has succinctly put it in this peace-through-strength way:

A United States that is weak is a United States that cannot stand by its alliance commitments is a United States whose credibility is open to question. Conversely, a United States that is strong, that is firm in its alliance commitments is much more likely to deter conflict.[11]

Even noted China moderates like Professor David Lampton of Johns Hopkins University agree with the important stabilizing and balancing functions of America's alliances in Asia. In his words:

If the United State precipitously weakened or disassociated itself from its Asian alliances, this would be very destabilizing. It would either force those countries to acquire their own forms of deterrence, which quite conceivably in some cases could mean nuclear weapons. Or it might lead these nations to conclude they need to go along with China on issues, economic and otherwise, that would be harmful to American interests. So, precipitous, disassociation from our alliances, I think would be catastrophic.[12]

Given the importance of America's alliances in Asia, the real question is how to best manage these relationships. American Enterprise Institute resident scholar Michael Auslin has provided arguably one of the most thoughtful and nuanced analyses of the present "worst of times" situation and how to make it right. To Auslin:

The issue is not whether America has enough men and women and planes and ships in the Pacific—it has had 300,000 troops forward deployed for close to half a century. The real question is: "What are we there for?" And the ultimate fear of our allies is that even with these 300,000 troops, America might not have the political will to uphold the very order that it helped create.[13]

As to why America's allies in Asia are increasingly fearful of an American abandonment, to Auslin, the problem goes far beyond any failed pivot and instead cuts to the very heart of the "what are we there for" matter. In his view:

It's not that our allies don't think we would come to their aid *in extremis*, in the case of war. It's that they understand that most of their lives are dealing not with war but of all those in between actions.[14]

Auslin paints these "in between actions" metaphorically as that "whole huge waterspace between just plain everyday diplomatic life that happens in the region on one end and all-out war on the other." In Auslin's view, it is within this huge waterspace that America's allies have concerns over all sorts of issues, from illegal fishing and pollution to oil drilling and territorial disputes.[15]

The problem to Auslin, however, is that America "doesn't seem to have a clear strategy." It thinks "just being in Asia with its massive might is simply enough." In sharp contrast, America's allies are saying: "You have to not only be here; you have to be involved."[16]

As to what such involvement might look like, Auslin cites the case of the Philippines—a frequent target of Chinese aggression in the South China Sea. While Auslin firmly believes it is not the job of America to protect Philippine territory, the United States can nonetheless come to the aid of the Philippines with far greater intelligence sharing and far more training, and by providing the Philippines with the kinds of weapons it needs to defend itself. Unfortunately, in Auslin's view, the United States has done none of that.

Ultimately, what Auslin worries about most with America's lack of a real fine-grained involvement in the waterspaces of Asia is the steady erosion of American influence and what it might portend. As Auslin puts it:

> When our political will prevents us from helping our Japanese friends in, say, the Senkaku Islands dispute or when in a much broader sense, it becomes increasingly clear to our allies that the America's "pivot" or "re-balance" to Asia is just rhetoric, the result is that US credibility gets undermined. And once America's credibility gets undermined, the next step is for its influence to drop.[17]

Of course, once America's influence drops, this opens the door to its allies going their own way—either bandwagoning with China to the detriment of the United States or acquiring their own nuclear arsenals to fend off an aggressive China. Either way, the result to Auslin is a "signal policy failure" with devastating consequences.[18]

✳✳✳✳✳

The bottom line from this surveying of expert opinion is clear: If there is to be a continuation of peace and prosperity in Asia, there must be a strong balancing alliance to offset the growing power of a rising China, and such a strong alliance can only exist if the United States engages with a much higher level of involvement in the region. Former ambassador to China Stapleton Roy has most broadly framed the strategic challenge:

> It is a fundamental interest of the United States to preserve the credibility of its alliances. [However,] China's military modernization program has the potential to erode US naval and air superiority and therefore to raise questions about the reliability of the United States as an alliance partner.[19]

To this warning Ambassador Roy adds:

> The United States cannot sit idly by if the Chinese create capabilities that erode the credibility of our alliances because of the allies' belief that the United States military can no longer operate in areas where it needs.[20]

The rub here, of course, is that the US military will not be able to "operate in areas" to protect its allies unless those allies welcome the United States with open arms and forward bases. This is ultimately why Potemkin-village pivots,[21] empty rhetoric, limited engagement, and distractions in other parts of the globe are so corrosive to peace in Asia. As Dean Cheng of the Heritage Foundation ultimately advises:

> We need to have a policy that stands by our allies so I would stop making commitments that we then walk away from. I think it was Lincoln who said: "Better to keep your mouth shut and have people think you're a fool than to open it and remove all doubt." So if we're going to make a commitment, we need to stand by it. And if we're not prepared to fulfill that [commitment], then keep our mouths shut.[22]

Chapter 45

DEFEATING THE
ENEMY THAT IS US

Question: Based on our investigation in this book, what is your final assessment of the claim that a rapidly militarizing China may represent a growing threat to peace and prosperity in Asia?

1. **It is a paranoid delusion designed by right-wing extremists to whip up support for massive defense spending.**
2. **It is a legitimate concern based on any rational assessment of China's possible revisionist intentions, rapidly growing military capabilities, and increasingly aggressive actions.**

The oft-referenced axiom "united we stand, divided we fall" is as true and relevant today as it was when it first appeared in the New Testament as "every city or house divided against itself shall not stand." The abiding fact here is that building peace in Asia through economic and military strength and keeping the peace by maintaining the requisite alliances can only take place within the context of a political consensus that a significant China security challenge may exist to begin with.[1]

The political hurdle, of course, is that actually building any such consensus may be far easier said than done. At the root of this "divided we fall" problem—nowhere more acute than in the United States—is the nature of democracy itself and the polyglot of competing interests that it breeds.

Just consider, for example, how the lucrative China trade has split American manufacturers into two distinct warring camps. On the one hand, there is a myriad of smaller domestic producers being mercilessly squeezed by illegal Chinese export subsidies; they have been crying out for an end to Chinese currency manipulation, the imposition of countervailing duties, and other appropriate remedies. On the other hand, there is a relatively small handful of large multinational corporations based in America—companies like Apple, Boeing, Caterpillar, General Motors, and IBM. These companies greatly benefit from China's illegal subsidies, sweatshop labor, tax loopholes, and lack of environmental controls when they offshore their production to China and then export their products back into American markets.[2]

So just what has been the political response to emerge from this particular clash of manufacturing interests? Simply that powerful lobbying groups like the National Association of Manufacturers and Business Roundtable, which are controlled by America's large multinationals, wind up *not* opposing Chinese mercantilism. These "see no China threat" lobbyists openly subvert any efforts at a crackdown by the White House or Congress.

Witness, too, this "divided we fall" spectacle at the individual industry level: When solar-panel manufacturers in America sought countervailing duties against illegally subsidized Chinese solar panels dumped into US markets, it wasn't China lobbying the hardest against such duties. Rather, it was red-blooded American solar-panel installers who feared losing business if the price of panels rose.[3]

Even in an American state like Ohio—arguably ground zero in China's mercantilist assault on a US manufacturing base critical to maintaining military strength—the electorate in this well-known presidential election "swing state" remains split. On one side of this particular Midwest house divided, the blue-collar factory workers of cities like Akron and Cleveland and Dayton and Youngstown—many of them now on the unemployment line—are all for tough government action against illegal Chinese subsidies. However, out in agricultural areas like Darke, Madison, and Wood Counties where farmers are growing bumper crops of corn and soybeans for lucrative export to China,[4] there is open opposition to any rebalancing of trade.

In fact, this particular swing-state struggle offers a perfect microcosm of the broader political problem that free and open democracies face in grappling with Chinese state capitalism. Just consider the bill offered up by Democratic Congressman Tim Ryan that would have cracked down on Chinese currency manipulation—Ryan represents the manufacturing cities of Youngstown and Akron. With no small irony, Ryan's bill was almost singlehandedly defeated by fellow Ohioan and Republican Majority Leader John Boehner.[5]

For Boehner, his political victory was a classic "two-fer": He greatly pleased the farmers from his mostly agricultural district—one of the largest farm-producing areas in the Buckeye state[6]—*and* Boehner got to reap more campaign contributions for himself and his party from the big multinationals offshoring to China.

Similar such divisions exist within groups ranging from organized labor and environmental groups to human rights activists. For example, because of quite-legitimate concerns about losing even more jobs offshore, trade unions strongly oppose any type of free-trade pacts with defense allies like Japan and South Korea. However, if properly structured, such free-trade pacts would help boost the economic growth of both the United States and its alliance partners—and thereby contribute to the comprehensive national power of the alliance and its efforts to build peace through both economic and military strength.

As for those pesky environmental and human rights activists in America, they tend to view the Pentagon through a proverbial dark lens and strongly oppose any increase in defense expenditures. The irony, of course, is that these activists wind up helping an authoritarian regime that may not only pose a rising national-security danger but, without question, is also one of the worst polluters and human-rights abusers on the planet.

Here's how Pentagon analyst Michael Pillsbury ultimately sums up this particular house-divided conundrum—while painting a clear picture of American interest groups playing checkers in a chess world:

> These eight or ten [critical interest] groups in America, and their representatives in Congress will not cooperate. In fact, they hate each other and would rather oppose each other on broad philosophical grounds. Tax cuts are good, or tax cuts are bad. Corporations are bad, or the labor unions are bad. They'd rather have this kind of bickering among themselves than focus on China as a challenge. And the Chinese view of this is "we've got to be sure we don't become a big subject in Washington. We've got to have a low profile, and not drive these groups together."[7]

✶✶✶✶✶

Unfortunately for the cause of peace through strength, the "divided we fall" syndrome facing democracies like the United States is not just a matter of a panoply of interest groups being far more eager to fight one another than to unite against a common threat. There is also the stark asymmetry between the far-ranging ability of an authoritarian China to influence the political process in open democracies versus the far more constrained ability of those competing democracies to similarly influence the closed and extremely opaque Chinese political process.

One of the most outspoken critics of such Chinese co-optation of the American political process has been Michael Wessel of the US-China Commission. As Commissioner Wessel frames this cooptation problem:

> China is advancing its comprehensive national power on every front; and here in Washington, they are looking at trying to advance political power. Chinese companies are spreading money around, they're hiring law firms, hiring lobbying firms, hosting parties, doing all the things that a normal special interest group trying to advance power in Washington would do. And they are very effective at it.[8]

As part of this "spreading money" around phenomenon, Wessel also notes with alarm the millions of hard advertising dollars that the Chinese government is pouring into efforts to ensure a softer media line on Chinese authoritarianism. Says Wessel:

> If you look at many of America's national papers, you'll find them stuffed with regular advertising inserts from faux [English-language] Chinese newspapers like the China Daily or China News, and many Americans unwittingly think these inserts represent real news rather than mere propaganda.[9]

✶✶✶✶✶

In pushing its own political narrative on Western soil, it's not just what the Chinese government is saying through its lobbyists and advertising dollars. It is also what the Chinese government has prevented journalists around the world from reporting to the public about China.

The taproot of what has become a pervasive form of self-censorship within the Western press is this particular turn of Beijing's Orwellian screw: To cover the news in China, the Western media must have correspondents with boots on the ground. However, the Chinese government has been using the visa process for decades to limit access to any journalists who take too hard a line against Beijing's policies or who dig too deep into news about such political "third rails" as corruption or pollution or democratic activism or worker unrest.

Just consider this confession of long-time China Hand Dorinda Elliot who was *Newsweek*'s bureau chief in Beijing and now is the global affairs editor at *Condé Nast Traveler*. Said Elliot: "I am ashamed to admit that I personally have worried about the risk of reporting on sensitive topics. . . . What if they don't let me back in?"[10]

Then there is the case of the *Atlantic*'s James Fallows—a well-known long-time dove on the possibility of an emerging China threat. Even Fallows has finally admitted that his reporting has been affected by his "knowledge of how thin-skinned the Chinese government might be."[11]

Visa denials are, however, hardly the only problem Western journalists face. While propagandists from China's government-run media are free to roam the world, Western reporters are routinely blocked from visiting large portions of China, and they are just as routinely subject to harassment, interference, and even physical violence in the field.[12]

To understand just how effective such pressures can be at inducing self-censorship, one need look no further than the stark case of Bloomberg News. After a Bloomberg report on Chinese corruption at high levels within the Communist Party, the Chinese government engineered a boycott of the purchase of Bloomberg's cash cow—its financial-market data terminals, which account for over 80 percent of the company's revenues. The next thing the world bore witness to was the retreat of Bloomberg from truly hard news coverage about China.[13] Said Bloomberg's groveling chairman Peter Grauer in acknowledging the vastness of the Chinese market: "We have to be there."[14]

✸✸✸✸✸

In thinking about this "divided we fall" failure of citizens in countries around the world to be adequately informed about a possibly emerging China threat, it's not just the news portion of the media that is a major culprit. One must also consider the equally pervasive self-censorship that is taking place within another key shaper of public opinion: the entertainment industry.

The obvious problem here is that any television or movie studio that wants to participate in the China market must be careful not to offend the Chinese government with any of its offerings. The tacit rule here is that any one single movie or TV show that portrays China in a negative light can mean a Chinese boycott of *all* the movies or shows in the studio's product line. It follows—at least in the minds of many self-censoring studio executives—that if a studio wants to successfully play in the vast Chinese market, *all* of its product line must cast China in a positive light.

To see that this is a very real concern, one need look no farther than MGM Studio's 2012 remake of the classic film *Red Dawn*. In the original 1984 rendition, the Soviet Union launches a surprise invasion of a small American town, and valiant American teens rise up to defeat the red menace—hence, the film's title.

In the remake, China was supposed to substitute for the now-defunct Soviet Union. However, after negative news stories about the remake began to surface in the Chinese press, MGM went to the film producers and had them digitally "de-Chinese" the invaders. What is perhaps ultimately most interesting about this particular example of self-censorship is that MGM made the change not because of any official complaints from the Chinese government—there were none—but rather, according to a spokesperson, simply to "give the film greater box office appeal in China, which has become one of the most profitable markets for American movies."[15]

✱✱✱✱✱

As a final comment on self-censorship, there is arguably its most surprising manifestation in what is supposed to be the ultimate repository of truth—the ivory tower of academia. Here is the overarching problem as Commissioner Wessel has described it:

> Academia is increasingly a business, and the fact is that universities are always looking for research dollars. Unfortunately, more and more of these research dollars are coming from Chinese entities—effectively allowing China to buy space at American universities. The unfortunate result has been a subtle form of self-censorship as university administra-

tors mute voices critical of China even as they hold their hands out for a fistful of yuan.[16]

This often self-censoring search for research dollars is not, however, the academy's only fall from ethical grace. There is also the disturbing matter of the proliferation of so-called Confucius Institutes not just on college campuses but at levels ranging from elementary to high school.[17]

While such Chinese-funded institutes help what are often cash-strapped American public schools offer Chinese language and culture courses, Chinese curriculum development, and even student-exchange programs free of charge, these Confucius Institutes have also been roundly criticized for feeding Chinese propaganda and doctrine right into the minds of America's youngest, and therefore most impressionable, citizens. Warns Commissioner Wessel:

> Such propaganda has had a dramatic effect on the writings of many pro-fessors and increasingly on the views of many students who are going to be the public policy leaders of tomorrow. It's smart, it's effective, and it's very detrimental to US interests.[18]

✶✶✶✶✶

The theme of this chapter—the last in our detective story—has been this: To peacefully counter the serious security challenges now being posed by a rapidly rising China, there must first be a political consensus on what the appropriate economic, military, and other actions are to take. However, achieving any such political consensus will obviously be difficult in free and open democracies where economic interests are divided by their stakes in the China trade, lobbying groups would rather fight each other than band together in common cause, an authoritarian Chinese government is able to exert significant media control over the China narrative outside Chinese borders, and both Western journalists and Western universities engage in systematic self-censorship.

In fact, this "house divided" assessment in our final chapter goes a long way toward explaining why democracies in the West—and America in particular—have been so slow to reach any real political consensus on the need to address the overarching "will there be war" question. Perhaps needless to say, if this head-in-the-sand trend continues, this is a story that can only end badly for all of us.

Of course, it is not too late to solve this detective story in a far better, and far more peaceful, way. In fact, there is great cause for hope if only the truth can truly bubble up to the surface so that all of us, both within and outside of China, can come to fully understand just how big the stakes are and just how large the scope for catastrophe may be.

This has been the ultimate purpose of our investigation—to explore these truths that need to become self-evident in order for peace to prevail. In this spirit, and to turn the rear-view wisdom of Spanish philosopher George Santayana on its head, let us end, then, with this: "Those who can truly see all of the possible futures have the best chance of choosing the best one and avoiding the worst."[19]

NOTES

Prologue

1. Stew Magnuson, "Anti-Ship Ballistic Missile Sparks Speculation," *National Defense*, April 2014, http://www.nationaldefensemagazine.org/archive/2014/April/Pages/Anti-ShipBallisticMissileSparksSpeculation,Concern.aspx (accessed January 7, 2015).

2. Bill Gertz, "China Conducts Test of New Anti-Satellite Missile," *Free Beacon*, May 14, 2013, http://freebeacon.com/national-security/china-conducts-test-of-new-anti-satellite-missile/ (accessed January 7, 2015).

3. Thomas Harding, "Chinese Nuclear Submarine Base," *Telegraph*, May 2008, http://www.telegraph.co.uk/news/worldnews/asia/china/1917167/Chinese-nuclear-submarine-base.html (accessed January 7, 2015).

4. James R. Holmes, "China's Underground Great Wall," *Diplomat*, August 20, 2011, http://thediplomat.com/2011/08/chinas-underground-great-wall/ (accessed January 7, 2015).

5. For a discussion of the evolution of the Peaceful Rise rhetoric, see, for example, Sujian Guo, ed., *China's Peaceful Rise in the 21st Century: Domestic and International Conditions* (Farnham, Surrey, UK: Ashgate Publishing, 2006).

Chapter 1: The Thucydides Trap Meets the "Security Dilemma"

1. This phrase appears to have been coined by Professor Graham Allison of the Kennedy School of Government, Harvard University. See, for example, Graham Allison, "Thucydides Trap Has Been Sprung in the Pacific," *Financial Times*, August 21, 2012, http://www.ft.com/intl/cms/s/0/5d695b5a-ead3-11e1-984b-00144feab49a.html#axzz3MUDvAjxS (accessed January 7, 2015).

2. For a quick guide to Thucydides, see "Thucydides' Critique of Empire: A Guide to Key Passages," website of Margaret Zulick at Wake Forest University, http://users.wfu.edu/zulick/300/thucyd/thucydidesguide.html (accessed on January 11, 2015).

3. Allison, "Thucydides Trap."

4. Ibid.

5. John J. Mearsheimer, *The Tragedy of Great Power Politics* (New York: W. W. Norton, 2001).

6. Mearsheimer's theory includes two additional assumptions—that all countries are "rational actors" and that "survival" is the most important goal.

7. Peter Navarro, *Crouching Tiger: Will There Be War with China?* www.crouchingtiger.net (documentary film series from DBC Productions, forthcoming 2016).

Chapter 2: China's Century of Humiliation and Its Homeland-Protection Imperative

1. This list also includes Austria-Hungary and Italy.

2. Taiwan was formerly known in Western languages as Formosa until the end of World War II.

3. See generally Diana Preston, The Boxer Rebellion: The Dramatic Story of China's War on Foreigners that Shook the World in the Summer of 1900 (New York: Berkley Books, 2001), and Joanna Waley-Cohen, The Sextants of Beijing: Global Currents in Chinese History (New York: W. W. Norton, 2000). See also Robert Bickers and R. G. Tiederman, eds., The Boxers, China, and the World (Lanham, MD: Rowman & Littlefield, 2007).

Chapter 3: Escaping a "Malacca Dilemma" and Guarding Trade Routes

1. The term "second revolution" was coined by Deng Xiaoping in March 1985. In a speech titled "Reform is China's Second Revolution," he explained as follows: "The reform we are now carrying out is very daring. But if we do not carry it out, it will be hard for us to make progress. Reform is China's second revolution." For a text of the speech, go to https://dengxiaopingworks.wordpress.com/2013/03/18/reform-is-chinas-second -revolution/ (accessed January 7, 2015).

2. China pulled ahead of the United States by at least one measure in 2014 known as "purchasing power parity." It compares countries on the basis of the real cost of living. As reported in the *Financial Times*, "The US is on the brink of losing its status as the world's largest economy, and is likely to slip behind China this year, sooner than widely anticipated, according to the world's leading statistical agencies. The US has been the global leader since overtaking the UK in 1872. Most economists previously thought China would pull ahead in 2019." Chris Giles, "China Poised to Pass US as World's Leading Economic Power This Year," *Financial Times*, April 30, 2014, http:// www.ft.com/intl/cms/s/2/d79ffff8-cfb7-11e3-9b2b-00144feabdc0.html#axzz3QJekHL3k (accessed January 30, 2015).

3. Mokhzani Zubir, "The Strategic Value of the Strait of Malacca" (unpublished manuscript), http://library.utem.edu.my/e-melaka/koleksi%20melaka/geografi/The strategicvalueoftheStraitofMalacca.pdf_(accessed January 7, 2015).

4. For analysis, see Ian Storey, "China's Malacca Dilemma," *China Brief*, Jamestown Foundation, December 31, 1969, http://www.jamestown.org/single/?no _cache=1&tx_ttnews%5Btt_news%5D=3943#.VJivWF4AAA (accessed January 7, 2015).

5. Ibid.

Chapter 4: America's Once and Future Embargo?

1. Captain Thomas R. Fedyszyn, "Renaissance of the Russian Navy," *US Naval Institute*, March 2012, http://www.usni.org/magazines/proceedings/2012-03/renaissance -russian-navy (accessed January 7, 2015).

2. "US Military Bases," MilitaryBases.com, http://militarybases.com/ (accessed January 7, 2015).

3. "Command Mission," COMLOG WESTPAC, http://www.clwp.navy.mil/mission .htm (accessed January 7, 2015).

Chapter 5: A "Revisionist" or "Status Quo" Power?

1. For a history of China's peaceful-rise rhetoric, see Zheng Bijian, "China's 'Peaceful Rise' to Great Power Status," *Foreign Affairs*, September/October 2005, http:// www.foreignaffairs.com/articles/61015/zheng-bijian/chinas-peaceful-rise-to-great-power -status (accessed January 7, 2015).

2. See, for example, C. N. Trueman, "The Air War in Vietnam," History Learning Site, http://www.historylearningsite.co.uk/air_warfare_vietnam.htm (accessed January 7, 2015).

3. Sun-Tzu Ping-Fa, *The Essential Art of War*, trans. Ralph D. Sawyer (New York: Basic Books, 2005), p. 19.

4. Andrew Osborn, "USSR Planned Nuclear Attack on China in 1969," *Telegraph*, May 13, 2010, http://www.telegraph.co.uk/news/worldnews/asia/china/7720461/USSR -planned-nuclear-attack-on-China-in-1969.html (accessed January 7, 2015).

5. For a chilling look at this massacre as it was captured on film, see "China vs. Vietnam: Johnson South Reef Skirmish of 1988," YouTube video, 3:30, posted by "JDUS2020," June 1, 2012, https://www.youtube.com/watch?v=uq30CY9nWE8 (accessed January 7, 2015).

6. Rodel Rodis, "Scarborough Will Not Be Mischief Reef Redux," Inquirer.net, May 2, 2012, http://globalnation.inquirer.net/35543/scarborough-will-not-be-mischief-reef -redux (accessed January 7, 2015).

7. Douglas Frison and Andrew Scobell, "China's Military Threat to Taiwan in the Era of Hu Jintao" (unpublished manuscript, January 31, 2004), http://people.duke .edu/~niou/teaching/FrisonScobell.pdf (accessed January 7, 2015).

Chapter 6: Some Sobering Military-Budget Math

1. There is controversy over just what China's exact number is because of numerous transparency issues. See "List of Countries by Military Expenditures," *Wikipedia*, http:// en.wikipedia.org/wiki/List_of_countries_by_military_expenditures (accessed January 7, 2015).

2. Shannon Tiezzi, "China's Grow Defense Budget: Not as Scary as You Think," *Diplomat*, February 5, 2014, http://thediplomat.com/2014/02/chinas-growing-defense -budget-not-as-scary-as-you-think/ (accessed January 7, 2015).

3. For an analysis of China's production cost advantages see, for example, Peter Navarro, "The Economics of the China Price," *China Perspectives*, Winter 2007, https://webfiles.uci.edu/navarrop/public/article%20hyperlinks/China%20Perspectives.pdf?uniq=-dqa51w (accessed January 7, 2015). Also appears in translation as: "L'avantage Concurrentiel Chinois: Entre Pratiques Déloyales et Avantages Comparatifs, *Perspectives Chinoises*, Winter 2007.

4. Jeremy Page, "China Clones, Sells Russian Fighter Jets," *Wall Street Journal*, December 4, 2010, http://online.wsj.com/news/articles/SB10001424052748704679204575646472655698844 (accessed January 7, 2015).

5. "Military Production during World War II," *Wikipedia*, http://en.wikipedia.org/wiki/Military_production_during_World_War_II (accessed January 7, 2015).

6. Ibid.

7. Peter Navarro, *Crouching Tiger: Will There Be War with China?* www.crouchingtiger.net (documentary film series from DBC Productions, forthcoming 2016).

8. Ibid.

Chapter 7: The Ghost of Admiral Liu Huaqing Haunting Asia

1. This is a distinctly Chinese way of expressing the Western idea that Liu could not "rest in peace" if China didn't build him some aircraft carriers.

2. James Holmes and Toshi Yoshihara, "Liu Huaqing, RIP," *Diplomat*, January 18, 2011, http://thediplomat.com/2011/01/liu-huaqing-rip/ (accessed January 7, 2015).

3. Ibid.

4. For an illustrative analysis of the Chinese literature, see generally Toshi Yoshihara and James R. Holmes, *Red Star over the Pacific* (Annapolis, MD: Naval Institute Press, 2010).

Chapter 8: The Game-Changing Aircraft-Carrier Killer

1. Eric Talmadge, Associated Press, "Chinese Missile Could Shift Pacific Power Balance," *Christian Science Monitor*, August 6, 2010, http://www.csmonitor.com/From-the-news-wires/2010/0806/Chinese-Missile-could-shift-Pacific-power-balance (accessed July 14, 2015).

2. Harry J. Kazianis, "Kazianis: China's Carrier-Killer Missile," *Washington Times*, October 31, 2013, http://www.washingtontimes.com/news/2013/oct/31/kazianis-chinas-carrier-killer-missile/ (accessed July 14, 2015).

3. Constructions costs for US carriers have steadily risen from around $5 billion to well over $10 billion for the latest ships. See "*Gerald R. Ford*-Class Aircraft Carrier," *Wikipedia*, http://en.wikipedia.org/wiki/Gerald_R._Ford-class_aircraft_carrier (accessed January 7, 2015).

4. Peter Navarro, *Crouching Tiger: Will There Be War with China?* www.crouchingtiger.net (documentary film series from DBC Productions, forthcoming 2016).

5. This "perception gap" between China's neighbors and China, which sees its military buildup as purely defensive in nature, and between China and the US, which sees that same buildup as offensive in nature, is examined in Linda Jakobson and Rory Medcalf, "The Perception Gap: Reading China's Maritime Objectives in Indo-Pacific Asia," Lowry Institute for International Policy, June 23, 2015, http://www.lowyinstitute.org/publications/reading -chinas-maritime-objectives-indo-pacific-asia-perception-gap (accessed July 14, 2015).

6. See, for example, Major Christopher J. McCarthy, "Anti-Access/Area Denial: The Evolution of Modern Warfare," US Naval War College, https://www.usnwc.edu/Lucent/ OpenPdf.aspx?id=95 (accessed July 14, 2015). See also Aaron L. Friedberg, *A Context for Supremacy: China, America, and the Struggle for Mastery in Asia* (New York: W. W. Norton, 2012).

7. Ibid.

8. Ibid.

Chapter 9: The Underground Great Wall of China

1. Hans M. Kristensen and Robert S. Norris, "Chinese Nuclear Forces, 2011," *Bulletin of the Atomic Scientists*, http://bos.sagepub.com/content/67/6/81.full.pdf+html (accessed January 7, 2015).

2. "The 10 Longest Range Intercontinental Ballistic Missiles (ICBM)," Army -Technology.com, November 4, 2013, http://www.army-technology.com/features/feature -the-10-longest-range-intercontinental-ballistic-missiles-icbm/ (accessed January 7, 2015).

3. "START I," *Wikipedia*, http://en.wikipedia.org/wiki/START_I (accessed January 7, 2015).

4. Left to the two treaty allies were choices about how each would meet those limits—for example, the mix of 700 ICBMs that would be deployed on land or at sea versus on heavy bombers. "New START," US Department of State website, http://www .state.gov/t/avc/newstart/index.htm (accessed January 7, 2015).

5. Peter Navarro, *Crouching Tiger: Will There Be War with China?* www .crouchingtiger.net (documentary film series from DBC Productions, forthcoming 2016).

6. Ibid.

7. See, for example, Michael Richardson, "China's Nuclear Program Still Shrouded in Secrecy," *Japan Times*, May 23, 2013, http://www.japantimes.co.jp/ opinion/2013/05/23/commentary/world-commentary/chinas-nuclear-program-still -shrouded-in-secrecy/#.VK_11WTF9oA (accessed January 9, 2015).

8. "Obama against Chinese Nuclear Great Wall," *PressTV*, January 25, 2013, http:// www.presstv.com/detail/2013/01/25/285419/obama-chinese-nuclear-great-wall/ (accessed January 7, 2015).

9. William Wan, "Georgetown Students Shed Light on China's Tunnel System for Nuclear Weapons," *Washington Post*, November 29, 2011, http://www.washingtonpost .com/world/national-security/georgetown-students-shed-light-on-chinas-tunnel-system -for-nuclear-weapons/2011/11/16/gIQA6AmKAO_story.html (accessed January 7, 2015).

Chapter 10: The Missiles "R" Us of the World

1. Peter Navarro, *Crouching Tiger: Will There Be War with China?* www
.crouchingtiger.net (documentary film series from DBC Productions, forthcoming 2016).

2. "China's Missiles," *Economist Online*, December 6, 2010, http://www.economist
.com/blogs/dailychart/2010/12/chinese_missile_ranges (accessed January 7, 2015).

3. Navarro, *Crouching Tiger*.

4. Ibid.

5. "China on Track to Aim 2,000 Missiles at Taiwan: Report," *Reuters*, July 19,
2010, http://www.reuters.com/article/2010/07/19/us-taiwan-china-idUSTRE66I13
F20100719 (accessed January 7, 2015).

6. Navarro, *Crouching Tiger*.

7. Japan calls them the Senkakus; China calls them the Diaoyus.

8. Navarro, *Crouching Tiger*.

9. Supersonic speed begins at Mach 5.

10. Bradley Perrett, Bill Sweetman, and Michael Fabey, "US Navy Sees Chinese
HGV as Part of Wider Threat," *Aviation Week*, January 27, 2014, http://aviationweek.com/
awin/us-navy-sees-chinese-hgv-part-wider-threat (accessed January 7, 2015).

11. Bill Gertz, "China Conducts Flight Test of New Mobile ICBM," *Free Beacon*,
October 2, 2014, http://freebeacon.com/national-security/china-conducts-flight-test-of
-new-mobile-icbm/ (accessed January 10, 2015).

Chapter 11: Any Ship Can Be a Minesweeper—Once

1. Scott Truver, "Taking Mines Seriously," *Naval War College Review* 65, no. 2
(Spring 2012) https://www.usnwc.edu/getattachment/19669a3b-6795-406c-8924
-106d7a5adb93/Taking-Mines-Seriously--Mine-Warfare-in-China-s-Ne (accessed January
7, 2015).

2. "USS Coral Sea (CVB 43)," Department of the US Navy, http://www.navy.mil/
navydata/nav_legacy.asp?id=59 (accessed January 7, 2015).

3. Frederick M. Sallagar, "Lessons from an Aerial Mining Campaign ('Operation
Starvation')," United States Air Force Project Rand, April 1974, http://www.rand.org/
content/dam/rand/pubs/reports/2006/R1322.pdf (accessed January 7, 2015).

4. Ibid.

5. Andrew S. Erickson, Lyle J. Goldstein, and William S. Murray, *Chinese Mine
Warfare*, Naval War College, https://www.usnwc.edu/Research---Gaming/China
-Maritime-Studies-Institute/Publications/documents/CMS3_Mine-Warfare.aspx (accessed
January 7, 2015).

6. Truver, "Taking Mines Seriously."

7. Ronald O'Rourke, "China Naval Modernization: Implications for US Navy
Capabilities—Background and Issues for Congress," Congressional Research Service,
June 1, 2015, https://www.fas.org/sgp/crs/row/RL33153.pdf (accessed July 19, 2015).

8. Andrew S. Erickson, Lyle J. Goldstein, and William S. Murray, "China's Undersea Sentries," *Undersea Warfare*, http://www.navy.mil/navydata/cno/n87/usw/issue_33/china.html (accessed January 7, 2015).

9. Erickson, Goldstein, and Murray. *Chinese Mine Warfare*.

10. Ibid.

11. These quotes are noted in Erickson, Goldstein, and Murray, *Chinese Mine Warfare*.

12. Ibid.

13. Ibid.

14. Ibid.

Chapter 12: Nukes at Sea and Sleepless in Seattle

1. Opinion varies on these submarines. Some sources claim there are three operational with two in development, and there is some debate as to whether these subs can carry only a single warhead or are fully "MRVed," that is, armed with multiple reentry vehicle warheads.

2. Peter Navarro, *Crouching Tiger: Will There Be War with China?* www.crouchingtiger.net (documentary film series from DBC Productions, forthcoming 2016).

3. Christian Conroy, "China's Ballistic-Missile Submarines: How Dangerous?" *National Interest*, November 18, 2013, http://nationalinterest.org/commentary/chinas-ballistic-missile-submarines-how-dangerous-9414 (accessed January 7, 2015).

4. Navarro, *Crouching Tiger*.

5. Ibid.

Chapter 13: Chinese Subs Lay in Wait—With Europe's Complicity

1. For example, the USS *Triton* nuclear sub conducted the first submerged circumnavigation of the globe in sixty days way back in the early 1960s—and that was on a mere shakedown cruise.

2. Posted by Chankaiyee2, "China to Build 15 More Yuan-class Submarines with German Engines," *China Daily Mail*, April 11, 2013, http://chinadailymail.com/2013/04/11/china-to-build-15-more-yuan-class-submarines-with-german-engines/ (accessed January 7, 2015).

3. Andrew Rettman, "China Tells EU to End Arms Ban," EUobserver, September 20, 2012, https://euobserver.com/defence/117614 (accessed July 19, 2015).

4. Stuart McMillan, "Europe's Arms Trade with China," ASPI Strategist, February 11, 2014, http://www.aspistrategist.org.au/europes-arms-trade-with-china/ (accessed July 19, 2015).

5. "EU States Strike Lucrative Military Contracts with China, Overriding Embargo—Report," *End the Lie*, April 30, 2014, http://endthelie.com/2014/04/30/eu-states-strike-lucrative-military-contracts-with-china-overriding-embargo-report/#jJZtT4tE72Rdwpbv.99 (accessed January 7, 2015).

6. Ibid.

7. "Vladimir Lenin," *Wikiquote*, https://en.wikiquote.org/wiki/Vladimir_Lenin (accessed July 19, 2015).

Chapter 14: Down to the Sea in Surface Ships

1. The debate over the importance of the role of the Liaoning is examined, for example, in Brian Killough, "Liaoning—Paper Tiger or Growing Cub?" *Diplomat*, September 28, 2012, http://thediplomat.com/2012/09/liaoning-paper-tiger-or -growing-cub/ (accessed July 19, 2015).

2. Ian Storey and You Ji, "China's Aircraft Carrier Ambitions," *Naval War College Review* 57, no. 1 (Winter 2004), https://www.usnwc.edu/getattachment/ffc60b3e-d2e6 -4142-9b71-6dfa247051f2/China-s-Aircraft-Carrier-Ambitions--Seeking-Truth- (accessed January 7, 2015).

3. A brief history of the Varyag's journey is available at "Liaoning (Varyag) Aircraft Carrier," SinoDefence, http://sinodefence.com/liaoning-varyag-class/ (accessed July 19, 2015). That the carrier was never intended to be a casino in Macao is covered in "China's First Aircraft Carrier: From Russia with Love," *Guardian*, August 10, 2011, http://www .theguardian.com/commentisfree/2011/aug/11/china-aircraft-leader (accessed July 19, 2015). For a fascinating account of the man behind the purchase, see also Minnie Chan, "The Inside Story of the Liaoning: How Xu Zengping Sealed deal for China's First Aircraft Carrier," *South China Morning Post*, January 19, 2015, http://www.scmp.com/ news/china/article/1681755/how-xu-zengping-became-middleman-chinas-deal-buy -liaoning (accessed July 19, 2015).

4. Associated Press in Beijing, "China's First Aircraft Carrier Completes Sea Trials," *Guardian*, January 2, 2014, http://www.theguardian.com/world/2014/jan/02/china -aircraft-carrier-completes-sea-trials (accessed July 19, 2015).

5. For how the "shootering" pose has evolved into a popular meme in China, see Brian Fung, "'Shootering' Is the New Eastwooding: China's Aircraft Carrier Gets a Meme," *Atlantic*, November 28, 2012, http://www.theatlantic.com/international/ archive/2012/11/shootering-is-the-new-eastwooding-chinas-aircraft-carrier-gets-a -meme/265678/ (accessed July 19, 2015).

6. Quoted in Harry Kazianis, "Why to Ignore China's Aircraft Carriers," *Diplomat*, January 28, 2014, http://thediplomat.com/2014/01/why-to-ignore-chinas-aircraft-carriers/ (accessed January 20, 2015).

7. Peter Navarro, *Crouching Tiger: Will There Be War with China?* www .crouchingtiger.net (documentary film series from DBC Productions, forthcoming 2016).

8. Toshi Yoshihara and James R. Holmes, "The Master 'PLAN': China's New Guided Missile Destroyer," *Diplomat*, September 4, 2012, http://thediplomat. com/2012/09/the-master-plan-chinas-new-guided-missile-destroyer/ (accessed January 7, 2015).

9. See, for example, James C. Bussert, "Catamarans Glide through Chinese Waters,"

Signal Online, December 2007, http://www.afcea.org/content/?q=node/1433 (accessed January 7, 2015).

10. Ibid.

Chapter 15: The Best Air Force Spies Can Steal

1. Douglas Frison and Andrew Scobell, "China's Military Threat to Taiwan in the Era of Hu Jintao" (unpublished manuscript, January 31, 2004), http://people.duke.edu/~niou/teaching/FrisonScobell.pdf (accessed January 7, 2015).

2. Carlo Kopp, "Just How Good is the F-22 Raptor?" *Air Power Australia*, September 1998, http://www.ausairpower.net/API-Metz-Interview.html (accessed January 7, 2015).

3. Ibid.

4. Peter Navarro, *Crouching Tiger: Will There Be War with China?* www.crouchingtiger.net (documentary film series from DBC Productions, forthcoming 2016).

5. For a discussion of the J-20 features, see, for example, "Chengdu J-20 Multirole Stealth Fighter Aircraft, China," Airforce-Technology.com, http://www.airforce-technology.com/projects/chengdu-j20/ (accessed July 19, 2015). For the J-31, see, for example, Jeffrey Lin and P. W. Singer, "New Chinese 5th Generation Fighter Jet--J31 Performs More Flight Tests," *Popular Science*, May 22, 2014, http://www.popsci.com/blog-network/eastern-arsenal/new-chinese-5th-generation-fighter-jet-j31-performs-more-flight-tests (accessed July 19, 2015).

6. Jeremy Page and Julian E. Barnes, "China Shows Its Growing Might," *Wall Street Journal*, January 12, 2011, http://online.wsj.com/news/articles/SB10001424052748704428004576075042571461586 (accessed January 7, 2015).

7. Elisabeth Bumiller and Michael Wines, "Test of Stealth Fighter Clouds Gates Visit to China," *New York Times*, January 11, 2011, http://www.nytimes.com/2011/01/12/world/asia/12fighter.html (accessed January 7, 2015).

8. Ibid.

9. Mail Foreign Service, "China Used Downed US Fighter to Develop First Stealth Jet," *Daily Mail*, April 19, 2011, http://www.dailymail.co.uk/news/article-1349906/Chengdu-J-20-China-used-downed-US-fighter-develop-stealth-jet.html (accessed January 7, 2015).

10. Sydney J. Freedberg Jr., "Top Official Admits F-35 Stealth Fighter Secrets Stolen, *Breaking Defense*, June 20, 2013, http://breakingdefense.com/2013/06/top-official-admits-f-35-stealth-fighter-secrets-stolen/ (accessed January 7, 2015).

11. Navarro, *Crouching Tiger*.

Chapter 16: Deny, Degrade, Deceive, Disrupt, and Destroy in Space

1. The exact body count for Iraq remains elusive, but estimates by various groups are consistent with the range. See "Gulf War: Casualties," *Wikipedia*, http://en.wikipedia .org/wiki/Gulf_War#Casualties (accessed January 7, 2015). It should also be noted that even though less than 300 American soldiers lost their lives in Iraq, as many as 250,000 of the roughly 700,000 troops who served became afflicted with the mysterious Gulf War Syndrome they brought home.

2. "National Security Space Strategy," US Department of Defense, http://www .defense.gov/home/features/2011/0111_nsss/ (accessed January 7, 2015).

3. Sonshi Group, trans., "Sun Tzu's *The Art of War*," Sonshi, https://www.sonshi .com/original-the-art-of-war-translation-not-giles.html (accessed July 19, 2015).

4. "On War," Clausewitz.com, http://www.clausewitz.com/readings/OnWar1873/ Bk5ch18.html (accessed July 19, 2015).

5. The 1967 Outer Space Treaty, which explicitly bans the weaponization of space, has been signed by over one hundred nations, including the United States and Russia. China is not among the signatories.

6. Walter Pincus, "Satellite Launches Were Forced Overseas," *Washington Post*, July 15, 1998, http://www.washingtonpost.com/wp-srv/politics/special/campfin/stories/ satellite071598.htm (accessed January 7, 2015).

7. These facilities include those at Jiuquan, Taiyuan, and Xichang. In addition, China has just completed its latest facility on Hainan Island—a preferred southern location for the launching of geosynchronous satellites because of its closer proximity to the equator.

8. The early definitive work on this problem is the controversial "Cox Report," which detailed the many ways China steals intellectual property to build out its weapons systems and satellite network. This report also indicates that US satellite manufacturers knowingly "transferred missile design information and know-how to the PRC without obtaining the legally required licenses." See "Overview," Select Committee United States House of Representatives, http://www.house.gov/coxreport/chapfs/over.html (accessed July 19, 2015).

9. Eileen Yu, "China's Satellite Network Aims for 'Centimeters' Accuracy," ZDNet, December 30, 2013, http://www.zdnet.com/article/chinas-satellite-network-aims-for -centimeters-accuracy/ (accessed July 19, 2015). See also Yang Jian, "Beidou to Cover World by 2020 with 30 Satellites," ShanghaiDaily.com, December 28, 2013, http://www .shanghaidaily.com/national/Beidou-to-cover-world-by-2020-with-30-satellites/shdaily .shtml (accessed July 19, 2015).

10. For the narrative, see "A New Policy Typology to Better Understand the Goals of China's Space Program," *Space Review*, http://www.thespacereview.com/article/1958/2 (accessed January 7, 2015).

11. This whole article is well worth a read as a glimpse into the Chinese war

mind. TL, LD, AF and AT, "How China Deals with the US Strategy to Contain China," Chinascope, February 19, 2011, http://chinascope.org/main/content/view/3291/92/ (accessed January 7, 2015).

12. This direct kill also shattered the satellite into thousands of pieces, thereby creating the single largest mass of space debris in Earth history. By one count, this debris consists of more than two thousand "pieces of trackable size (golf ball size and larger) and an estimated 150,000 debris particles." See "2007 Chinese Anti-Satellite Missile Test," *Wikipedia*, http://en.wikipedia.org/wiki/2007_Chinese_anti-satellite_missile_test (accessed January 7, 2015). This debris now poses a constant collision threat to other satellites in what has become an increasingly congested and polluted low-Earth-orbit transit-way.

13. Francis Harris, "Beijing Secretly Fires Lasers to Disable US Satellites," *Telegraph*, September 26, 2006, http://www.telegraph.co.uk/news/worldnews/1529864/ Beijing-secretly-fires-lasers-to-disable-US-satellites.html (accessed July 19, 2015).

Chapter 17: The Internet Meets Mephistopheles

1. See, for example, Richard Walters, "Gmail's China Block Adds Concerns over Internet Censorship," *Financial Times*, December 30, 2014, http://www.ft.com/cms/s/0/ c2b48a02-904e-11e4-b55d-00144feabdc0.html#ixzz3OHWXlifM (accessed January 7, 2015). Syracuse University professor Milton Mueller is quoted as saying: "The NSA revelations have not produced any major reforms yet. . . . At the same time, they have triggered a lot of discrediting of the internet freedom ideal. . . . We have lost a lot of moral authority."

2. "Training for Hackers Stirs Worry about Illegal Actions," *China View*, April 8, 2009, http://news.xinhuanet.com/english/2009-08/04/content_11821911.htm (accessed January 7, 2015). For a discussion of the role of educational institutions in China, see John Markoff and David Barboza, "2 China Schools Said to be Tied to Online Attacks," *New York Times*, February 18, 2010, http://www.nytimes.com/2010/02/19/ technology/19china.html?_r=0 (accessed January 7, 2015).

3. Geoffrey Ingersoll, "Hacking for the Chinese Army is a Competitive Job with Great Benefits," *Business Insider*, February 19, 2013, http://www.businessinsider.com/ chinese-hackers-get-great-benefits-2013-2 (accessed January 20, 2015).

4. Mandiant Consulting, "APT1: Exposing One of China's Cyber Espionage Units," http://intelreport.mandiant.com/Mandiant_APT1_Report.pdf (accessed January 7, 2015).

5. Ibid.

6. Ellen Nishima, "Confidential Report Lists U.S. Weapons System Designs Compromised by Chinese Cyberspies," *Washington Post*, May 27, 2013, http://www .washingtonpost.com/world/national-security/confidential-report-lists-us-weapons -system-designs-compromised-by-chinese-cyberspies/2013/05/27/a42c3e1c-c2dd-11e2 -8c3b-0b5e9247e8ca_story.html (accessed January 7, 2015).

7. Ibid.

8. Peter Navarro, *Crouching Tiger: Will There Be War with China?* www
.crouchingtiger.net (documentary film series from DBC Productions, forthcoming 2016).

9. David E. Sanger, David Barboza, and Nicole Perlroth, "Chinese Army Unit is
Seen as Tied to Hacking against US," *New York Times*, February 18, 2013, http://www
.nytimes.com/2013/02/19/technology/chinas-army-is-seen-as-tied-to-hacking-against-us
.html?pagewanted=all&_r=0&pagewanted=print (accessed January 7, 2015).

10. Ibid.

11. Colonel Qiao Liang and Colonel Wang Xiangsui, *Unrestricted Warfare* (New
Delhi, India: Natraj Publishers, 2007).

12. Peter Navarro, "Chinese Hacking and the Art of War," *Huffington Post*, March
21, 2013, http://www.huffingtonpost.com/peter-navarro-and-greg-autry/china
-hacking_b_2920096.html (accessed January 7, 2015).

13. John Reed, "Proof That Military Chips from China Are Infected?" *Defensetech*,
May 30, 2102, http://defensetech.org/2012/05/30/smoking-gun-proof-that-military-chips
-from-china-are-infected/#ixzz356TtQaOC (accessed January 7, 2015).

14. Ibid.

15. David Fulghum, Bill Sweetman, and Jen DiMascio, "Chinese Microchips Are
Considered Impossible to Regulate," *Aviation Week*. June 4, 2012, http://aviationweek
.com/awin/chinese-microchips-are-considered-impossible-regulate (accessed January 7, 2015).

16. Navarro, *Crouching Tiger*.

Chapter 18: The Dark Strategic Beauty of the Nonkinetic Three Warfares

1. Stefan Halper, "China: The Three Warfares," report Prepared for Andy Marshall,
director, Office of Net Assessment, Office of the Secretary of Defense, Washington, DC,
May 2013, p. 11, http://images.smh.com.au/file/2014/04/11/5343124/China_%2520The
%2520three%2520warfares.pdf?rand=1397212645609 (accessed January 7, 2015).

2. Ibid.

3. Ibid.

4. The term "cabbage strategy" was coined by Chinese general Zhang Zhaozhong
to describe pressing a territorial claim by gradually surrounding an area with flotillas
of military and civilian ships, thereby overwhelming the opposition. See, for example,
Brahma Chellaney, "China's Creeping 'Cabbage' Strategy," *Taipei Times*, December 1,
2013, http://www.taipeitimes.com/News/editorials/archives/2013/12/01/2003578036
(accessed July 19, 2015).

5. Personal interview with Stephan Halper, April 20, 2014.

6. Dean Cheng, "Winning without Fighting: Chinese Public Opinion Warfare and
the Need for a Robust American Response," *Heritage Foundation*, Backgrounder no.
2745, November 26, 2012, http://www.heritage.org/research/reports/2012/11/winning
-without-fighting-chinese-public-opinion-warfare-and-the-need-for-a-robust-american
-response (accessed January 7, 2015).

7. Harry Kazianis, "China's 10 Red Lines in the South China Sea," *Diplomat*, July 1, 2014, http://thediplomat.com/2014/07/chinas-10-red-lines-in-the-south-china-sea/ (accessed January 7, 2015).

Chapter 19: The Sum of All Chinese Capabilities

1. Garry Kasparov, "The Global War on Modernity," *Wall Street Journal*, January 23, 2015, http://www.wsj.com/articles/garry-kasparov-the-global-war-on-modernity -1421800948 (accessed January 27, 2015). This op-ed was written within the context of Russia's adventurism in the Ukraine and the Paris bombings of 2015 by Islamic extremists. However, as they say, "if the shoe fits . . ."

Chapter 20: The (Almost) Unsinkable Aircraft Carrier of Taiwan

1. Peter Navarro, *Crouching Tiger: Will There Be War with China?* www .crouchingtiger.net (documentary film series from DBC Productions, forthcoming 2016).
2. Ibid.
3. Peng Guangqian and Yao Youzhi, *The Science of Military Strategy* (Beijing: Military Science Publishing House, 2005), p. 443.
4. Michael D. Swaine, "Trouble in Taiwan," *Foreign Affairs*, March/April 2014, http://www.foreignaffairs.com/articles/59708/michael-d-swaine/trouble-in-taiwan (accessed January 7, 2015).
5. Mark Landler, "No New F-16's for Taiwan but US to Upgrade Fleet," *New York Times*, September 18, 2011, http://www.nytimes.com/2011/09/19/world/asia/us-decides -against-selling-f-16s-to-taiwan.html?_r=0 (accessed January 7, 2015).
6. Navarro, *Crouching Tiger*.
7. Ibid.
8. Ibid.
9. For how this phrase is often used in the Taiwan debate see, for example, Robert Green, "The Unsinkable Aircraft Carrier," Taiwan Today, May 1, 2005, http:// taiwantoday.tw/ct.asp?xItem=1080&CtNode=124 (accessed July 19, 2015).

Chapter 21: The Wild Child and Wild Card of North Korea

1. Richard Knight, "Are North Koreans Really Three Inches Shorter than South Koreans," *BBC News Magazine*, April 22, 2012, http://www.bbc.com/news/ magazine-17774210 (accessed January 7, 2015).
2. It is difficult to get an exact estimate of the numbers dead, but it likely runs into the several millions. This source places it at 3.5 million. "World: Asia-Pacific '3.5m North Koreans Starved to Death," *BBC News*. August 30, 1999, http://news.bbc.co.uk/2/hi/asia -pacific/433641.stm (accessed January 7, 2015).
3. Joshua Stanton and Sung-Yoon Lee, "Pyongyang's Hunger Games," *New York*

Times, March 7, 2014, http://www.nytimes.com/2014/03/08/opinion/pyongyangs-hunger -games.html?_r=0 (accessed January 7, 2015).

4. By contrast, South Korea's GDP is over a trillion dollars annually. "List of countries by GDP (Nominal)," *Wikipedia*, http://en.wikipedia.org/wiki/List_of_countries _by_GDP_(nominal) (accessed January 7, 2015).

5. Stanton and Lee, "Pyongyang's Hunger Games."

6. Beina Xu and Jayshree Bajoria, "The China-North Korea Relationship," *Council on Foreign Relations*, Backgrounder, http://www.cfr.org/china/china-north-korea -relationship/p11097 (accessed January 7, 2015).

7. Ibid.

8. Peter Navarro, *Crouching Tiger: Will There Be War with China?* www .crouchingtiger.net (documentary film series from DBC Productions, forthcoming 2016).

9. *Time*, "A New Lesson in the Limits of Power," Dean-Boys.com, April 25, 1969, http://www.dean-boys.com/shootdown/shoot.htm (accessed January 7, 2015).

10. "North Korean Torpedo San South's Navy Ship—Report," *BBC News*, May 20, 2010, http://www.bbc.co.uk/news/10129703 (accessed January 7, 2015). The attack near the disputed inter-Korean maritime border which killed forty-six sailors was denied by North Korea, but markings on the recovered torpedo parts allowed a match.

11. Jack Kim and Lee Jae-won, "North Korea Shells South in Fiercest Attack in Decades," *Reuters*, November 23, 2010, http://www.reuters.com/article/2010/11/23/ us-korea-north-artillery-idUSTRE6AM0YS20101123 (accessed January 7, 2015). This attack followed in the wake of a South Korean artillery exercise in the south and was the "heaviest attack" since the end of the Korean War.

12. VOA News, "S. Korea President Vows Strong Retaliation against North," *Voice of America*, April 1, 2013, http://www.voanews.com/content/south-korea-president-vows -strong-retaliation-against-north/1632828.html (accessed January 7, 2015).

13. "In Focus: North Korea's Nuclear Threats," *New York Times*, April 16, 2013, http://www.nytimes.com/interactive/2013/04/12/world/asia/north-korea-questions.html (accessed January 7, 2015).

14. "North Korea Timeline: Key Events in the Lead Up To and the Aftermath of the Iraq War," *Wisconsin Project on Nuclear Arms Control*, http://www.wisconsinproject.org/ countries/nkorea/Timeline.htm (accessed January 7, 2015).

15. Gopal Ratnam and Isabel Reynolds, "US to Boost Missile Defenses in Japan against North Korea Threat, *Bloomberg*, April 6, 2014, http://www.bloomberg.com/ news/2014-04-06/u-s-to-boost-missile-defenses-in-japan-against-n-korean-threat.html (accessed January 8, 2015).

16. David Randall, "North Korea Crisis: Kim Jong-un Threatens 'All-Out Nuclear War,'" *Independent*, March 31, 2013, http://www.independent.co.uk/news/world/asia/ north-korea-crisis-kim-jongun-threatens-allout-nuclear-war-8555350.html (accessed January 8, 2015).

17. Te-Ping Chen and Alistair Gale, "China Warns on Proposed New Missile Defense System for Seoul, *Wall Street Journal*, May 29, 2014, http://online.wsj.com/

articles/china-warns-on-proposed-u-s-missile-defense-system-for-seoul-1401277014 (accessed January 8, 2015).

18. Barbara Demick, "Seoul's Vulnerability Is Key to War Scenarios," *Los Angeles Times*, May 27, 2003, http://www.ph.ucla.edu/epi/bioter/seoulsvulnerability.html (accessed January 8, 2015).

19. Navarro, *Crouching Tiger*.

Chapter 22: On the Rocks in the East China Sea

1. "Anti-Japanese sentiment," *Wikipedia*, http://en.wikipedia.org/wiki/Anti-Japanese_sentiment (accessed January 7, 2015).

2. Peter Navarro, *Crouching Tiger: Will There Be War with China?* www.crouchingtiger.net (documentary film series from DBC Productions, forthcoming 2016).

3. Ibid.

Chapter 23: A Paracel Islands Prelude to the Next Vietnam War

1. J. R. Michael Fasham, ed., *Ocean Biogeochemistry: The Role of the Ocean Carbon Cycle in the Global Change* (New York: Springer, 2003), p. 80. The Mediterranean Sea is the second largest.

2. "On the Rocks," YouTube video, 2:16:29, recording of the April 12, 2013, Starr Forum, posted by "MIT CIS," June 12, 2013, https://www.youtube.com/watch?v=ieiRKW-BTnA (accessed January 8, 2015).

3. Peter Navarro, *Crouching Tiger: Will There Be War with China?* www.crouchingtiger.net (documentary film series from DBC Productions, forthcoming 2016).

4. For both a statement of the problem as well as the background history from the Vietnamese perspective, see, for example, "Vietnamese Take to Streets in Protest against China's Oil Rig Incursion," *Thanhnien News*, May 11, 2014, http://www.thanhniennews.com/politics/vietnamese-take-to-streets-in-protest-against-chinas-oil-rig-incursion-26159.html (accessed July 21, 2015). See also Hilary Whiteman, "How an Oil Rig Sparked Anti-China Riots in Vietnam," CNN, May 19, 2014, http://www.cnn.com/2014/05/19/world/asia/china-vietnam-islands-oil-rig-explainer/ (accessed July 21, 2015).

5. Staff Reporter, "Vietnam's Buildup in the South China Sea," *Want China Times*, April 8, 2012, http://www.wantchinatimes.com/news-subclass-cnt.aspx?id=20120804000010&cid=1101 (accessed January 8, 2015).

6. Ibid.

7. "Vietnam's Military Buildup," *Asia Times*, March 18, 2013, http://asitimes.blogspot.com/2013/03/vietnams-military-buildup-media-report.html (accessed January 8, 2015).

8. Staff Reporter, "Vietnam's Buildup in the South China Sea."

9. Navarro, *Crouching Tiger*.

Chapter 24: A Hungry Cow's Tongue in the South China Sea

1. It is about 680 miles to the Spratly Islands from Hainan, China. See "Distance between Hainan and the Spratly Islands," Evi, an Amazon company, http://www.evi .com/q/distance_between_hainan_and_the_spratly_island (accessed January 8, 2015).

2. While Brunei does not occupy any of the Spratly Islands, it has nonetheless staked a claim to the resources in some of the waters around them based on its declared Exclusive Economic Zone and continental shelf under the Law of the Sea Treaty. See, for example, Daniel J. Dzurek, "The Spratly Islands Dispute: Who's On First," International Boundaries Research Unit, Maritime Briefing 2, no. 1 (1996), p. 45.

3. Glenne B. Lagura, "Philippines' Ownership to Spratly Island," Academia.edu, http://www.academia.edu/1390813/Philippines_ownership_to_Spratly_Island_(accessed January 8, 2015).

4. Ibid.

5. The original line included eleven dots. However, it was reduced by Premier Zhou Enlai to nine dots in 1953 after a rare territorial accommodation with Vietnam in the Gulf of Tonkin. David Rosenberg, "How to Appease the Seas?" BienDong.net, August 1, 2013, http://www.southchinasea.com.cn/section/editorial/weekly-report/how-appease-seas (accessed January 8, 2015).

6. "Natuna Gas Field, Indonesia," OffshoreTechnology.com, http://www.offshore -technology.com/projects/natuna/ (accessed January 8, 2015).

7. Peter Navarro, *Crouching Tiger: Will There Be War with China?* www .crouchingtiger.net (documentary film series from DBC Productions, forthcoming 2016).

8. Keith Bradsher, "Philippine Leader Sounds Alarm on China," *New York Times*, February 4, 2014, http://www.nytimes.com/2014/02/05/world/asia/philippine-leader-urges -international-help-in-resisting-chinas-sea-claims.html?_r=1_(accessed January 8, 2015).

9. "A Game of Shark and Minnow," *New York Times Magazine*, slide and video presentation, October 27, 2013, http://www.nytimes.com/newsgraphics/2013/10/27/south -china-sea/ (accessed January 8, 2015).

10. Peter Navarro, "Speaking Honestly About China's Rising Military Could Get You in Hot Water," *National Interest*, November 24, 2014, http://nationalinterest.org/blog/ the-buzz/speaking-honestly-about-chinas-rising-military-could-get-you-11727 (accessed February 1, 2015).

11. It is interesting that the original hyperlink for Fanell's transcripted remarks was hacked and the URL then directed people to a Chinese website. This article provides some quotes and video. "Blunt Words on China from US Navy," *Interpreter*, February 5, 2013, http://www.lowyinterpreter.org/post/2013/02/05/Blunt-words-on-China-from-US-Navy. aspx (accessed January 8, 2015).

12. This metaphor has been popularized in Robert Kaplan, *Asia's Cauldron* (New York: Random House, 2014).

Chapter 25: China's New Monroe Doctrine for Asia

1. Ibid.

2. For a historical view of the debate between Grotius and Selden over an open or closed seas as it relates to China, see, for example, articles by Professor James Holmes of the US Naval War College, e.g., "China's Selective Access-Denial Strategy," National Interest, December 3, 2013, http://nationalinterest.org/commentary/chinas-selective -access-denial-strategy-9482 (accessed July 21, 2015); and "China's New Naval Theorist" *Diplomat*, July 11, 2013, http://thediplomat.com/2013/07/chinas-new-naval-strategist/ (accessed July 21, 2015).

3. A useful history of the evolution from the cannon-shot rule to the modern United Nations Convention on the Law of the Sea (UNCLOS) treaty is provided in "Law of the Sea: History of the Maritime Zones under International Law," NOAA, Office of Coast Survey, http://www.nauticalcharts.noaa.gov/staff/law_of_sea.html (accessed July 21, 2015).

4. Jeff M. Smith and Joshua Eisenman, "China and America Clash on the High Seas: The EEZ Challenge," *National Interest*, May 22, 2014, http://nationalinterest.org/feature/ china-america-clash-the-high-seas-the-eez-challenge-10513?page=3 (accessed January 8, 2015).

5. Steven Lee Myers and Christopher Drew, "US Aides Say Chinese Pilot Reveled in Risk," *New York Times*, April 6, 2001, http://www.nytimes.com/2001/04/06/ world/06FLIG.html (accessed January 8, 2015).

6. Craig Whitlock, "Pentagon: China Tried to Block US Military Jet in Dangerous Mid-Air Intercept," *Washington Post*, August 22, 2014, http://www.washingtonpost.com/ world/national-security/pentagon-china-tried-to-block-us-military-jet-in-dangerous-mid -air-intercept/2014/08/22/533d24e8-2a1b-11e4-958c-268a320a60ce_story.html (accessed January 8, 2015).

7. One part of the system involves a passive sonar array towed horizontally behind the ship by a 1,800-meter-long cable; this array can identify specific types of submarines up to 450 meters beneath the surface. The other part of the system is an active sonar array that hangs vertically under the ship.

Chapter 26: Bye, Bye to Hindi-Chini Bhai-Bhai

1. Peter Navarro, *Crouching Tiger: Will There Be War with China?* www .crouchingtiger.net (documentary film series from DBC Productions, forthcoming 2016).

2. Gurmeet Kanwai and Monika Chansoria, "China Preparing Tibet as Future War Zone," *Deccan Herald*, June 2, 2011, http://www.deccanherald.com/content/165996/ china-preparing-tibet-future-war.html (accessed January 8, 2015).

3. "Introduction to Satellite Map of Xinjiang-Uighur Autonomous region of China (P.R.C.)—1A," *China Report*, http://www.drben.net/ChinaReport/Xinjiang_Uyghur_AR/ Xinjiang-Uygur_AR-Sources/Xinjiang-AR-Maps/Map-Satellite-Xinjiang-Uighur _AR-1A.html (accessed January 8, 2015).

4. Kanwai and Chansoria, "China Preparing Tibet."

5. Ibid.

6. Jagannath P. Panda, "China's Designs on Arunachal Pradesh," *Institute for Defence Studies and Analyses*," March 12, 2008, http://idsa.in/idsastrategiccomments/ChinasDesignsonArunachalPradesh_JPPanda_120308.html (accessed January 8, 2015).

7. Swaminathan S. Anklesaria Aiyar, "Will China Eye Arunachal Pradesh's Shale Oil?" *Swaminomics*, September 25, 2011, http://swaminomics.org/will-china-eye-arunachal-pradesh%E2%80%99s-shale-oil/ (accessed January 8, 2015).

8. The definitive chronology is provided by Pacific Institute from which the examples that follow are drawn. As Excel spreadsheets go, it's a great read. "Water Conflict Chronology List," Pacific Institute, http://www2.worldwater.org/conflict/list/ (accessed January 8, 2015).

9. Sasha Ross, "Over the Water of the Nile," *Counterpunch*, July 9, 2013, http://www.counterpunch.org/2013/07/09/over-the-water-of-the-nile/ (accessed January 8, 2015).

10. See, for example, Ofira Seliktar, "Turning Water into Fire: The Jordan River as the Hidden Factor in the Six Day War," *Meria Journal*, June 4, 2005, http://www.gloria-center.org/2005/06/seliktar-2005-06-04/ (accessed on January 8, 2015).

11. Kim Wall, "Chinese Dam Concerns Raise Fears of Future Water Conflict," *South China Morning Post*, September 5, 2013, http://www.scmp.com/print/news/china/article/1303506/chinese-dam-concerns-raise-fears-future-water-conflict (accessed January 8, 2015).

12. Brahma Chellaney, "The Sino-Indian Water Divide," Project Syndicate, August 3, 2009, http://www.project-syndicate.org/commentary/the-sino-indian-water-divide (accessed January 8, 2015).

13. "Indo-China Water Dispute," *Indochina102*, March 1, 2012, http://indochina102.blogspot.com (accessed January 8, 2015).

14. Navarro, *Crouching Tiger*.

15. Jake Swearingen, "China Will Make the Dalai Lama Reincarnate Whether He Likes It or Not," *Wire*, September 10, 2014, http://www.thewire.com/global/2014/09/china-will-make-the-dalai-lama-reincarnate-whether-he-likes-it-or-not/380003/ (accessed January 8, 2015).

16. Navarro, *Crouching Tiger*.

Chapter 27: An Imploding China Wags the Dog

1. For a humorous take, see Philip Coppens, "Wag the Dog," *Conspiracy Times*, http://www.philipcoppens.com/wagthedog.html (accessed January 8, 2015).

2. See, for example, David Sobek, "Rallying around the Podesta: Testing Diversionary Theory across Time," *Journal of Peace Research* 44, no. 1 (January 2007): 29–45; Karl DeRouen, "Presidents and the Diversionary Use of Force: A Research Note," *International Studies Quarterly* 44, no. 2 (June 2000): 317–328; and Thomas S. Mowle,

"Worldviews in Foreign Policy: Realism Liberalism, and External Conflict." *Political Psychology* 24 no. 3 (September 2003): 561–592.

3. Peter Navarro, *Crouching Tiger: Will There Be War with China?* www .crouchingtiger.net (documentary film series from DBC Productions, forthcoming 2016).

4. See, for example, "Corruptions Perceptions Index 2013," *Transparency International*, http://www.transparency.org/cpi2013/results (accessed January 8, 2015).

5. Edward Wong, "Survey in China Shows a Wide Gap in Income," *New York Times*, July 19, 2013, http://www.nytimes.com/2013/07/20/world/asia/survey-in-china-shows -wide-income-gap.html?_r=0 (accessed January 8, 2015).

6. Jonathan Watts, "The Big Steal," *Guardian*, May 26, 2006, http://www .theguardian.com/world/2006/may/27/china.comment (accessed January 8, 2015).

7. Max Fisher, "How China Stays Stable despite 500 Protests Every Day," *Atlantic*, January 5, 2012, http://www.theatlantic.com/international/archive/2012/01/how-china -stays-stable-despite-500-protests-every-day/250940/ (accessed January 8, 2015).

8. "Water Pollution in China," *Facts and Details*, http://factsanddetails.com/china/ cat10/sub66/item391.html (accessed January 8, 2015).

9. In November of 2013, the Chinese Communist Party loosened the one-child policy so that families can now have two children if at least one parent was an only child. However, this new policy is unlikely to solve China's looming demographic problem. See, for example, Christina Larson, "Why China's Second-Baby Boom Might Not Happen," Bloomberg, August 1, 2014, http://www.bloomberg.com/bw/ articles/2014-08-01/with-end-of-chinas-one-child-policy-there-hasnt-been-a-baby-boom (accessed July 21, 2015).

Chapter 28: Madison's "Mischief of Factions" with Chinese Characteristics

1. Notes Johns Hopkins University professor David Lampton on this point: "There are a number of theories or perspectives that try to explain what drives Chinese foreign policy behavior and certainly one whole area of theory would be they have a master plan and they're implementing it." Peter Navarro, *Crouching Tiger: Will There Be War with China?* www.crouchingtiger.net (documentary film series from DBC Productions, forthcoming 2016).

2. The "mischief of factions" is a phrase attributed to American Founding Father James Madison who used it to describe how special interests in a democracy might put their own interests above that of the nation. For a history of the issue see, for example, Alan Lockard, "Controlling the Mischief of Factions: Before and After Madison," *FJHP* 24 (2007), http://www.flinders.edu.au/sabs/fjhp-files/2007/Lockard1.pdf (accessed January 8, 2015).

3. Navarro, *Crouching Tiger*.

4. Ibid.

5. Ibid.

6. Ibid.

7. Ibid.

8. Barry Leonard, *Congress and Foreign Policy* (Collingdale, PA: Diane Publishing, 1996).

Chapter 29: The Emerging China-Russia Threat Vector

1. Jeremy Page, "Why Russia's President is 'Putin the Great' in China," *Wall Street Journal*, October 1, 2014, http://online.wsj.com/articles/why-russias-president-is-putin-the-great-in-china-1412217002 (accessed January 8, 2015).

2. Lldd11, "Where are the natural resources in Russia?" Answers.com, http://wiki.answers.com/Q/Where_are_the_natural_resources_in_russia (accessed July 23, 2015).

3. See, for example, Loro Horta, "From Russia without Love: Russia Resumes Weapons Sales to China," December 12, 2013, http://www.realcleardefense.com/articles/2013/12/12/from_russia_without_love_russia_resumes_weapons_sales_to_china__106998.html (accessed January 8, 2015).

4. For an interesting discussion of these themes, see Zhao Huasheng, "Does China's Rise Pose a Threat to Russia?" April 26, 2013, http://www.ciis.org.cn/english/2013-04/26/content_5908664.htm (accessed January 8, 2015).

Chapter 30: When Quantity Has a Quality of Its Own

1. "Satchel Paige Quotes," Satchel Paige: The Official Website, http://www.satchelpaige.com/quote2.html (accessed July 21, 2015).

2. Peter Navarro, *Crouching Tiger: Will There Be War with China?* www.crouchingtiger.net (documentary film series from DBC Productions, forthcoming 2016).

3. Ibid.

4. Ibid.

5. "Talk:Joseph Stalin," *Wikiquote*, https://en.wikiquote.org/wiki/Talk:Joseph_Stalin (accessed July 21, 2015).

6. Ibid.

Chapter 31: The Forward Base as a Soft, Fixed Target

1. Peter Navarro, *Crouching Tiger: Will There Be War with China?* www.crouchingtiger.net (documentary film series from DBC Productions, forthcoming 2016).

2. Ibid.

3. Ibid.

4. Ibid.

5. Ibid.

6. Ibid.

7. Ibid.

8. Ibid.
9. Ibid.
10. Ibid.
11. Ibid.
12. Ibid.
13. Ibid.
14. Ibid.

Chapter 32: The Ongoing Battle over Air-Sea Battle

1. Perhaps the most vocal of these critics has been Professor Amitai Etzioni of George Washington University.

2. For example, see James R. Holmes, "AirSea Battle vs. Offshore Control: Can the US Blockade China?" *Diplomat*, August 19, 2013, http://thediplomat.com/2013/08/airsea-battle-vs-offshore-control-can-the-us-blockade-china/ (accessed January 8, 2015).

3. Andrew F. Krepinevich et al., "AirSea Battle: A Point-of-Departure Operational Concept," *Center for Strategic and Budgetary Assessment*, May 28, 2010, http://www.csbaonline.org/publications/2010/05/airsea-battle-concept/ (accessed January 8, 2015).

4. Ibid.

5. Ibid.

6. Ibid. Krepinevich et al. also offer this example, which explicitly highlights the targeting of the Chinese mainland: "Air Force long-range penetrating strike operations to destroy PLA ground-based long-range maritime surveillance systems and long-range ballistic missile launchers (both anti-ship and land-attack) to expand the Navy's freedom of maneuver and reduce strikes on US and allied bases and facilities."

7. Amitai Etzioni, "AirSea Battle: A Dangerous Way to Deal with China," *Diplomat*, September 3, 2013, http://thediplomat.com/2013/09/air-sea-battle-a-dangerous-way-to-deal-with-china/ (accessed January 8, 2015).

8. Peter Navarro, *Crouching Tiger: Will There Be War with China?* www.crouchingtiger.net (documentary film series from DBC Productions, forthcoming 2016).

9. Ibid.

10. To Hammes, these Scud launches should have been very easy targets. They were liquid-fueled rockets that took as much as a half an hour to prepare; and as they sat out in the open for launch, they were readily visible by satellite. In contrast, as we discussed during our analysis of China's Great Underground Wall of missiles, China's new generation of missiles are solid-fueled rockets that can be quickly launched. Moreover, within the tunnel systems of the Great Underground Wall, China's missiles can be moved rapidly to different points.

Chapter 33: A Net Assessment of Offshore Control

1. Victor Robert Lee, "Japan's Defense Minister Kept Busy as Obama Visits Asia," *Diplomat*, April 24, 2014, http://thediplomat.com/2014/04/japans-defense-minister-kept-busy-as-obama-visits-asia/ (accessed January 8, 2015).

2. Nien-Tsu Alfred Hu and Ted L. McDorman, eds., *Maritime Issues in the South China Sea* (Farnham, Surrey, UK: Ashgate, 2014), pp. 36–37. There is also the Karimata Strait that connects first with the Java Sea and then to the Lombok and Sunda Straits. Still other choke points include the Balabac Strait, the Mindoro Strait, the Verde Island Passage, and the Bashi and Balintang Channels.

3. As noted earlier, the Hughes version is called "War by Sea." For details see Jeffrey E. Kline and Wayne P. Hughes Jr., "Between Peace and the Air-Sea Battle," *Naval War College Review* 65, no. 4 (Autumn 2012), https://www.usnwc.edu/getattachment/e3120d0c-8c62-4ab7-9342-805971ed84f4/Between-Peace-and-the-Air-Sea-Battle--A-War-at-Sea.aspx (accessed January 11, 2015).

4. Ibid., pp. 35–36.

5. T. X. Hammes, "Offshore Control Is the Answer," *US Naval Institute Proceedings Magazine*, December 2012, http://www.usni.org/magazines/proceedings/2012-12/offshore-control-answer (accessed January 8, 2015).

6. Kline and Hughes, "Between Peace and Air-Sea Battle."

7. "Who Authorized Preparations for War With China?" YouTube video, 1:39:15, from a panel discussion on the Pentagon's Air-Sea Battle concept hosted by the Sigur Center for Asian Studies at the George Washington University, posted by "Amitai Etzioni," July 25, 2013, https://www.youtube.com/watch?v=kibpu7qHVLY (accessed January 7, 2015).

8. T. X. Hammes, "Offshore Control is the Answer."

9. Ibid.

10. Mark Morris, "AirSea Battle vs. Offshore Control: Which Has a Better Theory of Victory?" November 26, 2013, http://warontherocks.com/2013/11/airsea-battle-vs-offshore-control-which-has-a-better-theory-of-victory/ (accessed January 8, 2015).

11. Kline and Hughes, "Between Peace and Air-Sea Battle."

12. "China's Ambitions in Xinjiang and Central Asia: Part 1," *Stratfor Global Intelligence*, September 30, 2013, http://www.stratfor.com/analysis/chinas-ambitions-xinjiang-and-central-asia-part-1#axzz37BLM4mxU (accessed January 8, 2015).

13. James R. Holmes, "AirSea Battle vs. Offshore Control: Can the US Blockade China?" *Diplomat*, August 19, 2013, http://thediplomat.com/2013/08/airsea-battle-vs-offshore-control-can-the-us-blockade-china/ (accessed January 8, 2015).

14. It may well be worth noting here that some critics of Offshore Control even argue that the "distant blockade" aspect of the strategy may be almost as escalatory as strikes on the mainland themselves. For this more nuanced view of a "War-at-Sea" variation, see, for example, Andrew S. Erickson, "Deterrence by Denial: How to Prevent China from Using Force," *National Interest*, December 16, 2013, http://nationalinterest

.org/commentary/war-china-two-can-play-the-area-denial-game-9564?page=2 (accessed on January 11, 2015).

15. Peter Navarro, *Crouching Tiger: Will There Be War with China?* www .crouchingtiger.net (documentary film series from DBC Productions, forthcoming 2016).

Chapter 34: What Might "Victory" Look Like?

1. Peter Navarro, *Crouching Tiger: Will There Be War with China?* www .crouchingtiger.net (documentary film series from DBC Productions, forthcoming 2016).

2. "Who Authorized Preparations for War With China?" YouTube video, 1:39:15, from a panel discussion on the Pentagon's Air-Sea Battle concept hosted by the Sigur Center for Asian Studies at the George Washington University, posted by "Amitai Etzioni," July 25, 2013, https://www.youtube.com/watch?v=kibpu7qHVLY (accessed January 7, 2015).

3. Personal communication with Toshi Yoshihara, January 7, 2015.

4. Ibid.

5. Here, for example, is Princeton scholar Aaron Friedberg: "First and foremost, the regime, the current regime wants to maintain the control of the Communist Party. That's their principle objective. Everything that they do, internally and externally, is intended to serve the purpose of preserving CCP rule in China." Navarro, *Crouching Tiger: Will There Be War with China?*

Chapter 35: Should America Beat a Neoisolationist Retreat?

1. Peter Navarro, *Crouching Tiger: Will There Be War with China?* www .crouchingtiger.net (documentary film series from DBC Productions, forthcoming 2016).

2. Ibid.

3. Ibid.

4. Ibid.

5. Ibid.

6. Ibid.

7. Ibid.

8. Ben Bland and Robin Kwong, "Supply Chain Disruption: Sunken Ambitions," *Financial Times*, November 3, 2011, http://www.ft.com/intl/cms/s/0/6b20d192-0613 -11e1-ad0e-00144feabdc0.html#axzz3Dltnddgn (accessed January 8, 2015).

9. "South Korea," *NTI*, http://www.nti.org/country-profiles/south-korea/ (accessed January 8, 2015).

10. Navarro, *Crouching Tiger.*

Chapter 36: Will Economic Engagement Keep the Peace?

1. These quotes were frequently uttered by the president in his stump speeches on behalf of China's entry into the WTO. For sample clips, see *Death by China*, a 2012 Netflix documentary film, http://deathbychina.com (accessed January 8, 2015).

2. Ibid.

3. The more formal name is the US-China Economic and Security Review Commission. We use the short form throughout the text for brevity.

4. Peter Navarro, *Crouching Tiger: Will There Be War with China?* www .crouchingtiger.net (documentary film series from DBC Productions, forthcoming 2016).

5. "Economic Engagement Promotes Freedom," *USA*Engage*, http://archives .usaengage.org/archives/studies/engagement.html (accessed January 8, 2015).

6. Ibid.

7. Ibid.

8. Ibid.

9. For a history and compelling first person account, see Hongda Harry Wu, *Laogai: The Chinese Gulag* (Boulder, CO: Westview, 1992). China has recently vowed to end the Laogai system; however, this appears to be more of a name change than a change in its penal system.

10. An in-depth analysis of the role of foreign corporations in helping to build China's "Great Firewall" is offered in Robert McMahon and Isabella Bennett, "US Internet Providers and the 'Great Firewall of China,'" Council on Foreign Relations, February 23, 2011, http://www.cfr.org/internet-policy/us-internet-providers-great-firewall -china/p9856 (accessed July 21, 2015).

Chapter 37: Will Economic Interdependence Prevent War?

1. In the field of international relations, a "liberal" is not the same as a Liberal in American politics. "Liberals" in this international sense are associated with a commitment to free trade, which is often anathema to the Left in America.

2. Baron De Montesquieu, *The Spirit of the Laws*, vol. 1 (New York: Hafner, 1975), p. 316.

3. This pop phrasing is ubiquitous in the economic interdependence literature. See, for example, Gregory Bresiger, "Trade Trumps War," Antiwar.com, March 3, 2000, http:// www.antiwar.com/orig/bresiger1.html#2 (accessed January 8, 2015).

4. For reportage, see, for example, Ian Storey, "China's Malacca Dilemma," *China Brief*, http://www.jamestown.org/single/?no_cache=1&tx_ttnews%5Btt_news %5D=3943#.VK8OSmTF9oA (accessed January 8, 2015).

5. Dale C. Copeland, "Economic Interdependence and War: A Theory of Trade Expectations," *International Security* (Spring 1996), https://www.mtholyoke.edu/acad/ intrel/copeland.htm (accessed January 8, 2015).

6. Christopher Helman, "China Thwarts U.S. 'Containment' with Vietnam Oil Rig Standoff," *Forbes*, May 8, 2014, http://www.forbes.com/sites/ christopherhelman/2014/05/08/china-thwarts-u-s-containment-with-vietnam-oil-rig -standoff/ (accessed January 20, 2015).

7. Copeland, "Economic Interdependence and War."

8. Ibid.

9. Peter Navarro, *Crouching Tiger: Will There Be War with China?* www .crouchingtiger.net (documentary film series from DBC Productions, forthcoming 2016).

10. Ibid.
11. Ibid.
12. Ibid.

Chapter 38: Will Nuclear Weapons Deter Conventional War?

1. "Chinese and Soviet Statements on Frontier Question," *Keesing's Record of World Events*, November 1969, http://web.stanford.edu/group/tomzgroup/pmwiki/uploads/0349-1969-11-K-c-EYJ.pdf (accessed January 8, 2015).

2. Kenneth Waltz, "The Spread of Nuclear Weapons," *Adelphi Papers*, 1981, https://www.mtholyoke.edu/acad/intrel/waltz1.htm (accessed January 20, 2015). Note that Waltz passed away in 2013.

3. This example is adapted from an example in Jeffrey Kimball, "Did Thomas C. Schelling Invent the Madman Theory?" *History News Network*, October 24, 2005, http://hnn.us/article/17183 (accessed January 20, 2015).

4. James Rosen and Luke A. Nichter, "Madman in the White House," *Foreign Policy*, March 25, 2014, http://www.foreignpolicy.com/articles/2014/03/25/madman_in _white_house_nixon_russia_obama (accessed January 8, 2015).

5. Ibid.

6. Jeffrey Kimball, "Did Thomas C. Schelling Invent the Madman Theory?"

7. Peter Navarro, *Crouching Tiger: Will There Be War with China?* www .crouchingtiger.net (documentary film series from DBC Productions, forthcoming 2016).

8. Ibid.

9. See, for example, Ankit Panda, "China's Military May Have Gone 'Rogue' After All," *Diplomat*, September 23, 2014, http://thediplomat.com/2014/09/chinas-military -may-have-gone-rogue-after-all/ (accessed January 8, 2015).

Chapter 39: Can We Negotiate Our Way out of the Thucydides Trap?

1. Peter Navarro, *Crouching Tiger: Will There Be War with China?* www .crouchingtiger.net (documentary film series from DBC Productions, forthcoming 2016).

2. Ibid.

3. Ibid.

4. Ibid.

5. Ibid.

6. Ibid.

7. Ibid.

8. See, for example, Canwest News Service, "China Blocks Efforts to Sanction Sudan over Darfur Crisis," Canada.com, May 30, 2007, http://www.canada.com/story .html?id=4bb2ff74-12a6-4a92-a3c4-2bf5c2ec1481 (accessed July 22, 2015).

9. Ibid.

10. Ibid.

Chapter 40: Is a "Grand Bargain" with China Feasible?

1. Peter Navarro, *Crouching Tiger: Will There Be War with China?* www
.crouchingtiger.net (documentary film series from DBC Productions, forthcoming 2016).
2. Ibid.
3. Ibid.
4. Ibid.
5. Ibid.
6. Ibid.
7. Ibid.
8. Ibid.
9. Ibid.
10. Ibid.
11. Ibid.
12. Ibid.
13. Ibid.
14. "Can the US and China Build a New Model of Major Power Relations?"
YouTube video, 1:26:52, from a conference streamed live on December 5, 2013, from the
Woodrow Wilson Center, posted by "WoodrowWilsonCenter," https://www.youtube.com/
watch?v=oNuYgJfr6eA (accessed January 8, 2015).

Chapter 41: The Logic and Architecture
of Peace through Strength

1. Thucydides, *History of the Peloponnesian War*, trans. Rex Warner (New York:
Penguin Classics, 1972).
2. Deng Xiaoping, quoted in a *People's Daily* article from February 26, 1990.
3. Peter Navarro, *Crouching Tiger: Will There Be War with China?* www.
crouchingtiger.net (documentary film series from DBC Productions, forthcoming 2016).
4. Ibid.
5. Sun Tzu, *The Art of War* (Minneapolis, MN: Filiquarian, 2007).
6. For discussion, see, for example, "Geopolitical Power Calculations,"
DistribuTECH2015, http://fas.org/nuke/guide/china/doctrine/pills2/part08.htm (accessed
January 8, 2015).
7. Navarro, *Crouching Tiger*.
8. General Wesley Clark, "Getting Real about China," *New York Times*, October
10, 2014, http://www.nytimes.com/2014/10/11/opinion/sunday/getting-real-about-china.
html?_r=0 (accessed January 8, 2015).
9. Navarro, *Crouching Tiger*.
10. For a history and timeline, see Piero Scaruffi, "A Timeline of the Mongols,"
Scaruffi.com, 1999, http://www.scaruffi.com/politics/mongols.html (accessed January 8,
2015).

11. Navarro, *Crouching Tiger*.

12. Ibid.

Chapter 42: On the Primacy of Peace through Economic Strength

1. Peter Navarro, *Crouching Tiger: Will There Be War with China?* www
.crouchingtiger.net (documentary film series from DBC Productions, forthcoming 2016).

2. Ibid.

3. Ibid.

4. Ibid. However, note that China has periodically allowed some upward "float" of its currency. When the Chinese economy has softened, China has typically allowed the yuan to once again weaken to stimulate its economy at the expense of its trading partners. See, for example, Lingling Wei, "China Intervenes to Lower Yuan," *Wall Street Journal*, February 26, 2014, http://www.wsj.com/articles/SB1000142405270230407100457940681 0684766716 (accessed July 22, 2015).

5. Navarro, *Crouching Tiger*.

6. Ibid.

7. Ibid.

Chapter 43: Toward a New Strategy for Peace through Military Strength

1. This quote may be found in chapter 3 in the list at "Sun Tzu," *Wikiquote*, http://en.wikiquote.org/wiki/Sun_Tzu (accessed January 8, 2015).

2. Peter Navarro, *Crouching Tiger: Will There Be War with China?* www
.crouchingtiger.net (documentary film series from DBC Productions, forthcoming 2016).

3. Ibid.

4. Ibid.

5. Ibid.

6. Ibid.

7. Ibid.

8. Ibid.

9. Ibid.

10. Ibid.

11. Ibid.

Chapter 44: Pivot Softly and Carry a Firm Alliance Stick

1. For the history, see Kenneth Lieberthal, "The American Pivot to Asia," *Foreign Policy*, December 21, 2011, http://www.foreignpolicy.com/articles/2011/12/21/the _american_pivot_to_asia (accessed January 8, 2015).

2. Kirk Spitzer, "USA Upgrading in Asia, But 'Pivot' Questioned," *USA Today*, December 17, 2013, http://www.usatoday.com/story/news/world/2013/12/17/us-japan-asia-security-strategy/4049517/ (accessed January 8, 2015).

3. Kris Osborn, "Navy's Plan for 306-Ship Fleet Fading Away," Military.com, July 31, 2013, http://www.military.com/daily-news/2013/07/31/navys-plan-for-306-ship-fleet-fading-away.html (accessed January 8, 2015).

4. Peter Navarro, *Crouching Tiger: Will There Be War with China?* www.crouchingtiger.net (documentary film series from DBC Productions, forthcoming 2016).

5. Ibid.

6. Ibid.

7. Ibid.

8. Ibid.

9. Ibid.

10. Ibid.

11. Ibid.

12. Ibid.

13. Ibid.

14. Ibid.

15. Ibid.

16. Ibid.

17. Ibid.

18. Ibid.

19. "Who Authorized Preparations for War With China?" YouTube video, 1:39:15, from a panel discussion on the Pentagon's Air-Sea Battle concept hosted by the Sigur Center for Asian Studies at the George Washington University, posted by "Amitai Etzioni," July 25, 2013, https://www.youtube.com/watch?v=kibpu7qHVLY (accessed January 7, 2015).

20. Ibid.

21. As noted by the Free Dictionary, http://www.thefreedictionary.com/Potemkin+village (accessed July 22, 2015), a "Potemkin village" is "something that appears elaborate and impressive but in actual fact lacks substance."

22. Navarro, *Crouching Tiger*.

Chapter 45: Defeating the Enemy That Is Us

1. This first signs of this threat were identified more than a decade ago. See Bill Gertz, *The China Threat* (Washington, DC: Regnery Publishing, 2000).

2. For an analysis of the origins of the "China Price" and the contribution of illegal export subsidies, lack of adequate health-and-safety regulations, and lax pollution controls to the bottom line of both Chinese and multinational companies see, for example, Peter Navarro, "The Economics of the 'China Price,'" *China* Perspectives, November–December 2006, http://chinaperspectives.revues.org/3063 (accessed July 22, 2015).

3. See, for example, David R. Baker, "Tariffs Could Dim Solar Energy's Rapid

Growth," *SFGATE*, July 9, 2014, http://www.sfgate.com/business/article/Tariffs-could
-dim-solar-energy-s-rapid-growth-5538030.php (accessed January 8, 2015).

4. "2011 Ohio Corn and Soybean Yield Numbers by County," *Ohio's Country Journal*, February 24, 2012, http://ocj.com/2012/02/2011-ohio-corn-and-soybean-yield -numbers-by-county/ (accessed January 8, 2015).

5. See, for example, this account: Dave Johnson, "Important Bipartisan Currency Bill Introduced in House," *Huffington Post*, May 20, 2013, http://www.huffingtonpost .com/dave-johnson/important-bipartisan-curr_b_2918910.html (accessed January 8, 2015).

6. As Speaker Boehner notes on his official government website: "Ohio's 8th Congressional District is one of the largest agricultural districts in the Buckeye State. It boasts more than 6,000 farms, growing grains, produce and raising livestock on nearly 1 million acres." See "Farm Forum," John Boehner, 8th District of Ohio, http://boehner .house.gov/services/farm-forum/ (accessed January 8, 2015).

7. Peter Navarro, *Crouching Tiger: Will There Be War with China?* www .willtherebewarwithchina.com (documentary film series from DBC Productions, forthcoming 2016).

8. Ibid.

9. Ibid.

10. Emily Parker, "China's Government is Scaring Foreign Journalists into Censoring Themselves," *New Republic*, December 9, 2013, http://www.newrepublic.com/ article/115851/censorship-china-how-western-journalists-censor-themselves (accessed January 8, 2015).

11. Ibid.

12. Andrew Jacobs, "Foreign Journalists in China See Decline in Reporting Conditions," *New York Times*, September 12, 2014, http://sinosphere.blogs.nytimes .com/2014/09/12/foreign-journalists-in-china-see-decline-in-reporting-conditions/? _php=true&_type=blogs&_r=0 (accessed January 8, 2015).

13. Neil Gough and Ravi Samaiya, "Bloomberg Hints at Curb on Articles about China, *New York Times*, March 20, 2014, http://www.nytimes.com/2014/03/21/business/ international/bloomberg-should-have-rethought-articles-on-china-chairman-says.html (accessed January 8, 2015).

14. Ibid.

15. Chris Schrader, "'Red Dawn' Villains Switched from China to North Korea," *Screen Rant*, http://screenrant.com/red-dawn-villains-china-north-korea-schrad-106177/ (accessed January 8, 2015).

16. Navarro, *Crouching Tiger*. The "yuan" is the Chinese currency, also known as the renminbi.

17. Here's a typical website describing Confucian Institute K–12 activities: http:// usm.maine.edu/confucius/programs (accessed January 8, 2015).

18. Navarro, *Crouching Tiger: Will There Be War with China?*

19. The original Santayana quote is, of course: Those who cannot remember the past are condemned to repeat it. See "George Santayana," *Wikiquote*, https://en.wikiquote.org/ wiki/George_Santayana (accessed July 22, 2015).

INDEX

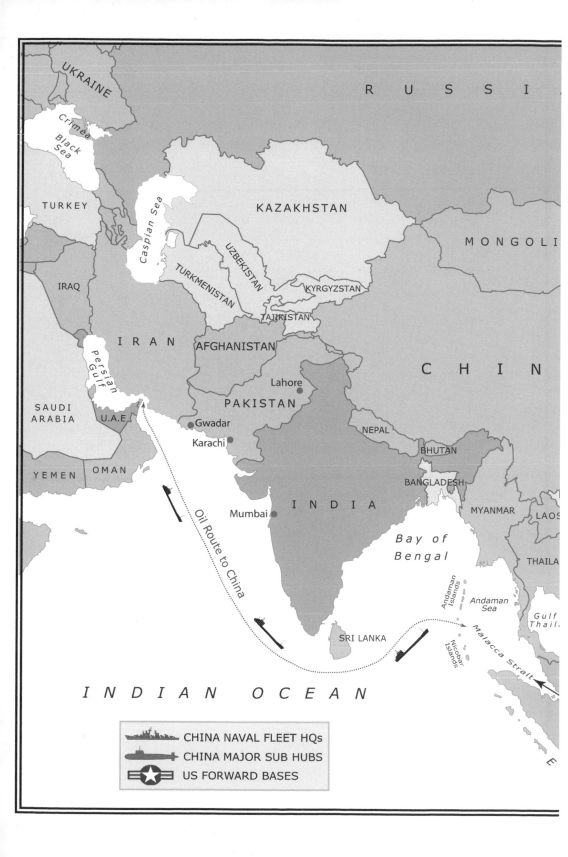